Blessed Margaret of Castello:
Servant of the Sick and the Outcast

Mary Elizabeth O'Brien, OP

Foreword by
Bro. Gerard Thayer, OP

NEW PRIORY PRESS
EXPLORING THE DOMINICAN VISION
Chicago, IL

The scripture quotations contained herein are from The New Revised Standard Version Bible: Catholic Edition, copyright © 1993 and 1989 by the Division of Christian Education of the National Council of the Churches of Christ in the U.S.A. Used by Permission. All Rights reserved.

Copyright © 2017 by the Dominican Province of St. Albert the Great (U.S.A.). All rights reserved.
Published by New Priory Press
1910 S. Ashland Avenue
Chicago, IL 60608

Contents

Foreword by Bro. Gerard Thayer, OP vii
Preface ix
Acknowledgements xi
Prologue xiii
"O Lustrous Pearl"
    Fr. Andrew Hofer OP xiv

Chapter 1. "A Lasting Beauty"
Margaret's Early Spirituality 1
The Legend 2
    Documentation of Sources 3
    Hagiography 12
    The "Lunettes" 13
"Little Margaret"'s World (1287-1320) 16
    Parental Rejection 17
The Baptism 17
    A Blessed "Pearl" 19
Medieval Castle Life 19
    The Castle Chaplain 21
Parisio's Decision 23
    St. Veridiana 24

Chapter 2. "The Darkness is Not Dark"
A Young Anchoress 29
A Medieval Anchorhold 32
    Margaret's Cell 32
The Anchoress Vocation 37
    Ancrene Wisse 38
    Margareta Contracta (Lame Margaret of Magdeburg) 42
    Hildegard of Bingen 48

    Julien of Norwich 51
The Spirituality of Solitude 53

Chapter 3. "He Will Not Break a Bruised Reed"
The Failed Miracle **59**
Mercatello 64
    The Palazzo Vault 64
Citta di Castello 71
    The Failed Miracle 71
Trust in God's Providence 73
    Forgiveness 76

Chapter 4. "The Strength that God Supplies"
A Saint of the Streets **81**
Homelessness 82
    A Family of the Streets 85
"Monastero di Santa Margherita" 91
    Monastic Rejection 94
Seeds of Ministry to the Sick and Outcast 96
    The Spirituality of Disability 98

Chapter 5. "A Holy Calling"
The Mantellata **105**
A Holy Calling 106
    A Vocation of Service 106
The Sisters of Penance of St. Dominic 108
    The *Mantellata* 116
The Tertiary Vocation 121
    Catherine of Siena (1347-1380) 121
    Rose of Lima (1586-1617) 124
    Pier Giorgio Frassati (1901-1925) 128

Chapter 6. "Love One Another"
Serving the Sick and the Outcast 133
Margaret as Mystic 134
 "If only you knew what I carry in my heart" 134
Mysticism 140
 Saint Catherine de Ricci 144
 Blessed Henry Suso 145
 Mechthild of Magdeburg 147
Margaret as Minister 148
 A "Wounded Healer" 148
Ministry to Outcasts 156
 Medieval Prisoners 156

Chapter 7. "Unless a Grain of Wheat Falls"
The Healing Miracles 165
Beatification 168
 Incorruptibility 169
 The Healing Miracles 169
Ministries Dedicated to Blessed Margaret 175
 "L'IstitutoBeata Margherita Cieca della Metola" (Blessed Margaret of Metola Institute for the Blind), Citta di Castello, Perugia, 1920 175
 "Dis-abilita Associazione Sportiva Dilettantistica Beata Margherita" (Blessed Margaret Amateur Sports Association) Program for the Physically Challenged, Citta di Castello, Perugia 176
 "Castello Nursing Simulation Learning Center", Aquinas College School of Nursing, Nashville, Tennessee, 2015 176
 Religious Shrines to Honor Blessed Margaret of Castello in the United States:
  St. Patrick Church, Columbus, Ohio 180
  St. Louis Bertrand Church, Louisville, Ky. 180
 Religious Shrines to Honor Blessed Margaret of Castello in Italy:
  La Chiesa di San Domenico, Citta di Castello, Perugia . 184

   La Cappella Beata Margherita, Metola 184
Margaret's Legacy 185
   Memorialization in Art: Painting, Sculpture and Stained Glass 185

Epilogue 189
Index 191

Foreword

It was several years ago, while in conversation with my dear friend Sister Mary Elizabeth, that she first brought up the idea of writing about Blessed Margaret of Castello, inquiring as she did, what I thought of the idea. As a Dominican friar for well over 50 years, Blessed Margaret was no stranger to me. I had been introduced to her while still a novice. It was at a point in the world of religious formation, when spiritual reading more often than not centered on getting to know the "family," so to speak. It was also an age when the lives of those holy men and women were most often presented through a hagiographic lens. It was a style that quite honestly, I found a bit off-putting. Presented, as the genre suggests, with undue reverence, I found that my ability to identify with those early Dominicans was, over all, a bit of a stretch.

As the idea of writing this book started to move forward, from conception to gathering sources, I remember challenging Sister to "let Margaret speak to us." What you hold in your hand is that challenge met and one that you will find far exceeds what even I had in mind when suggesting it. In advocating for that approach, my thought was that Margaret needed not only to speak to those who shared her afflictions, the blind, the lame, and those living with other physical challenges, by helping them to embrace their infirmities as a grace, but to go beyond that as well. We, who are not so physically challenged need to hear Blessed Margaret speak to us also, helping us to acknowledge our own, often denied, spiritual blindness and the lameness with which we embrace our faith.

What has so refreshingly happened is that this seasoned author has taken us on a journey. It is a journey that allows us to identify, in a very tangible sense, the anxiety and fear that Margaret worked through in search of her Beloved. Chapter by chapter, experience by experience, challenge by challenge, we are first allowed to share young Margaret's life of confinement; then we journey on through the 14th-century streets of *Citta di Castello* with Margaret as she sought her heart's desire, Him whom she loved unreservedly, and who she discovered in the faces of those she encountered on the fringes of society.

Sr. Mary Elizabeth's fingerprints are all over the many delightful discoveries throughout the book where readers will find themselves skillfully provided with a color commentary about the life, customs, and rituals that made up the medieval secular and religious worlds that were home to Blessed Margaret.

Blessed Margaret of Castello

Each of the chapters leads off with a fitting scripture quote and a simple, yet strikingly beautiful, poem that both focuses and embraces the chapter's theme, setting the stage for what is to unfold. It is a style that provides a unifying thread that runs through all seven chapters.

Too often, in a work such as this, the reader encounters a passing cast of characters presented by the author as a backdrop or foil to help unfurl the principal character's story. In *Blessed Margaret of Castello: Servant of the Sick and the Outcast*, that is not the case. There is an intimacy created that travels the length of the work, binding Margaret, those whose lives crossed her own, the many scholars quoted throughout the book, and the reader.

Here you will encounter a Blessed that you will come to love as your own sister and you will view the world through different eyes for you will begin to see the face of Christ through Margaret's blindness.

Brother Gerard Thayer OP

Preface

Several years ago I was introduced to the legend of Blessed Margaret of Castello, a 13th/14th-century Dominican Tertiary, by the members of my Lay Dominican community. I was deeply moved by Margaret's loving and grace-filled acceptance of having been born with serious physical challenges. Because of her fragility, Blessed Margaret was rejected by her parents, subjected to an early life of solitude and later cast into the streets as a beggar, yet she never lost her deep and abiding trust in God. Ultimately, Margaret became a beloved "wounded healer," ministering to the sick poor in the streets and in their homes, as well as to prisoners incarcerated in the *Citta di Castello* jail.

This book is written to open a 21st-century window into the medieval world, life and ministry of Blessed Margaret. The goals are twofold: to explore Margaret's spirituality and apostolic activities as a Dominican Tertiary, focusing specifically on her care of the sick and of prisoners, and to understand and interpret Margaret's spirituality and ministry as providing models for contemporary society. The work will, I believe, be of interest to a variety of today's ministers to the ill and infirm, including nurses, physicians, chaplains, social workers and pastoral care team members in parishes, as well as to those with personal physical challenges who seek to minister to others. Blessed Margaret's prison ministry is also an exemplar for individuals providing care and ministry to those imprisoned in a variety of settings.

Chapter One begins with documentation of Margaret's legend, or *vita*, describing the author's sources, and exploring "Little Margaret"'s world while hidden in her parent's castle for the first six years of life. Also identified is her burgeoning spirituality guided by the family chaplain, Fra Giacomo Cappellano, and her parental rejection resulting in enclosure in an anchoritic cell. In Chapter Two, Blessed Margaret's life as a "young anchoress," from ages six to eighteen, is examined comparing her spiritual regimen to those of historical anchoresses Hildegard of Bingen, Lame Margaret of Magdeburg, and Julien of Norwich. Chapter Three describes Margaret's response to a failed miracle at *Citta di Castello*, and Chapter Four explores the young woman's life as a beggar, as well as her experience of a painful expulsion by a monastic community of women. In Chapter Five, Blessed Margaret's formal calling to become a Lay Dominican, or *Mantellata*, is described and the third-order vocation is explained using examples of other well-known Dominican Tertiaries: Catherine of Siena, Rose of Lima, and Pier Gorgio

Frassati. Chapter Six considers Blessed Margaret as both mystic and minister; it also explores her role as "a wounded healer" and focuses on her care for the sick in their homes and her ministry to prisoners. And, in Chapter Seven, a number of miracles associated with and following Margaret's death are identified and her beatification is documented; also included are examples of Blessed Margaret's memorialization in art reflected in such media as paintings, sculpture and stained glass.

In the preface to Ubaldo Valentini's 1988 work, *Beata Margherita De La Metola: Una Sfida Alla Emarginazione*, Pietro Cardinal Palazzini posed a rhetorical question: "Why a new life of Blessed Margaret?" The Cardinal's response noted that "the riches of the saints are inexhaustible mines" in which one should "dig deep" for lessons "still unpublished or little explored."[1] The same question might be posed today, almost 30 years later, and the response would be similar. In this era of the 21st Century, rife with the challenges of war, poverty, disease and a variety of destructive "isms," such as egoism and materialism, love of God and love of neighbor, the "riches" exemplified in the life of Blessed Margaret, are desperately needed. "Little Margaret" of Metola, now Blessed Margaret of Castello, is indeed a treasured role model for the contemporary Christian in this third millennium.

---

[1] Pietro Cardinal Palazzini, "Preface" (pp. 7-11) in Ubaldo Valentini, *Beata Margherita De La Metola: Una Sfida Alla Emarginazione* (Perugia, Italy: Petruzzi Editore, 1988), 7.

Acknowledgements

To thank all of the individuals involved in creating this book seems an impossible task. Nevertheless, I must try, as its completion is only due to the many Dominican "shoulders" on which I stand. First, I must express deep gratitude to Father Gabriel O'Donnell, OP, of the Pontifical Faculty of the Immaculate Conception, Dominican House of Studies (Washington, DC). His advice and guidance continually lead me to a deeper understanding of and love for the teachings of Saint Dominic and the Dominican spirituality, which guided the life and ministry of Blessed Margaret of Castello. Next, I thank Brother Ignatius Perkins, OP, recipient of the "St. Catherine of Siena Chair in Catholic Health Care Ethics" at the Pontifical Faculty of the Immaculate Conception and "Director, Office of Health Services" for the Dominican Province of St. Joseph, whose love of Blessed Margaret inspired me to learn of her ministry to the sick and the outcast. From the conception of the research undergirding this work, I was blessed by the ongoing support of Brother Gerard Thayer, OP, Aquinas College (Nashville, Tennessee), who advised me to "let Margaret speak to us."

There are a number of other mentors who assisted in a variety of ways as the story of Blessed Margaret's passionate care for the sick and the outcast began to take shape. Father Andrew Hofer, OP, Master of Students at the Dominican House of Studies shared his prayerful meditation, "O Lustrous Pearl" to introduce Margaret's legend; Sister Mary Justin Haltom, OP, graciously gave permission to reproduce her beautiful photograph of an image of Blessed Margaret in stained glass; and Sister Anna Wray, OP, supported the work with her thoughtful advice and her prayers.

Special thanks go also to Robert C. MacDonald, Assistant to the Archivist for the Dominican Province of St. Joseph at Providence College (Providence, Rhode Island) for excerpts from Dominican Fr. William R. Bonniwell's letters to his Prior Provincial, Fr. T.S. McDermott, OP, documenting Fr. Bonniwell's research exploring the life and ministry of Blessed Margaret of Castello.

I am deeply grateful, as well, to dear friends and colleagues who gave of their precious time to review a first draft of the book manuscript: Brother Ignatius Perkins, OP, PhD, RN, FAAN, ANEF, FRSM, FNYAM; Brother Gerard Thayer, OP; Sister Margaret Anne Masiello, OP; and Dr. Patricia McMullen, PhD, RN, J.D, CRNP, FAANP, FAAN, Dean of The Catholic University of America School of Nursing.

Heartfelt and loving gratitude go to Joan Butler, OP, President, and the members of my Lay Dominican Community, who supported the writing with their caring and their prayers. A particular debit of thanks is owed to LaVerne Atiba, OP, who guided our study of Blessed Margaret's life and ministry.

I am especially appreciative of the dedication of Terry L. Jarbe, production editor at New Priory Press, who enthusiastically embraced the concept of Blessed Margaret's ministry to the sick and the outcast, and gently shepherded the manuscript to publication.

I am continually gifted by the witness and prayers of the Dominican Priests and Brothers of the Priory of the Immaculate Conception and the Dominican Sisters of St. Cecilia who inspire me by their loving commitment to follow the spiritual path set forth by our Holy Father Dominic. Ultimately, my deepest gratitude is to God the Father, the source of my strength and the center of my life, to His Divine Son, Our Lord Jesus Christ, whose love nourishes my soul and to the Holy Spirit of wisdom and understanding, without whose guidance the following pages would never have seen the light of day. To God be the glory!

Prologue

Blessed Margaret of Castello may be considered not only the patroness of those with physical challenges, but also the patroness of those, who despite such afflictions, devote their lives to the service of others. Margaret was both contemplative and caregiver, mystic and minister. She looked on God with a deep and abiding love and she looked on her neighbor as a reflection of God's love. As a true follower of St. Dominic, "Little Margaret" embraced a motto of the Dominican Order which she may never have personally known: *"Contemplare et Contemplata Aliis Tradere"*- "To contemplate and to give to others the fruits of contemplation."

Blessed Margaret's early life of solitary enclosure, dedicated to prayer and penance, as well as the caring she later received from a "family of the streets," prepared her abundantly to contemplate the love and mercy of God and to share His gifts in ministry to the poor, the sick, and the outcast.

The purpose of the present exploration of Margaret of Castello's "Legend" is to allow Blessed Margaret to speak to us from the across the centuries; to speak to us of her love, her faith, and her courageous ministry to those in need.

Margaret was beatified in 1609 and was indeed blessed of the Lord; she was, in the words of the Dominican Sisters of St. Cecilia, truly "a beauty in God's sight."[2]

---

[2] "A Beauty in God's Sight: The Story of Blessed Margaret of Castello," *Veritas, Dominican Sisters of St. Cecilia Newsletter*, Spring, 2009, 5.

Blessed Margaret of Castello

"O Lustrous Pearl"

In honor of Blessed Margaret of Castello
Fr. Andrew Hofer, OP

O lustrous pearl in heaven's light,
prepared by God for glory's sight,
how loved and wanted by the King
that to His courts He did you bring.

Unworthy of your precious name,
the world despised your fragile frame.
Abandoned, blind, forgotten, lame,
you suffered greatly for the Name.

And what the world was blind to see
laid deep within as mystery.
For you the hidden would suffice:
the finest Pearl of greatest price.

O Blessed Margaret, priceless jewel,
amidst the world so cold and cruel,
now teach us how to bear our cross
with joyful grace when all seems lost.

O lustrous pearl in heaven's light,
do pray that we may have your sight
to praise with you the Father, Son,
and Spirit Blest, your Three in One.

Chapter 1. "A Lasting Beauty"

Margaret's Early Spirituality

"Let your adornment be the inner self with the lasting beauty of a gentle and quiet spirit, which is very precious in the Lord's sight."

1 Peter 3:4

Child of God

Rejected by man, but beloved
of God,
This blessed child they would
name a "pearl."
So weak and helpless the tiny
newborn,
So hopelessly challenged, so
cruelly unwanted.

Survival alone seemed fraught
with anguish,
For what could she become,
this dear child of God?
What could give life to her
Fragile existence?

"If only you knew what I carry
in my heart," was
Margaret's answer;
"If only you knew what I carry
in my heart," became
Margaret's strength.

Blessed Margaret of Castello, sometimes identified as Margaret of Metola, was a 14th-century Dominican Tertiary, a Sister of Penance of St. Dominic. Blessed Margaret is frequently described as the patroness of persons living with physical challenges; this patronage is related to the fact that Margaret was born blind, lame and with a severe curvature of the spine. She was also very small in stature resulting in the occasional descriptor "Little Margaret."

Despite her physical afflictions, Margaret was blessed with a powerful and profound spirituality. Her love of the Lord was initiated as a small child under the guidance of a devoted priest chaplain. Because of the multiple deformities, obvious at birth, Margaret was rejected by her parents and ultimately secluded in a small cell attached to a chapel in the forest. Between the ages of approximately six to eighteen years, young Margaret lived a life similar to that of a religious anchoress, enclosed in the stone cell or "anchorhold"; her days were organized around study, prayer, Mass and reception of the Eucharist.

As adulthood approached, Margaret's parents removed her from the enclosed cell, first to an underground vault in Mercatello and then to visit the tomb of a holy Franciscan Brother in *Citta di Castello* where numerous healing miracles were said to have occurred; such a healing was the family's hope for their afflicted daughter. Failing the wished for miracle, Margaret was abandoned by her parents at Castello.

Following this second rejection by her family, and later by a monastic community of nuns, and after spending some months as a beggar in the streets of *Citta di Castello*, Blessed Margaret was accepted by a Lay Dominican community, the Sisters of Penance of St. Dominic, and began ministering to the sick in the streets, in their homes, and in the prisons.[1,i]

The Legend

The "legend," or life, of Blessed Margaret of Castello was initially communicated verbally. The story of this fragile Italian child, born with severe physical challenges, rejected by noble parents, cast into the streets as a beggar, yet ultimately beatified as a holy woman "precious in the Lord's sight," captivated all who heard of her.

In the era of the late 13th and early 14th Centuries, however, the time in which Margaret lived, the writing of a "legend," or *vita*, even that of a holy person, was not entered into lightly. We are told by Blessed Margaret's first medieval biographer that he initially hesitated to write of her for three reasons: first, he "doubted the credibility of a story passed down by word of mouth"; secondly, he was concerned about Margaret's association with the order of preaching Brothers who he

---

[1] *Blessed Margaret of Castello OP: A Medieval Biography* (Trans. Carolina Accorsi) (Fatima, Portugal: Dominican Nuns of the Perpetual Rosary, 1994); William R. Bonniwell, *The Life of Blessed Margaret of Castello:1287-1320"* (Charlotte, N.C.: Tan Books, 2014).

believed gave undue praise to their "holy ones"; and finally, because Blessed Margaret had not been canonized by the Church.[2]

The same medieval biographer, did, nevertheless, after research, come to identify a number of reasons why he later decided to proceed with relating a brief account of Margaret's life; these included Blessed Margaret's obvious sanctity, her commitment to God's service, and her lifelong consecration to virginity.[3]

The aim of the present exploration of Margaret of Castello's "Legend" is to allow Margaret to speak to us from across the centuries; to speak to us of her love, her faith, and her courageous ministry to those in need. The ultimate goal of this study is to allow Blessed Margaret to model for today's world her tender care and compassion for the most fragile and marginalized members of our society: the poor, the sick and the outcast.

Documentation of Sources

In order to provide a contemporary understanding of Blessed Margaret's life and ministry, a number of literary sources were reviewed. A primary reference was the anonymously-authored work, *Blessed Margaret of Castello OP: A Medieval Biography*, translated from the Latin by Carolina Accorsi and published in English, in 1994, by the Dominican Nuns of the Perpetual Rosary, Fatima, Portugal. Accorsi's translation "was made from a Latin transcription provided by Marie Hyacinthe Laurent, O.P., in his work entitled, "La Plus Ancienne Legende de la B. Margherita."[4] This "Medieval Biography," believed to have been authored by a Canon of the Cathedral in *Citta di Castello*, is reported to predate other early accounts of Margaret's life; these include a Latin biography published by the Bolandistes and an Italian text authored by Fra Tommaso D'Antonio da Siena (Fra Tommaso Caffarini) around 1400.[5,ii]

Important secondary sources for the present study were the English language biography/hagiography, *The Life of Blessed Margaret of Castello: 1287-1320*, written by William R. Bonniwell, O.P., (1952; 1979;

---

[2] *Blessed Margaret of Castello OP: A Medieval Biography* (Trans. Carolina Accorsi) (Fatima, Portugal: Dominican Nuns of the Perpetual Rosary, 1994), 11-12.

[3] Ibid., 13-14

[4] Editor's Note, A Medieval Biography, p. xiii; Reference: M.H. Laurent, "La Plus Ancienne Legende de la B. Margherita de Citta di Castello," *Archivum Fratrum Praedicatorum*, Volume 10 (1940: 109-115).

[5] *Le Legendae di Margherita da Citta di Castello*. Ed. Maria Lungarotti (*Spoleto: Centro Italiano di Studi sull'Altro Medioevo*, 1994), cited in Maiju Lehmijoki-Gardner, *Domenican Penitent Women*. Mahwah, N.J.: Paulist Press, 2005, P. 245.)

1983/2014),[6] and two Italian works: *Beata Margherita De La Metola: Una Sfida Alla Emarginazione*, authored by Ubaldo Valentini (1988)[7] and *Beata Margherita di Citta di Castello* by Barbara Sartori (2011).[8] A number of other books, chapters, and journal articles containing material relevant to the medieval era, and to the life, spirituality, and ministry of Blessed Margaret, were reviewed as well.

 The primary source of Margaret's legend, the anonymously authored publication entitled, in the English version, *Blessed Margaret of Castello OP: A Medieval Biography*, is considered to be the first account of Margaret's world, her spirituality and her calling to a life of prayer and penance. The original Latin manuscript of this oldest legend of Blessed Margaret is preserved in the archives of St. Dominic in Bologna, Italy.[9] Author Ubaldo Valentini included the "Introduction" and entire XXVI (26) chapters of the "Medieval Biography," in both Latin and Italian, labeled "A Code 'Cividale'" in the appendix of his work: *Beata Margherita de la Metola: Una Sfida Alla Emarginazione*.[10]

 Valentini validates the assumption that this "Medieval Biography," the oldest of the Dominican Tertiary, was probably written by a Canon of *Citta di Castello*; he notes that other accounts of Margaret's legend, contained in the Vatican library and archives of the Dominicans at Santa Sabina, are "nothing more than a summary."[11] This *Legenda*, he adds, is called "Maior," while the others are called "Minor." Ubaldo Valentini considers the *Legenda*, the "Medieval Biography," to be the work of a "religious" because of the emphases on Margaret being a member of a Third Order, the recording of miracles occurring through her intervention, and the description of the "sanctity of the blessed."[12]

 An introduction to the English translation of the "Medieval Biography" also reinforces the claim that this was the first written Legend of Blessed Margaret; it is asserted that other early accounts of her life were "probably written with this text 'under the eyes' or 'in the hands'" of the authors.[13] It is also reported that Fr. William Bonniwell

---

[6] William R. Bonniwell, *The Life of Blessed Margaret of Castello:1287-1320* (Charlotte, N.C.: Tan Books, 2014).
[7] Ubaldo Valentini, *Beata Margherita De La Metola Una Sfida Alla Emarginazione* (Perugia, Italy: Petruzzi Editore, 1988).
[8] Barbara Sartori, *Beata Margherita di Citta di Castello* (Milano, Italy: Paoline Editorale Libri, 2011).
[9] Valentini, 203.
[10] Ibid., 203-228.
[11] Ibid., 203.
[12] Ibid.
[13] *Blessed Margaret of Castello OP*, viii.

"relied heavily on this work when writing his book" on the life of Blessed Margaret.[14]

Although brief, the "Medieval Biography," nevertheless, documents significant occurrences in Blessed Margaret of Castello's life such as: Margaret's physical challenges, parental rejection and the creation of an anchoritic "cell" by her father Parisio; Margaret's spirituality (prayer and penance) and mysticism; the failed miracle at *Citta di Castello*; reception and expulsion by a monastery of nuns and several publicly witnessed miracles. The brevity of the work is defended by the author's comment: "I think more could be told in truth about the life and sanctity and virtues of Margaret...(but) the tale must be narrated piously, devoutly and truthfully."[15]

In the introductions to later editions (1979, 1983) of a secondary source, William R. Bonniwell's "life" of Blessed Margaret of Castello, the Dominican author notes that his book was based on three medieval works: the earlier described "Medieval Biography" composed by a Canon Regular of the Cathedral of Castello, which appeared in 1345; an account of Margaret's life by a Dominican Priest published in 1347 in classical Latin; and a 14th-century Italian translation authored by Dominican Friar, Tommaso Caffarini. Bonniwell commented that all three works were still extant at the time of his initial writing and that "all three were used to compile" his book.[16] Fr. Bonniwell added, however, that whenever he would speak of "the Medieval Biographer," it would be the Canon to whom he was referring, as, he noted: "he is the chief source of our knowledge of Margaret."[17]

In introductory remarks to the first (1952) edition of Fr. Bonniwell's book which was entitled: "The Story of Margaret of Metola," the author confirmed that "The first important biography of Margaret was written... by an unknown Canon of the Cathedral of *Citta di Castello*": "That Canon biographer "probably saw Margaret many times" as a boy but seriously doubted "the extraordinary anecdotes" about her life and was "determined to refute them."[18]

Bonniwell described the Canon's research:

---

[14] Ibid., ix.
[15] Ibid., 31-32.
[16] Bonniwell, xiii.
[17] Ibid.
[18] William R. Bonniwell, *The Story of Margaret of Metola* (New York, N.Y.: P.J. Kennedy & Sons, 1952), viii.

There were still living in Castello many persons who had known Margaret well; these he sought out and cross-examined. Next, he searched the records at the town hall, where he found many official documents pertaining to her. When he had completed his investigation, he was obliged to admit that the anecdotes were true. Thereupon, perhaps in reparation for his former disbelief, he wrote Margaret's biography.[19]

Fr. Bonniwell added: "Because of his skepticism he (the Canon) makes an invaluable witness" and concluded that because of the existence of this *vita* of Blessed Margaret, as well as the other biographies identified earlier, "it is now possible, for the first time in five hundred years, to reconstruct the true and complete story of Margaret of Metola."[20]

Father Bonniwell's account of Blessed Margaret's life, crafted as an historical novel, contains myriad details not, however, found in the Canon's manuscript. One must assume that these data were obtained from the other two early biographies, as well as having been discovered through Bonniwell's extensive research conducted in Rome, Paris, Metola, Margaret's birthplace, and *Citta di Castello*, the setting for Blessed Margaret's ministry to the sick and the outcast. While Fr. Bonniwell does not share specific details of the research in his book, he speaks in the 1983 edition's "introduction" of numerous visits to *Citta di Castello* and Metola and offers gratitude "to the many persons in *Citta di Castello* for their unstinted efforts to assist me in my researches every time I visited their city."[21] He asserted: "In the region once called Massa Trabaria (the region neighboring the Castle at Metola), the eager cooperation given me resulted in unearthing valuable data not given by the medieval biographers."[22]

Father Bonniwell's work appears, thus, to be a compilation of facts describing Blessed Margaret's life gleaned from the writings of three medieval biographers: first, a work written, in barbarous Latin "about the year 1360 by an unknown Canon of the Cathedral of *Citta di Castello*"; second, "an account written by a Dominican Friar who saw the first manuscript and "rewrote the life in classical Latin" in 1397; and a third biography written in 1400, in Italian, by Dominican Thomas

---

[19] Ibid.
[20] Ibid.
[21] Bonniwell, 2014, xiv.
[22] Ibid.

D'Antonio Caffarini.[23] The legend is fleshed out and expanded by data reflecting narrative accounts of Margaret's spirituality and ministry supplied by the author's Italian "assistants," as well as by written documents discovered during his research visits to Rome, Paris, Metola and *Citta di Castello*.

Detailed information descriptive of Fr. Bonniwell's research and early publication efforts is revealed in a series of letters to his Dominican Provincial, Fr. T.S. McDermott OP, dating from February 1, 1949 to June 1, 1951. Importantly, these letters serve to explain why Fr. Bonniwell was forced to convert his research-based "fact-filled," manuscript into an historical novel style manuscript in order to facilitate publication. These letters, from which the following data have been excerpted, are currently housed in the "Dominican Provincial Archives," St. Joseph's Province, Providence College, Providence, Rhode Island.[iii]

In a letter of February 1, 1949, Bonniwell reported:

> I am now at work on my next work: "The Life of Blessed Margaret of Castello OP. I expect to have the rough copy of the manuscript ready by summer. I am greatly hampered in the writing of this book by my ignorance of what Castello (where she lived) and Metola (where she was born) are like. They are such small places that I cannot find any descriptions, although I have gone to the greatest of pains in searching various libraries. This blind girl lead (sic) so remarkable a life that I hope to make this work the best thing I have ever written."

During the summer of 1949, a joint European trip was proposed for Fr. William Hinnebusch, OP, who would do research on the history of the Dominican Order, and Fr. Bonniwell, who sought to expand the research for his book on Blessed Margaret. An undated "Memorandum" was submitted to the Master of the Order, identifying Bonniwell's proposed research efforts:

> Although we have written her (Margaret's) life, there are some important points which need additional light, information which a year's steady correspondence with priests in Italy has failed to obtain:
>> 1. A good description of what Margaret looked like, especially her features. This, no biographer gives; all

---

[23] Bonniwell, 1952, ix.

the pictures of her falsify what her earliest biographer says of her. As Margaret's body is still incorrupt, conversations with the priest who witnessed the verification of her body in September 1920, should give me that information. Many of these priests still live. Moreover, there should be at *Citta di Castello* or in Rome three different descriptions of her body, the first written in 1743, the next in 1844 and the last in 1920. I would like to find all three if I can.
2. For accurate and realistic telling of Margaret's story, I need an accurate knowledge of the country around Metola and *Citta di Castello*.
3. The few dates given by Margaret's earliest biographer conflict with the dates given by modern writers. As Pere M.H. Laurent, in Rome, has made a study of Margaret's life, discussions with him could clear up this tangle.
4. In Metola, a house is shown today as the place where Margaret was born. It is certain that she was born in the castle but this may be the place she was imprisoned; a few days' sojourn in Metola would enable me to settle this point.
5. As the ruins of Parisio's castle are still extant, a determination of its size and shape would assist in settling several points regarding Margaret's life.
6. We earnestly desire to obtain copies of the latest miracles obtained through her intercession.
7. There may be other documents in the Sacred Congregation's files which would be of assistance in completing our story of Margaret.
8. Both the "Reale Societa Romana di Storia Patria" and the "Archivo Storico Italiano" have in recent years published many original documents of *Citta di Castello*, its laws in the middle ages, and similar documents. These would be invaluable...in describing the condition of the city prison which Margaret regularly visited. But unfortunately these volumes (some twenty or twenty-five) are not in the United States.

Apparently the research expedition was approved, for on December 3, 1949, Fr. Bonniwell wrote to his provincial from Spain: "Our trip across the Atlantic was smooth and uneventful."

After discovering that Spanish data files on Blessed Margaret had been stolen, Bonniwell then went on to Rome, where he continued his letter of December 3rd:

> Everybody here has given every assistance, and Bl. Margaret of Metola is working overtime to furnish me with all the material I want. I got into the files of the Sacred Congregation only to discover that their files too had been looted during the Napoleonic Wars. Then I went to *Citta di Castello* where I saw Bl. Margaret's body; it is still incorrupt but has become a brown color. I then went to Mercatello and saw from a distance the town of the castle...I discovered in the Episcopal Archives at *Citta di Castello* the medical reports on Margaret that I have been seeking for over a year! In the Vatican Library, too, I am finding much material about her; books which I thought had long ago perished.

On January 1, 1950, Bonniwell added, "I went to make a final check in the Archives, and I found several documents which the Bollandists and the writers here of the Archivum Historicum believed to have perished centuries ago! Two more ancient 'Lives' of Bl. Margaret and descriptions of the various 'translations' of her body! Immediately, I postponed my flight for another week, as these documents are of the highest importance to me."

Father Bonniwell then traveled to Paris and, on January 19,1950, reported: "After five days digging here at the Bibliotheque Nationale, I found the document concerning Bl. Margaret but alas, it is not her Processus. It is simply a number of papers referring to the granting of an extension of her feast"; and on January 25, he wrote: "I am anxious to get back and re-write my life of Margaret." On February 25, 1950, Fr. Bonniwell informed his Provincial that he had arrived in New York, but added: "I have been too exhausted to notify you of my arrival... I am afraid the life of Bl. Margaret is due for a prolonged delay."

That "delay" was indeed "prolonged," for in the next letter, almost eight months later, dated October 9, 1950, Father Bonniwell wrote of his concern that "on submitting a first manuscript to the literary critics, they pointed out... the lack of any real information concerning the persons who played a big part in the life of Blessed Margaret. A most desperate search of all available foreign libraries failed to bring any more such information, though I did learn a lot about new miracles and the topography of *Citta di Castello*. The only alternative was to include her miracles in the book; that is what I am now doing. I expect to have this new copy ready in another month."

A letter written on February 2, 1951, expressed great disappointment in not having "yet found a publisher for 'Margaret of Metola.'" Bonniwell lamented: "I have wasted the last two months trying to find a publisher who will even read the manuscript! They are not interested because she (Margaret) is unknown to the public... so it looks as if the two years I spent on the biography is love's labor lost."

Father Bonniwell apparently continued his search, nonetheless, because on April 2, 1952, two months following the report of his failure to find a publisher, he admitted: "the latest of a string of editors had just refused the honor of publishing 'Margaret of Metola,'" noting that the editor said "the same thing all the other publishers say: 'No one has ever heard of Margaret of Metola' and 'The biography is too factual.'" Bonniwell added: "They want it fictionalized; that is the rage in biographies just now." Within yet another two months, on June 1, 1951, he wrote: "I finally got the 'popularized' version of my book typed."[iv]

Fr. William Bonniwell's "popularized," or historical, novel account of Blessed Margaret's life was finally published in 1952 by P.J. Kennedy & Sons of New York; it was entitled "The Story of Margaret of Metola." Bonniwell concluded the "introduction" to the 1952 edition of his life of Blessed Margaret with a defense of its novelistic style: "The results of my researches were embodied in a critical study of Margaret's life but her story is too wonderful to remain buried under a mass of historical discussions about manuscripts and dates. For that reason, the present account has been written."[24]

The title "The Story of Margaret of Metola" was later changed to "The Life of Blessed Margaret of Castello: 1287-1320" and released in second and third English language editions (1979; 1983) by different publishers.

Another secondary source of information about Blessed Margaret is the work, *Beata Margherita de la Metola: Una Sfida Alla Emarginazione*, written by Italian author Ubaldo Valentini and published in 1988.[25] Valentini's book provides further details of Margaret's legend identifying ministries dedicated to her memory such as the "L' Istituto Beata Margherita Cieca della Metola" ("The Blessed Margaret of Metola

---

[24] Bonniwell, 1952, x.
[25] Valentini.

Institute for the Blind"), founded in Italy by Msgr. Giacinto Faeti in 1920, as well as describing a variety of Italian shrines, paintings and statues memorializing Blessed Margaret. Valentini also documented numerous healings which occurred through the intercession of Margaret after her death; and, of notable importance, is his account and pictorial inclusion of 32 Seventeenth-century lunettes depicting significant incidents in the blessed's life.

A twenty-first century (2011) Italian account of Blessed Margaret's legend is the work, *Beata Margherita di Citta di Castello*, by journalist Barbara Sartori.[26] The book's publisher commented that although Margaret's legend includes "aspects of the culture of an era long gone from us," it's importance, nevertheless, is the description of an "incredible experience of a person humanly disadvantaged living with serenity and abandonment to God."[27] Barbara Sartori notes that, in writing her account of Margaret's life, two versions of the *"Legenda"* provided information; they are described as the two Latin works "renamed 'maior' and 'minor' legends."[28] These, Sartori asserted, are "different texts by different authors but they contain "substantially identical content."[29]

Sartori also commented on use of the word "legend" to describe the life, or *vita*, of Blessed Margaret, noting that "the term 'legend' in our contemporary thought suggests a fairytale or (the) imaginary but scholars who have dealt with the examination of the two writings (described above) never doubted their historicity with regard to the biographical data and (data) essential to the spiritual life of Margaret."[30] B. Sartori adds, however, "of course we must not forget that we are facing two hagiographic texts, not two chronicles."[31]

In discussing hagiography and the lives of the saints, Michael Goodich asserted, nevertheless, that the legend of Margaret of *Citta di Castello* is "documented by three nearly contemporary biographies based on notarized statements testifying to her virtuous life and miracles"; in particular Goodich cites the works of M.H. Laurent, "La plus Ancienne Legende de la B. Marguerite de Citta di Castello," *Archivum Fratrum Praedicatorum*, 10 (1940), pp. 109-131; "Vita Beatae Margaritae Virginis de Civitate Castelli Sororis Tertii Ordinis de Paenitentia Sancti

---

[26] Sartori.
[27] Sartori, Back Cover
[28] Sartori, 10.
[29] Ibid.
[30] Ibid.
[31] Ibid.

Dominici," *Analecta Bollandiana*, 19 (1900), pp. 22-36; and William R. Bonniwell, *The Life of Margaret of Castello*, Dublin, U.K.: Clonmore and Reynolds, 1955.[32]

Barbara Sartori's book also includes photographs of chapels, altars, statues and paintings, created in both Italy and the United States, to honor the memory of Blessed Margaret.

As well as the above publications, considered as primary and secondary sources for the present exploration of Blessed Margaret's life and ministry, a number of other books, chapters and journal articles were reviewed for material descriptive of and relevant to Margaret's medieval world, to her spirituality and to her service to the sick and the outcast. These included works related to such topics as: life in a medieval castle, the medieval church (including the role of the priest as castle chaplain), the anchoress vocation, the spirituality of solitude, mystical spirituality, the tertiary vocation (the Sisters of Penance of St. Dominic), the role of a "wounded healer," medieval medicine (care of the sick in their homes), life and ministry in medieval prisons, and healing miracles in the medieval era.[v]

Hagiography

It must be admitted that the early biographical writings about Margaret of Castello may be said to fall into the genre of hagiography; that is, the authors presented numerous positive virtues attributed to Blessed Margaret without acknowledging spiritual failings or weaknesses. Nevertheless, extant literature suggests that there is historical confirmation of the many anecdotes recorded in these hagiographical works.

Such inspirational accounts of the lives of holy people, especially those written during the middle ages, generally do describe only the positive virtues of an individual while notably omitting mention of faults. Thus, these hagiographical writings are sometimes criticized as being biased and inaccurate. If, however, one understands that the purpose of a work is in fact to inspire and uplift the reader, hagiography can be accepted in the spirit in which it is written.

In an early work entitled *The Legends of the Saints: An Introduction to Hagiography*, it is asserted that "in order to be strictly hagiographic, the document should be of a religious character and should aim at

---

[32] Michael E. Goodich, *Lives and Miracles of the Saints: Studies in Medieval Latin Hagiography* (Burlington, Vt.: Ashgate Publishing, 2004), 130.

edification."[33] The author adds: "The term may only be applied therefore to writings inspired by devotion to the saints and intended to promote it."[34]

Hagiographical sources of this kind can be useful "to expand the theological tradition," especially for the period of the Middle Ages "when more obvious sources are wanting."[35] Unfortunately, "anachronistic ideas of hagiography and genre have obscured the creativity of many works."[36] Nevertheless, medieval hagiographies, such as those written about Margaret of Castello, seem to have been the most beloved by the faithful.[37]

The Lunettes

As noted earlier, a significant contribution to Blessed Margaret's legend is Ubaldo Valentini's description and pictorial reproduction of 32 lunettes depicting significant occurrences in the blessed's life. The existence of these lunettes, commissioned in the mid-17th Century by the Prior of a Dominican Convent in *Citta di Castello*, represent critically important data as they contain both visual and written identification and validation of key occurrences in the spiritual life and ministry of Blessed Margaret.

In art or architecture, a lunette is identified as a half-moon or crescent shaped space or painting; lunette shaped panels were characteristic of medieval paintings.[38] The lunettes pictured in Valentini's work reproduce a series of crescent shaped paintings located in the lower level of the cloister of a 17th-century Dominican convent adjacent to the now deconsecrated church of San Domenico in *Citta di Castello*. Valentini described the convent cloister noting that "in the gallery below there were painted 32 lunettes illustrating the life and miracles of the blessed."[39] Five of the paintings (Lunettes 3, 4, 5, 9, and

---

[33] Hippolyte DeLehaye, *The Legends of the Saints: An Introduction to Hagiography* (London, U.K.: Longmans, Green and Co., 1907), 2.

[34] Ibid.

[35] Marie A. Mayeski, "New voices in the Tradition: Medieval Hagiography Revisited," *Theological Studies* 63:4 (2002), 690-710, 690.

[36] Anna Taylor, "Hagiography and Early Medieval History," *Religion Compass* 7:1 (2013): 1-14, 1.

[37] Thomas J. Heffernan, *Sacred Biography: Saints and their Biographies in the Middle Ages* (New York: Oxford University Press, 1988).

[38] Victor M. Schmidt, "The Lunette-Shapted Panel and Some Characteristics of Panel Painting," *Studies in the History of Art* 61:1 (2002): 82-101; Edward J. Olszewski, "A Possible Source for the Triptych, Lunette and Tondo Formats in Renaissance Paintings," *Notes in the History of Art* 28:2 (2009): 5-11.

[39] Valentini, 118.

10) were attributed to the artist Giovanni Battista Pacetti (Lo Squazzino); the remaining 27 lunettes (circa 1662) were painted by Salvi Castellucci.[40] The artwork was commissioned by the convent's Dominican Prior, Master Lorenzo Giustini, and financed by donations from local families as well as by alms that Prior Giustini "collected during his popular sermons, as evidenced by an inscription."[41]

It is reported that "the same Father Prior then wrote next to each bezel a legend in Latin for scholars and in Italian for the people."[42] In Valentini's pictorial reproduction of the lunettes one can see the inscriptions beneath each painting with both the Latin and Italian narratives of the occurrence depicted. The value of such lunettes and their narrative images is reflected in the comments of an art historian who noted that from the early Christian era "visual imagery served an important role in communication as well as embellishment."[43] This was related to the fact that the audience "was not always capable of or concerned with reading texts."[44]

The series of Blessed Margaret of Castello lunettes begins with "The Birth of the Blessed," in 1287.[45]

The second lunette depicts Margaret's "Prayer (for a miraculous healing) before the Tomb of Blessed Giacomo" in *Citta di Castello*.[46]

Lunette number three illustrates Margaret's consecration of her life to God and reception of the habit of a Sister of Penance of St. Dominic;[47] and lunette four pictures Blessed Margaret in ecstasy, levitating above the floor.[48]

Lunettes five, six, and seven all describe miraculous occurrences at the home of two of Margaret's hosts in *Citta di Castello*, Venturino and Grigia, the extinguishing of a serious fire by covering the flames with Blessed Margaret's mantle; the teaching and correcting of lessons, although herself blind, of Venturino and Grigia's children; and the healing of a bedridden young relative of the family.[49]

---

[40] Ibid.
[41] Ibid.
[42] Ibid., 118-119.
[43] James Snyder, *Medieval Art, Painting, Sculpture, Architecture, 4th-14th Century* (N.Y.: Harry N. Abrams Inc., 1989), 15.
[44] Ibid.
[45] Valentini, 121.
[46] Ibid., 122.
[47] Ibid., 123.
[48] Ibid., 124.
[49] Ibid., 125-127.

Lunette eight depicts yet another miraculous healing, that of curing the diseased eye of Sister Venturella.[50]

Lunette number nine reflects an oft repeated anecdote telling of the newly deceased Blessed Margaret's healing of a mute and crippled girl brought to her casket in the Dominican church of Santa Maria della Carita. Margaret is said to have raised her hand and touched the child who immediately stood up and shouted: "I am healed by the power of Blessed Margaret."[51]

Lunettes ten and eleven also picture healings, one of a man bitten by a bear while cutting firewood in the forest, the other of a child drowned in the river and thought to be dead.[52]

Lunette twelve displays a famous quotation engraved on Margaret's tomb: "If only you knew what I carry in my heart"; also pictured are three stones, one imprinted with an image representative of the child Jesus, the second with an image reminiscent of the Blessed Virgin, and the third stone containing an image identified as that of St. Joseph; these were reportedly found in Margaret's heart on autopsy.[53]

Lunettes thirteen, fourteen, fifteen, and sixteen also depict Margaret's healings including relief of a man with an incurable shoulder wound, curing of an arthritic with joint infirmities, healing of a child ill with a pestilential fever and cure of a woman with cancer of the face.[54]

Lunette seventeen pictures the transference of Blessed Margaret's body to a new urn in the presence of numerous clergy; it was reported to have been "found whole, beautiful and blew a most sweet odor."[55]

The eighteenth lunette illustrates a scenario in which a Governor of the city, who had criticized the incensing of Margaret's body, was ultimately restored to health by her intercession.[56]

Lunettes 19 through 31 depict a series of miraculous healings obtained through Blessed Margaret's intercession after her death; these include the healings of: a young man who fell from a high window and was thought dead; a blind man, not healed earlier for little faith; a woman with breast cancer; a Sister with a chest problem and swollen face; a woman entering into a dangerous childbirth; a man tormented by evil spirits; a man with an abdominal hernia; a man with a severely

---

[50] Ibid., 128.
[51] Ibid., 129.
[52] Ibid., 130-131.
[53] Ibid., 132.
[54] Ibid., 133-136.
[55] Ibid., 137.
[56] Ibid., 138.

broken leg; four paralyzed persons; a child with shrunken limbs; two brothers, one with loss of hearing and speech, the other experiencing severe headaches and fever; a 4 year old who had an accidental fall; and a man unjustly imprisoned for whom the prison doors suddenly opened.[57]

Finally, lunette number thirty-two, the last of the series, illustrates the preserved state of Blessed Margaret's incorrupt body despite exposing the interior of her burial urn to the open air.[58]

A number of the above identified anecdotes of Margaret's legend are described in detail in the following chapters.

"Little Margaret"'s World

The "Medieval Biographer" tells us that Blessed Margaret's "origen was spiritual and timely"; her father Parisio, was "Lord of the 'Castle Metola' in the region of Massa Trabaria," Italy.[59] Parisio was a "Capitaneus," or captain, a distinguished military title; his young wife was named "Emilia." Massa Trabaria was a 13th-century papal state adjacent to which, on a high peak, was the Castle of Metola. In this era, Italy was a fledgling country "experiencing continual warfare among its various regions."[60] Margaret's parents to be, Parisio and Emilia, were "members of the upper echelons of the Italian nobility... their family name has never been revealed."[61]

Parisio and Emilia, as Lord and Lady of the Castle Metola, were in the spring of 1287, anxiously awaiting the birth of their first child. As a noble couple, they had planned an extravagant celebration to honor the birth as well as the forthcoming Baptism; it was hoped that the infant would be a son and heir to the family fortune. The Castle staff had been kept "on alert" for some days in order to have adequate food and wine prepared for guests and visiting dignitaries as soon as the birth was announced.

The birth of a child is almost always considered by the family to be a cause for celebration. In the middle ages the occasion was even more valued for "birth in the pre-modern era could be a hazardous affair."[62]

---

[57] Ibid., 139-151.
[58] Ibid., 152.
[59] *Blessed Margaret of Castello OP*, 15.
[60] Janice McGrane, *Saints to Lean On: Spiritual Companions for Illness and Disability* (Cincinnati, Ohio: St. Anthony Messenger Press, 2006), 2.
[61] Ibid.
[62] Louis Haas, "Women and Childbearing in Medieval Florence," in (pp. 88-99) Cathy J. Itnyre (Ed) *Medieval Family Roles* (N.Y., N.Y.: Garland Publishing Inc., 1996), p. 94-95, 94.

Because of lack of prenatal care, both mother and infant might be afflicted with a variety of complications both prior to and immediately after the birth. Thus, the mother was to be greatly congratulated and comforted after a successful delivery and "relief, joy and sense of accomplishment (were evident) in letters that were sent announcing a new arrival."[63] Clearly, Parisio and Emilia must have been anticipating sharing that "joy" and "sense of accomplishment" in birth announcements which would be sent to friends and neighbors.

Parental Rejection

Sadly, however, there was no rejoicing at the Castle Metola on the day the child was born. There would be no birth announcements. There was to be no party, no grand celebration, for the newborn child, a girl, "was dreadfully deformed."[64] Parisio and Emilia's horror was accompanied by denial and immediate rejection of the little one. In the words of the Medieval Biographer: "Both her parents, when they observed their daughter was born small and deformed, were caused by very much grief to rid themselves of her."[65] But, the biographer added: Little Margaret was beautiful in God's eyes and "thus, the one whom the world began to despise, Divine Goodness decreed to restore."[66]

Fr. Bonniwell reported that the infant was so small that it appeared she would "never reach normal height... In addition, she was hunchbacked. As the right leg was much shorter than the left, it was also obvious that the girl would be lame...and...a week or so after her birth the parents discovered that...she was totally blind."[67] Because of embarrassment over the child's physical challenges, her parents determined to simply announce that the newborn was frail and not expected to live; this would explain their grief and serve as a cover for their complete and absolute rejection of the less than perfect infant. The child was immediately handed over to the care of a trusted castle nursemaid.

The Baptism

Despite the parents' rejection of the child, and much to the consternation of Parisio and Emilia, the Castle Chaplain, Fra Giacomo Cappellano, insisted that the baby be baptized; infant baptism was

---

[63] Ibid., 95.
[64] Bonniwell, 2014, 6.
[65] *Blessed Margaret of Castello OP,* 15.
[66] Ibid., 16.
[67] Bonniwell, 2014, 7.

considered a serious responsibility of the priest in the 13th Century.[68] Because of the dangers associated with childbirth and infancy in the medieval era, "a newborn infant was immediately prepared for Baptism, lest it die in a state of original sin";[69] in the Middle Ages, "Baptism was usually carried out between the first and the third day of life."[70] The sacrament of Baptism was "considered vitally important as the Church taught that the unbaptized could not enter heaven,"[71] the effect of Baptism being "the remission of original and actual sin and removal of the penalty."[72]

Baptism, usually performed by a priest at the parish church was, in the medieval era, "not merely a religious occasion. In a society where church and community were so closely associated, religious observances invariably became important social events. After the Baptism, it was common to have some sort of celebration involving the child's family and their friends and the occasion was often marked by gift giving."[73] Medieval Baptisms also generally involved the participation of godparents, who, after the infant had been blessed by the priest, would offer "a profession of faith for the child."[74] The godparents "made the Christian renunciations and promises on the child's behalf and were thereafter related by 'spiritual affinity.'"[75] This medieval spiritual affinity or spiritual kinship "was an important social glue which created networks of friends and allies beyond those provided by common ancestry and marriage."[76]

Considering both the Church's and the community's religious and social expectations associated with an infant's reception of the sacrament of Baptism, a dilemma arose as to how to respond to the Castle Chaplain's insistence on Baptism and yet not bring shame to the noble parents, Parisio and Emilia. Parisio was especially averse to any suggestion that his child be baptized at a nearby church where her

---

[68] Kevin E. Lawson, "Baptismal Theology and Practices and the Spiritual Nurture of Children, Part I: Early and Medieval Church," *Christian Education Journal* 8:1 (2011): 130-145.

[69] Frances Gies and Joseph Gies, *Life in a Medieval Village* (N.Y. Harper & Row, 1990), 117.

[70] Joseph Lynch, *The Medieval Church: A Brief History* (London: Longman, 1992), 276.

[71] Jeffrey L. Singman, *The Middle Ages: Everyday Life in Medieval Europe* (N.Y.: Sterling, 2013), 20.

[72] Roland H. Bainton, *The Medieval Church* (N.Y.: Van Nostrand, 1962), 145.

[73] Singman, 21.

[74] Gies and Gies, 119.

[75] Margaret Deanesly, *A History of the Medieval Church* (London, U.K.: Routledge, 1989), 201.

[76] Lynch, 277.

infirmities would be on public display. It was thus decided that the nursemaid, into whose care the little one had been entrusted, would bring her to be baptized privately at a distant parish.

A Blessed "Pearl"

A scholar of medieval religion noted that "one of the most important elements of the Baptismal Ceremony was the assigning of a name."[77] He added: "the child at Baptism received only a single name; the term 'Christian name' still survives today"[78] and pointed out that the parents chose the baptismal name which often was the name of an honored saint or "a traditional name from the child's family."[79] Clearly, these options would not have been acceptable to Parisio and Emilia; thus, the choosing of their infant's name was left to the decision of the nursemaid who presented her for the sacrament. The nurse chose the name Margherita (Margaret). In commenting on the nursemaid's choice, Fr. William Bonniwell wryly observed: "In so doing she surely did not reflect on the meaning of the word, for Margherita means 'pearl.'"[80]

Did the nurse truly "not reflect on the meaning of the word"? Now, over seven centuries later, we cannot determine why Lady Emilia's servant chose the name of Margaret for her small charge, but we might speculate. Perhaps the nursemaid did indeed reflect on the meaning of the name Margherita and selected it purposely as a gift for the desperately fragile infant whose life, she recognized, would not be easy, if survival were even possible. It may have been that the nurse's loving eyes saw in "Little Margaret" only the beauty of a precious child of God rather than only the physical deformities which had so repelled her parents. In fact, the newborn being named "Margherita" was a blessed gift of God who alone knew the appropriateness of the name for His beloved child.

Medieval Castle Life

For the first six years of her life, "Little Margaret" lived comfortably in the family castle under the guidance and supervision of her nursemaid and the other servants; she was also blessed by the religious tutelage of the castle chaplain, Fra Giacomo Cappellano.[81] Thus, it is helpful to

---

[77] Singman, 21.
[78] Ibid.
[79] Ibid.
[80] Bonniwell, 2014, 8.
[81] Ibid.

briefly explore the environment and atmosphere of the medieval castle where Margaret's early spirituality was formed and blossomed.

Italian Castles in the Middle Ages, "castellum," were "fortified residences usually those of a local Lord."[82] As they often stood on "irregular terrain, the castles of northern Italy were influenced by military models."[83] The first castles were built of wood but "from the twelfth century onward, castles were generally built of stone."[84] A number of castles were "constructed within or adjacent to towns by their feudal overlords, serving at once as protection and as a reminder of the lord's authority."[85] "Little Margaret"'s father, Parisio, identified earlier as a "Capitanus," indeed had a "lord's authority" over the local citizenry.

By the era of the Twelfth Century, "the castle was beginning to take on much more of the shape of a permanent residence…housing a variety of different people."[86] The castle residents included administrators and clerks who ran the estate; next in importance were the "religious representatives; some of these would be administrators also."[87] Authors of *Life in a Medieval Castle*, Joseph and Frances Gies, provide a description of one 12th-century castle as having two stories containing storerooms, as well as common rooms for the residents and servants; sleeping rooms for the lord and lady and a dormitory for the children.[88]

One of the most important architectural structures of the medieval castle was the chapel. The castle chapel was viewed as "an indispensable feature where the lord and his family heard morning Mass."[89] Often the chapel was built two stories high "with the nave divided horizontally; the family sat in the upper part…while the servants occupied the lower part."[90] Some castles had two chapels "and an attached sacristy for housing liturgical objects."[91]

---

[82] Clemente Manenti, *Castles in Italy: The Medieval Life of Noble Families* (Cologne, Germany: Konemann, 2001), 76.
[83] Ibid.
[84] Singman, 122.
[85] Ibid
[86] Philip Warner, *The Medieval Castle* (London: Penguin Books, 2001), 191.
[87] Ibid., 191-192.
[88] Joseph Gies and Frances Gies, *Life in a Medieval Castle* (N.Y.: Harper Perennial, 2015), 57-58.
[89] Ibid., 70.
[90] Ibid.
[91] Singman, 134.

Usually the "castle household was astir at daybreak" at which time servants began their rounds of chores prior to Mass and breakfast.[92] A schedule described for one medieval castle household suggested that the lady of the family might "rise at 7AM to hear Matins followed by a Mass, and a prescribed second Mass toward midday"; such regular devotions were considered "routine in the high middle ages."[93] If the castle of Captain Parisio and his wife Emilia was similar in architecture and daily schedule to those described, it is understandable that, as is noted later, little Margherita learned to love spending time in prayer, even as a small child.

The Castle Chaplain

During Margaret's early years, the Metola Castle Chaplain, Fra Giacomo Cappellano, "began to teach (Margaret) the rudiments of religion" and recognized her "remarkable intelligence"; this was communicated to her parents but they remained "cold and uninterested."[94] The "Medieval Biographer" explained that the "angels in heaven" had early taken "Little Margaret" under their care as she was "lucid in zeal and beautiful and gracious to God."[95] Margaret, he asserted, "was born deprived of physical eyes, for fear that she would see the world; she was nourished by Divine light, so that standing on earth, she might see heaven; she was formed in a very small body, so that she would thoroughly enjoy a mind protected by sublime humility."[96] Thus, Blessed Margaret was born prepared to receive the religious teaching provided by the kind and caring castle chaplain.

A castle chaplain or chancellor is described as a "priest or monk in charge of the chapel and of the secretarial department of the castle";[97] in fact, the chaplain may have been one of the few castle residents who could write. The chaplain, as a priest, was expected to have some degree of literacy.[98] While the specific duties of chaplains serving in medieval castles varied, the role was one of significant prestige for the religious life of the community of residents. Although castle chaplains were often administrators and teachers, as well as pastors, their ministry was welcomed by noble families and servants alike.

---

[92] Ibid., 109-111.
[93] Ibid., 151.
[94] Bonniwell, 2014, 8.
[95] *Blessed Margaret of Castello OP,* 16.
[96] Ibid.
[97] Gies and Gies, *Life in a Medieval Castle,* 229.
[98] Ibid.

While the chaplain or chancellor "was in charge of the chapel or chancel (the altar area of a church)...the chaplain and his assistants" might also assume secretarial duties.[99] As well as presiding at Mass, "the chaplain kept the lord's seal and wrote his business and personal letters...his clerk took charge of the vessels and vestments for Mass (and)...other clerks assisted with the accounts, ran errands and made purchases."[100] Another important duty of the chaplain's staff was taking charge of "offerings to the poor."[101] The almoner distributed all leftover castle food to those in need in the local village.[102]

When considering the prestige and the variety of important duties which fell within the purview of the castle chaplain, it is not difficult to understand why Fra Cappellano's earlier noted demand that Margaret be baptized, had to be honored by her parents. Parisio and Emilia could not find a reason to countermand the specific order of the castle's religious and administrative leader.

While a few castle chaplains may have had some university education, many did not. They prepared for their ministry by "reading, by attending a local cathedral school, by hearing sermons and by living in a clerical group."[103] Those who had the opportunity of attending "cathedral schools, monastic schools and the universities were more likely to become teachers, church officials or secretaries in noble households."[104] Regardless of educational background a primary function of the priest was that of instruction: "He was to teach the children the Creed, the Lord's Prayer, the Ave and the Ten Commandments."[105]

Children of the castle "did their lessons under the guidance of a tutor, commonly the chaplain."[106] Thus, it was natural that, despite her physical challenges, "Little Margaret" would begin to be taught her religious duties and other lessons by the castle chaplain, Fra Cappellano. One might determine, from his role in teaching Margaret, that Fra Cappellano had received some degree of theological or spiritual education. As spiritual teacher and guide, Fra Cappellano viewed the young Margaret as having a keenly intelligent mind with which she understood her present suffering, and, it was believed that a time would

---

[99] Gies and Gies, *Life in a Medieval Castle*, 95-96.
[100] Ibid., 105
[101] Ibid.
[102] Ibid.
[103] Lynch, 296
[104] Gies and Gies, *Life in a Medieval Village*, 169.
[105] Ibid.
[106] Ibid., 112.

come when she would "bless the day she was born blind and deformed."[107] Fr. Bonniwell posits that Fra Cappellano might have explained Little Margaret's burdens of physical challenge and parental rejection as part of her road to loving and serving God; that to love God one does not need "eyesight, or a normal body, or the love and affection of fellow man, agreeable and pleasant as all these things are."[108]

Citing a possible observation of Fra Cappellano, Bonniwell mused: "Little Margaret understands...that one of the most efficacious ways in which love can be deepened, strengthened and purified, is by suffering. Our Savior taught us that the royal road to perfect love is the Cross. Everyone has noticed how contented and cheerful Margaret has always been; the reason is that she regards her handicaps and deformities as being merely the means by which she can surely reach her God."[109]

Such an explanation of Little Margaret's spirituality, coming from the castle chaplain, would have carried weight for castle residents as, in the 13th Century, the church was a "society" in which clergy "directed the thoughts and activities of a receptive laity-kings, magnates and peasants alike."[110]

Parisio's Decision

In the Castle, Margaret, because of her physical challenges, was, at least during part of the day "sequestered in a room under the care of a nurse."[111] Although many biographers have criticized Margaret's family "for the cruel treatment accorded her...at an early age, she allegedly devoted herself to religious self-denial" and prayer.[112] "Little Margaret" found comfort and joy in these religious practices as well as through the spiritual support and teaching of her mentor and guide Fra Giacomo Cappellano.

At around the age of six, however, a problem arose to destroy Margaret's peaceful existence in the Castle at Metola. A visitor to the castle engaged "Little Margaret" in conversation, and the child, unwittingly, almost disclosed her noble parentage. Fortunately, the exchange was overheard by a servant who quickly whisked Margaret away to her room before the guest could ask any more questions.

---

[107] Bonniwell, 2014, 17.
[108] Ibid., 16.
[109] Ibid.
[110] R.W. Southern, *Western Society and the Church in the Middle Ages* (N.Y.: Penguin Books, 1976), 38.
[111] Goodich, 130.
[112] Ibid.

Unfortunately, the incident reached the ears of Parisio and Emilia who were horrified on hearing of the encounter. They were terrified at the thought of word going out to all the neighbors that the Lady of the Castle Metola had given birth to a seriously disabled child and determined that something had to be done immediately or their carefully kept secret would be discovered.

In an imagined conversation between Parisio and Emilia, Fr. Bonniwell described Parisio's solution: that of enclosing Margaret in a small cell to be constructed adjacent to a chapel in the forest named "The Church of St. Mary of the Fortress of Metola."[113] Parisio argued that Margaret would be safe there and out of sight as very few parishioners visited the chapel. Thus, he reasoned, Little Margaret could have the joy of spending long hours in the chapel praying from morning to night, which, he observed, would make their daughter happy. As a rationale for his suggestion, Parisio reminded his wife, Emilia, of the account, related to them by Fra Cappellano, concerning the enclosed life of prayer and penance undertaken by an anchoress named St. Veridiana.

Emilia is thought to have possibly recounted the incident as follows: "The chaplain said that this saint (Veridiana) wanted to do penance so she had a small cell built next to a church...The cell had a tiny window through the church wall so that the recluse could see the altar and attend Mass but could not be seen by the congregation. On the other side of the cell was another small window through which food was passed to the saint...the chaplain said that she lived there for over thirty years."[114]

St. Veridiana

St. Veridiana, lived from 1182 to 1242 in Castelfiorentino, near Florence, Italy; she was born into a noble family, the Attavani. According to her legend, she had, at the age of twelve, while assisting some relatives, distributed to the poor a great quantity of food which had been stored in her uncle's warehouse. Unbeknownst to the young woman, the food had already been promised to a local buyer. When the uncle found his warehouse empty he reproached his niece angrily. Veridiana, in sorrow for her mistake, prayed all night and in the morning found the room again filled with food.

When the neighbors heard of the miracle they began to besiege Veridiana for help. In order to avoid publicity and acclaim, Veridiana went on pilgrimage to Rome but, on return, she was begged not to leave again. Ultimately Veridiana agreed if "She could live like an anchorite

---

[113] Bonniwell, 2014, 12.
[114] Ibid., 11.

(hermit). The town erected a small cell next to a church, and it became Veridiana's home for the next 34 years."[115]

Veridiana, sometimes called "Verdiana," was "not formally canonized but Pope Clement VII approved devotion to her in 1533. She is referred to as "saint" in most Franciscan histories,[116] and it is believed that St. Francis once visited her in her cell.

In discussing "Anchorites in the Italian Tradition", Mario Sensi noted that little was known about the anchoritic "liturgy of reclusion" in medieval Italy.[117] He comments, however, that in a *vita* of Veridiana of Castelfiorentino, we do find a description of her liturgy explaining that on returning from the pilgrimage to Rome, she was formally enclosed in a cell that had been prepared for her: "When the day of her clothing ceremony was fixed, the people were called together and the parish priest, after having received her vow of obedience...blessing the habit and the veil, he dressed and veiled her, and put his Canon in charge of her in order that he might lead her in, after which she was accompanied by a procession to her cell and was walled in."[118] Veridiana, is considered an "Italian Ancillae" or "Servant of God."[119]

Fr. William Bonnewill's account of Blessed Margaret's seclusion in a religious cell or "anchorhold" is supported by that of the Canon of *Citta di Castello* in his medieval biography: "Fearing that the noble daughter, so deformed, would be seen by visitors, a certain cell was prepared by her father in which the innocent and kind girl was enclosed."[120] The Medieval Biographer explained: "And, thus, through the serious transgression of her father, Margaret was invited to penitence; there was kindness in her penitence, though, because she appealed to God in behalf of sinners, offering her suffering for them."[121]

Shocking as the decision of "Little Margaret"'s parents may seem today, there was some precedent, in the medieval era, for committing a small child, for spiritual reasons, to life in a religious setting outside of the family home. One example is that of Saint Hildegard of Bingen whose parents felt, that as she was their "tenth" child, she should be "tithed" to the church. Thus, Hildegard was apprenticed to live with a Benedictine

---

[115] Sarah Gallick, *The Big Book of Woman Saints* (N.Y.: HarperSanFrancisco, 2007), 63.
[116] Ibid., 413.
[117] Mario Sensi, "Anchorites in the Italian Tradition," pp. 62-90 in Ed. Liz Herbert McAvoy, *Anchoritic Traditions in Medieval Europe* (Rochester, N.Y.: The Boydell Press, 2010), 71.
[118] Ibid.
[119] Goodich, 131.
[120] *Blessed Margaret of Castello OP*, 16-17.
[121] Ibid., 17.

anchoress at the age of only 8 years (Hildegard of Bingen's experience as a child "anchoress" is explored in the following chapter).

And, in discussing "Children and their Parents from the Ninth to the Thirteenth Century," Mary McLaughlin validates the practice that some children were, for religious reasons, made "exiles" from their homes at an early age. In one example, McLaughlin recounts the lament of a male child sent to a monastery to fulfill a vocation chosen by his father: "So weeping my father gave me away, a weeping child, into the care of the Monk Reginald, and sent me away into exile for love of Thee and never saw me again."[122]

Another important point, when considering the removal of young children from their homes was the medieval understanding of childhood. In discussing "The Matter of the Medieval Child," J. Allan Mitchell identified an early attitude toward children as a 'marginalization' of infancy in the medieval mental life,' proof that in 'Une Societe Adultocentriste,' children were bound to be abject or indifferent members."[123] For some in the middle ages "children under seven did not count for much because of their immaturity and expendability."[124] While Jeffrey Singman admits that the first six years of life "did constitute a recognizable stage in the life of a medieval child", he adds that "during this time, the child had virtually no responsibilities. Life consisted of a daily round of food, sleep and play. It was not common for a child to be sent to school before the age of seven, although basic tutoring might begin earlier."[125] This perception of the minimal productivity and low expectations of the medieval child may have supported a decision to move a child from the bosom of the nuclear family into the environment of a religious community where a virtuous life might be embraced.

In the case of "Little Margaret" of Castello's removal from the "bosom of the nuclear family," while ostensibly carried out to support development of her childhood spirituality, the underlying rationale was parental rejection. Margaret's physical afflictions were an embarrassment to her noble parents. With their child safely enclosed in an anchoress' cell, Parisio and Emilia could now deny her existence in their daily lives, and, they hoped, for many years to come.

---

[122] Mary M. McLaughlin, "Survivors and Surrogates: Children and Parents from the Ninth to the Thirteenth Centuries" (PP. 20-124), in (Ed.) Carol Neel, *Medieval Families: Perspectives on Marriage, Household & Children* (Toronto: University of Toronto Press, 2004), pp. 45-46, 46.

[123] J. Allan Mitchell, *Becoming Human: The Matter of the Medieval Child* (Minneapolis: University of Minnesota Press, 2014), 33.

[124] Ibid.

[125] Singman, 25.

As well as providing documentation of the literary sources for *Blessed Margaret of Castello: Servant of the Sick and the Outcast*, this chapter has described important components of Blessed Margaret's Legend: her early spirituality, parental rejection, Baptism and naming, medieval castle life, the pastoral role of the castle chaplain and Parisio and Emilia's decision to enclose their daughter in an anchoritic cell at age six.

In the following chapter young Margaret's next 13 years, lived as a religious anchoress, is explored.

ENDNOTES for Chapter 1. "A Lasting Beauty"

[i] Blessed Margaret is sometimes identified as "Margaret of Metola." She was born in a castle in Metola, Italy, a small, mountainous village neighboring *Citta di Castello*, a city in the Province of Perugia. Margaret lived in Metola, first in the family castle until the age of six, and then, for the next thirteen years, enclosed in a small cell next to a chapel in the forest of Metola. Her parents removed her from the enclosure because of local warfare and placed her, for a time, in an underground vault in the family *palazzo* in Mercatello; she was later taken to a Francisan Shrine in *Citta di Castello* in hope of a miraculous cure of her afflictions. When the miracle did not occur, Margaret was abandoned in *Citta di Castello*, where she ultimately became a Dominican Tertiary ministering to the sick and the outcast during the final decade of her life. Thus, today, Margaret is more frequently identified as "Margaret of Castello," rather than "Margaret of Metola." *Citta di Castello* is the home of *La Chiesa di San Domenico* where the incorrupt body of Blessed Margaret is currently venerated.

[ii] "In the absence of contemporaneous documentary claims directly connected to Margaret, it should be noted that certain references in her hagiographic story have real historical confirmation. It is certain, for example, that the (Order of) Preachers were in Citta di Castello at least since 1270 and before the 13th and 14th centuries consolidated their position...furthermore (the names of) four preachers explicitly mentioned in the *recensiones* for their presence at the time of the discovery of the three stones in Margaret's heart...seem to be found in the Acts of the late Thirteenth century" (Ref.: Giovanna Casagrande, "Margherita da Citta di Castello." In *Dizionario Biografico degli Italiani*, Volume 70, 2008, pp. 660-687, Pub. Istituto dell'Enciclopedia Italiana (Bologna, Italy). Cited in
http://www.Treccani.it/enciclopedia/margherita-da-citta-di-castello_(Dizionario-Biografico)/.

[iii] Permission was received to cite from Fr. William Bonniwell's letters to his Provincial, Fr. T.S. McDermott OP, dating from February 1, 1949 to June 1, 1951, as housed in the "Dominican Provincial Archives," St. Joseph Province, Providence College, Providence, Rhode Island, July, 2016).

[iv] In the early to mid-Twentieth Century, when Fr. William Bonniwell was seeking a publisher for his work on Blessed Margaret, books describing the lives of Catholic saints and blesseds tended to be written in the style of popular piety. That is, the lives of these holy persons frequently fell into the genre of historical novel rather than that of history or biography. Classic examples are works of Louis De Wohl, such as *"The Quiet Light,"* a historical novel which depicts the life of St. Thomas Aquinas,

published in 1950 and Taylor Caldwell's well known novel of St. Luke entitled: *Dear and Glorious Physician,* published in 1959.)

ᵛ : Some examples of the books reviewed include: *Saints to Lean on: Spiritual Companions for Illness and Disability* (Janice McGrane); *Saints for the Sick* (Joan C. Cruz); *The Legends of the Saints: An Introduction to Hagiography* (Hippolyte DeLehaye); *Hunters of Souls: Dominican Saints and Blesseds* (Mary Jean Dorcy); *The Medieval Castle* (Philip Warner); *Life in a Medieval Castle* (Joseph and Frances Gies); *Castles in Italy: The Medieval Life of Noble Families* (Clementi Manenti); *Life in a Medieval Village* (Joseph and Frances Gies); *Medieval Family Roles* (Cathy J. Itnyere); *Medieval Children* (Nicholas Orme); *The Medieval Church* (Ronald H. Bainton); *Ancrene Wisse: Guide for Anchoresses* (anonymous); *Anchoretic Traditions in Medieval Europe* (Liz Herbert McAvoy); *Anchoretic Spirituality* (Anne Savage); *Dominican Penitent Women* (Mariju Lehmijoki-Gardner); *Women of the Medieval World* (Julius Kirshner & Susan Wemple); *Women Mystics in Medieval Europe* (Emilie Z. Brunn); *The Mystic Mind: The Psychology of Medieval Mystics and Ascetics* (Jerome Kroll); *Christian Healing in the Middle Ages and Beyond* (Frank C. Darling); *Miracle Cures: Saints, Pilgrimages and the Health Powers of Belief* (Roberta A. Scott); *The Wounded Healer* (Henri J.M. Nouwen); *Miracles and the Medieval Mind* (Benedicta Ward); *Medicine in the Middle Ages* (Ian Dawson); *The Medieval Prison: A Social History* (Guy Geltner); *Summary of the Rule of the Third Order* (Domenicans); *The Dominican Secular Third Order in the West* (Paul N. Zammit); *Manual of the Brothers and Sisters of the Third Order of Penance of St. Dominic* (Jean Baptiste Feuillet); and *The Dominican Order Convocation: A Study of the Growth and Representation in the Thirteenth Century* (Ernest Barker).

Examples of journal articles reviewed included such titles as: "Re-reading the Relationship between Devotional Images, Visions and the Body: Clare of Montefalco and Margaret of Citta di Castello" (Cordelia Warr); "Spiritual Devotion: Late Medieval Mysticism" (Gary Evans); "Enclosure and Solitude of the Heart" (Gail Fitzpatrick); "Holy Feast, Holy Fast: The Religious Significance of Food to Medieval Woman" (Caroline Bynum); "Woman of the Medieval Anchorhold" (Natalie Grinnell); "The Anchorhold as Symbolic Space in Ancrene Wisse" (Bob Hassenfratz); "True Anchoresses are Called Birds: Asceticism and Ascent and Purgative Mysticism of the Ancrene Wisse" (Mary A. Edsall); "Did the Middle Ages Believe in Miracles" (Steven Justice); "On Saints and Miracles" (Judy Rowley); "Representing Wonder in Medieval Miracle Narratives" (Axel Ruth); "Dimensions of Belief About Miraculous Healing" (Andrew Village); "The Resiliency of Children and Spirituality" (Annemie Dillen); "Children as Mystics, Activists, Sages and Holy Fools: Understanding the Spirituality of Children" (Joyce A. Mercer); "Nurturing a Child's Spirituality" (Rita Pfund); "Women Healers of the Middle Ages" (William L. Minkowski); "The Wounded Healer" (Serge Daneault); "The Dilemma of the Wounded Healer" (Noga Zerubavel and Margaret O. Wright); "Coping in Medieval Prisons" (Guy Geltner); and "Hagiography and Early Medieval History" (Ann Taylor).

Chapter 2. "The Darkness is Not Dark"

A Young Anchoress

"Even the darkness is not dark to you; the night is as bright as the day."
Psalm 139: 12

Christ's Light

Solitude guided young Margaret's path,
Yet no darkness permeated her prayerful day.

For the light of Christ shone in her heart,
And the love of Christ illumined the way.

The Potter was molding a sacred urn,
Blessed Margaret became His obedient clay.

Unfortunately, we do not have a detailed account of Blessed Margaret's entrance into her cell as described for St. Veridiana in the preceding chapter. We may trust, however, that the enclosure was done simply, with modest support from Little Margaret's mother, Emilia, who, Fr. Bonniwell mused, had been instructed to "explain to Margaret what a great privilege" was being bestowed upon her: "she'll be able to pray from morning to night without anyone disturbing her."[1] Her father, Parisio seems to have rationalized the enclosure with words to the effect that it would be for Margaret's own good, keeping her out of danger and preventing injuries which might have occurred had she remained in the environment of the castle fortress of Metola.

---

[1] William R. Bonniwell, *The Life of Blessed Margaret of Castello:1287-1320* (Charlotte, N.C.: Tan Books, 2014), 12.

Fr. Bonniwell briefly described Margaret's entrance to her new home as being carried out "with scant ceremony"...she was "thrust" into the cell and the mason "was ordered to wall up the doorway."[2]

While we can only guess at "Little Margaret"'s anxiety and lack of understanding of her sudden and unexpected seclusion, the teaching of Chaplain Cappellano must have taken root in her young heart. Fra Cappellano is described as going to visit Margaret and finding her in tears yet, on discovering the reason, was deeply moved. In imagined words, which Margaret, now a child anchoress, might have spoken, we hear: "Father, when they brought me here this morning, I did not understand...why did God let this happen to me. But now He has made it clear. Jesus was rejected even by His own people, and God is letting me be treated the same so that I can follow our dear Lord more closely."[3] Regardless of "her young age, Margaret's heart was ready to live the scandalous mystery of the Cross; to give herself, in her innocence as a child, as He had done, that Jesus who she so desired to love."[4]

Many writers have applauded Blessed Margaret's intelligence and "luminosity" of mind which was evident even in her early years:

> Margaret was remarkable for clarity of mind and for infused contemplation. She willingly embraced the cross because she saw suffering through the eyes of faith. She did not know why God permitted her to have so many afflictions; but what she did know, was that He never permits one single misfortune without good reason. Margaret often wondered why people pitied her since she viewed her suffering as the expression of Christ's love for her and her means to gain heaven.[5]

Although most biographers/hagiographers do not formally identify Blessed Margaret of Castello as an "anchoress," she did indeed experience an enclosed anchoritic religious life from ages six to eighteen years. Margaret's early vocation as an anchoress is, however, reflected in the writings of some medieval scholars. In his work *Cities of God: The Religion of the Italian Communes, 1125-1135*, historian Augustine

---

[2] Ibid.
[3] Ibid., 17
[4] Barbara Sartori, *Beata Margherita di Citta di Castello* (Milano, Italy: Paoline Editorale Libri, 2011), 26.
[5] Ronda Chervin, Terri V. Nichols and the Marian Women in Ministry, *Woman to Woman: Handing on our Experiences of the Joyful, Sorrowful and Glorious Mysteries of Life* (San Francisco: Ignatius Press, 1988), 124.

Thompson, O.P., asserted that "enclosure in an anchorhold did not prevent service to neighbor," and added medieval "women's *legendae* give glimpses of those who visited them and their requests."[6] Among Thompson's examples was one from Blessed Margaret's legend, which reported: "Donna Grigia asked Margherita of *Citta di Castello* to be godmother for her granddaughter and she agreed."[7]

Admittedly, the young Margaret did not herself choose anchoritic enclosure, but, with the support and teaching of a priest chaplain, she lovingly and joyfully accepted the enforced life of solitude as God's gift in drawing her closer to Him.

Anchoresses were "a frequent feature of medieval life...anchorites and anchoresses were enclosed...the word itself signifying one who dwelt in a cell 'beside the choir.'"[8] While a few male "anchorites" undertook the rigors of the enclosed religious vocation in the middle ages, the great majority of solitaries who embraced the life were women "anchoresses." Men, seeking a contemplative lifestyle, seemed more drawn to the peripatetic vocation of the "hermit"; the women leaned toward the stability of the cell or anchorhold.

In describing Italian anchorites, author Mario Sensi admits that "there is no proper history of the...eremitic movement."[9] There is, however, an appreciable body of literature about a number of individuals who lived as hermits or anchorites with or without professed vows. For some penitential women, such as Margaret of Cortona and Angela of Foligno, one finds biographies and testimonials, but for many others written history "did not go beyond the compilation of their vitae."[10] An example of the latter group Sensi identifies is "Margaret of *Citta di Castello*, 'the blind woman of Metola' (d. 1320), whose Legenda was written in a Dominican milieu by an anonymous friar at the end of the fourteenth century."[11] Mario Sensi pointed out that for some time such women were "understood as single phenomena...(and) venerated

---

[6] Augustine Thompson, *Cities of God: The Religion of the Italian Communes, 1125-1325* (University Park, Pa.: The Pennsylvania State University Press, 2005), 197.
[7] Ibid., 197.
[8] Margaret Deanesly, *A History of the Medieval Church* (London, U.K.: Routledge, 1989), 211.
[9] Mario Sensi, "Anchorites in the Italian Tradition," pp. 62-90 in Ed. Liz Herbert McAvoy, *Anchoritic Traditions in Medieval Europe* (Rochester, N.Y.: The Boydell Press, 2010), p. 62.
[10] Ibid., 64.
[11] Ibid

as saints and blessed (they were, however) only the conspicuous manifestations of a vast penitential movement with deep social roots."[12]

Although, as observed earlier, most biographers have not identified Blessed Margaret as an "anchoress," it is important to note that a 2010 work, *Anchoritic Traditions in Medieval Europe*, edited by contemporary medieval scholar Liz Herbert McAvoy, contains a chapter entitled "Anchorites in the Italian Tradition," in which Mario Sensi identifies Margaret of Castello as among those laywomen who were part of the "penitential movement." Most of the women, as Margaret *of Citta di Castello*, were mystics "bound to their city and its concerns."[13] Blessed Margaret's thirteen-year anchoritic experience, in the small cell attached to the Church of St. Mary of the Fortress of Metola, was the spiritual "proving ground" for her later apostolic ministry to the sick and the outcast in the impoverished homes and desolate prisons of *Citta di Castello*.

A Medieval Anchorhold
Margaret's Cell

There is no documentation identifying the physical architecture of Blessed Margaret's cell, or anchorhold, nor is there a description of her daily regimen of devotions. We can, however, gain some understanding of this important period in the young blessed's life by exploring the anchoress vocation as experienced by others during the later medieval period. It has been reported that, during the 12th, 13th, and 14th Centuries, over 200 European women devoted their lives to solitude as religious anchoresses; while admittedly rare, the vocation was not an unheard of calling for a single woman of the era.

Within the past decade, there has been a resurgence of interest in the anchoritic traditions of the Middle Ages among contemporary medieval scholars. This is evidenced by the publication of 21st-century books on the topic such as: *Lives of the Anchoresses: The Rise of the Urban Recluse in Medieval Europe*, written by Anneke B. Mulder-Bakker, 2005;[14] and *Anchoritic Traditions of Medieval Europe*, edited by Liz Herbert McAvoy, 2010.[15]

---

[12] Ibid

[13] Ibid., 65.

[14] Anneke B. Mulder-Bakker, ed. *Lives of the Anchoresses: The Rise of the Urban Recluse in Medieval Europe* (Translated by Myra Heerspink Scholz) (Phila: University of Pennsylvania Press, 2005).

[15] Liz H. McAvoy, Editor, *Anchoritic Traditions in Medieval Europe* (Woodbridge, U.K.: The Boydell Press, 2010).

This sub-field of medieval studies has, in fact, generated enough interest to bring about the formation of an "International Anchoritic Society," which has held biennial conferences, attended by medieval scholars, in such locations as: Wales (2005), Hiroshima (2008), and the United States (2011 and 2014). Conference topics have included: "Rhetorics of the Anchorhold"; "Mapping of the Medieval Anchorhold"; "The Anchoritic Vocation"; and "Anchorites in their Communities."

In following the earlier identified aim of the present book, to allow Blessed Margaret to speak to us from across the centuries, let us travel back in time to the age of the medieval "anchorhold," the anchoress vocation and the spirituality of solitude as encountered in the later middle ages. These topics will be explored not only in the Legend of Margaret of Castello, but also in the lives of other well-known 12th, 13th, and 14th-century religious figures, including Hildegard of Bingen, who was apprenticed to an anchoress when only eight years old; "Margareta Contracta," or Lame Margaret of Magdeburg, who became an anchoress and urban recluse at the age of twelve; and Julien of Norwich, a distinguished 14th-century anchoress.

Discussions of the solitary vocation, or medieval eremitism, have occasionally resulted in confusion because of interchangeable use of the terms "hermit" or "hermitess" and "anchorite" or "anchoress." There is a difference:

> The hermit has been defined as a solitary who can both live alone or within a community of other hermits and who is often peripatetic; indeed his/her ability to move about is paradigmatic of the vocation. In contrast the anchorite is one who has made a solemn vow of stability of place before the Bishop or his representative and lives out his or her life in a locked or walled-up cell.[16]

It is pointed out, nonetheless, that both have "opted for the solitary life for the purposes of spiritual development and both undertake important work on behalf of the community which, discursively at least, they have left behind."[17]

Another important distinction between the hermit and the anchorite is the fact that often hermits lived in isolated rural locations and many "begged for or grew their own food," while the anchorite, enclosed in a

---

[16] Liz H. McAvoy, "Introduction" (pp. 1-21) in Ed. Liz H. McAvoy, *Anchoritic Traditions in Medieval Europe* (Rochester, N.Y.: The Boydell Press, 2010), 2.
[17] Ibid.

cell attached to a church, "usually lived in the middle of villages or towns."[18] While Blessed Margaret's cell was not in a town or village, its location next to the Church of St. Mary of the Fortress of Metola in the forest was not too distant from the castle of her parents.

A final difference in the two solitary vocations is related to the religious rituals associated with the embrace of the calling. For many medieval hermits "the only essentials were the intention to live a holy life and the wearing of the hermit's habit."[19]

Because of the commitment to lifelong enclosure, anchorites and anchoresses "shared at least one primary definition of their vocation: that their way of life was a living death."[20] Thus, the liturgy of enclosure often included prayers for the dying, at times even an excerpt from the Requiem Mass, with the Bishop or priest administering extreme unction to the candidate as he or she entered the anchorhold, "never, in theory, to leave it alive."[21] Some potential recluses "underwent a burying ceremony, symbolizing (their) worldly death...the cell became a metaphorical tomb in which the rest of the anchoress' physical life would be spent."[22] For many anchoresses the door was sealed or walled up from the outside; this was the case for Blessed Margaret's cell in which the door had been sealed after her entry. And, for some anchoresses, even a grave was prepared at the time of enclosure. One imagines that this kind of permanent solitude, surrounding both life and death, is what Blessed Margaret's father was anticipating for his physically challenged offspring.

The medieval anchoress' cell, or anchorhold, in which she was enclosed, consisted of a single room, or sometimes two or more connected rooms, physically attached to the side wall of a church or chapel. The location of the architecture being next to the church was critical in allowing a window to be created opening into the chancel or altar space; this was necessary so that the anchoress could hear Mass, receive the sacraments of Penance and the Eucharist, and offer prayers before the Tabernacle containing the Blessed Sacrament.

The window opening into the chapel was called a "hagioscope," or "squint." A hagioscope, (Greek "holy"; "to see") "in architecture, is an

---

[18] Anne Savage, *Anchoritic Spirituality: Ancrene Wisse and Associated Works* (Mahwah, N.J.: Paulist Press, 1991), 16.
[19] Ibid.
[20] Ibid.
[21] Ibid.
[22] Michelle M. Sauer, "Violence, Isolation and Anchoritic Preparation: Dorothy of Montau, Anchoress of Marianwerder," *Magistra* 21:1 (2015): 132-150, 545.

opening through the wall of a church in an oblique direction, to allow the worshippers in the transepts or other parts of the church, from which the altar was not visible, to see the elevation of the Host."[23] While the hagioscope allowed the anchoress access to the chancel, members of the congregation could not see the solitary. Some chapel squints were round or square; others were described as "cruciform" in shape. Most apertures were located fairly high on the anchorhold wall with a ledge beneath on which the anchoress could kneel for her devotions.

On the far side of the cell, a window, open to the outside, was located through which food and other supplies were passed to the occupant. Some anchoresses, especially those described as "urban recluses," also used the exterior window as a place to receive and counsel visitors seeking spiritual guidance. This window was generally "covered with a curtain with a large cross on it" to signify its designation as a place for conversation with visitors.[24]

A number of medieval anchoresses had servants tasked to supply food and other necessities for daily living. In the case of young Margaret, we might assume that her faithful chaplain, Fra Cappellano, was a frequent visitor providing support and religious guidance as Margaret matured on her spiritual journey. Possibly the castle nursemaid, into whose hands the infant Margaret had initially been entrusted, delivered material sustenance. And, the literature also suggests that Margaret's mother Emilia may have been an occasional visitor.

No detailed description of the interior of Blessed Margaret's cell has been found, but from the comments of both Fr. William Bonniwell and the Medieval Biographer we may trust that it was similar to the usual religious anchorhold of the Middle Ages as described above. Fr. Bonniwell recalled Margaret's father as using the legend of St. Veridiana as a model for creating Margaret's cell, and the Medieval Biographer simply tells us that Parisio caused a "certain cell" to be prepared. As we are told that "Little Margaret"'s anchorhold was to be attached to a chapel so that she could attend Mass and receive the Eucharist, and also that her mother visited occasionally, the cell must have had the interior and exterior windows usual in such medieval enclosures.

Some anchorholds of the Middle Ages had a large enough exterior window to allow sunlight and fresh air to enter the cell. Fr. Bonniwell must have believed the latter to have existed in Margaret's cell for he reflected poignantly:

---

[23] http://en.wikipedia.org/wiki/Hagioscope
[24] Deansley, 211.

One morning during her 13th year in Prison, Margaret realized with a start that it was now some time since the wintry winds had been howling and screaming through the snow-laden trees of the forest; their place had been taken by soft gentle breezes. She became conscious of the excited gurgling of the mountain freshets created by the melting snow, and she inhaled the fragrant aroma of the pine trees which came stealing into her cell, as if to share her imprisonment. But, above all, it was the lusty singing of the countless thrushes which filled her heart to overflowing, for the birds seemed to be telling her how they hurried back from the south, as soon as the weather permitted, to be with their little blind friend.[25]

Fr. Bonniwell's musing concluded: "To Margaret it was God who was talking to her through the many voices of nature, and she was deeply moved by these delicate attentions of her Divine lover."[26]

As described by Sister Janice McGrane, Blessed Margaret's "companions were the foxes and the birds, and the plenteous fir trees that carried the mountain breezes to her small cell. Margaret loved God dearly. Her life in the castle (had been) imbued with the doctrine and faith of the Catholic Church."[27] McGrane added that because, in her new setting of the small cell, Margaret "was able to hear Mass and receive the sacraments and Padre Cappellano was able to visit her, these (gifts) along with her deep faith in God and her prayer life, greatly helped Margaret endure the hardships and isolation of her enclosure."[28]

Another commentary explained the importance of a variety of "windows" in Blessed Margaret's anchorhold:

> Two small windows were her saving grace. One window faced the adjacent church, and here she would receive the sacrament from Padre Cappellano. The other small aperture was used to pass Margaret her daily meals. Her truest window (however) was her inner window to God, for although she couldn't understand the actions of her parents, she opened her inner

---

[25] Bonniwell, 2014, 23.
[26] Ibid.
[27] Janice McGrane, *Saints to Lean On: Spiritual Companions for Illness and Disability* (Cincinnati, Ohio: St. Anthony Messenger Press, 2006), 6.
[28] Ibid.

sight to the omnipresence of God and found solace in that joyful experience.[29]

The Anchoress Vocation

The solitary anchoress vocation was not entered into lightly; the spiritual calling was embraced only after significant prayer and discernment on the part of the potential recluse and in collaboration with a spiritual director or Bishop. Clearly, for "Little Margaret," the initial enclosure in an anchorhold was not her choice but a religious lifestyle chosen for her. Thus, some authors who write about Margaret's 13 years in the cell, describe the setting as a "prison" and lament the decision of her parents, especially that of her father Parisio, to have chosen the forced enclosure.

Blessed Margaret herself, would, I believe, disagree with the concept of her cell being a "prison." After initial anxiety and confusion, as revealed earlier in this chapter, "Little Margaret" was blessed with the grace to view her enclosure as a gift from God rather than a punishment from her parents. This is validated in the words of the Medieval Biographer who, we must remember, actually met people who had known and interacted with Margaret. The biographer admits that it was through the "transgression" of her father that Margaret was "invited to penitence," but added "there was kindness in her penitence, though, because she appealed to God on behalf of sinners, offering her suffering for them."[30] He asserted: "From infancy she was freed for Divine training, and in her childhood years she delighted in penance because she thought herself chosen by God...and her tender mind was radiated by the light of God."[31] This does not sound like the soul of a prisoner, unless we consider Blessed Margaret a prisoner of love; a prisoner of the love of Christ which delighted her soul rather than causing it suffering.

Young Margaret's faith and understanding were extraordinary. "This was partly due to the instruction given her by the patient chaplain. But there can be no question that it was, in a far greater degree, due to Divine grace": The religious teaching Margaret received was so completely internalized that "years later she astonished the Dominican

---

[29] James Heater and Coleen Heater, *The Pilgrim's Italy: A Travel Guide to the Saints* (Nevada City, Ca.: Inner Travel Books, 2008), 207.
[30] *Blessed Margaret of Castello OP: A Medieval Biography* (Trans. Carolina Accorsi) (Fatima, Portugal: Dominican Nuns of the Perpetual Rosary, 1994), 17.
[31] Ibid.

Friars at *Citta di Castello* with the extent and depth of her theological knowledge."[32]

Once Margaret accepted the fact that God had blessed her by the calling to a solitary life, she wanted to give herself over as completely as possible to His love; to do this "with her whole heart, her whole soul and her whole mind."[33] This commitment was supported by her chaplain whose teaching "filled the child with joy and hope."[34] Because Margaret wanted to follow Jesus as closely as possible, in imitating his pain and suffering, she undertook penances additional to those of the reclusive lifestyle of the anchorhold. Even as a young child "Little Margaret" initiated a monastic-style fast, sometimes only taking bread and water for nourishment for several days at a time.[35] She also began to secretly wear a hairshirt under her clothes, hidden from the view of any who might visit, especially her mother, Emilia.

Blessed Margaret's penances were described in the words of the Medieval Biographer: "I find the fact that when this one was seven years of age, or thereabouts, she began to weaken her little body by fasting. And over a period of time she increased her fasting and abstinence to such a great extent that it is written, even from the Holy Feast of the Cross to Easter, she fasted continuously. And at other times she fasted four days in the week...on bread and water...and secretly wore a haircloth (which she would hide) because she feared her mother."[36]

Ancrene Wisse

Precisely because the Medieval Biographer, who first documented Margaret's legend, took great care not to include imaginary information, we have no specific details of the young blessed's devotions during her years as a recluse in the cell next to the "Church of St. Mary of the Fortress of Metola." The biographer admitted that he based his biography of Blessed Margaret of Castello on details transmitted primarily by "word of mouth" as well as some sketchy documents. Neither did Fr. Bonniwell attempt to describe Blessed Margaret's spiritual or religious practices during her period of solitude.

As Margaret had, however, been taught by Fra Giacomo Cappellano to practice the faith during her early years, it may be trusted that the castle

---

[32] Bonniwell, 2014, 19.
[33] Ibid.
[34] Ibid.
[35] Caroline W. Bynum, *Fragmentation and Redemption: Essays on Gender and the Human Body in Medieval Religion* (N.Y.: Zone Books, 1991), 142.
[36] *Blessed Margaret of Castello OP*, 17-18.

chaplain continued his spiritual guidance during her anchorhold enclosure. Aside from hearing daily Mass and participating in reception of the sacraments of Penance and the Eucharist on specified occasions, the daily horarium of medieval anchoresses seemed to vary according to individual preference and/or direction from the recluse's spiritual advisor. Prayer, spiritual reading, meditation and the reciting of the liturgy of the hours were usual religious practices.[37]

There were several written sets of guidelines to direct the medieval anchoress' daily schedule; the most well-known of these directives was entitled: *Ancrene Wisse*, which translates simply as "Guidelines for Anchoresses." *Ancrene Wisse* was a "thirteenth-century text that for many years was held up as the template for anchoritic discipline, particularly for female practitioners."[38] The work contains, as well as the anchoress' "prayers and devotions, the structure of the anchoritic cell...the squint is defined as a window that provides viewing access to the high altar and the consecration (Mass) without causing the anchoress to leave her cell or expose herself in any way."[39]

The *Ancrene Wisse*, which some authors suggest was originally written for three medieval anchoresses, contains eight main chapters, which focus on different aspects of the solitary life; these include: 1. Devotions; 2. Protecting the Heart through the Senses; 3. Birds and Anchorites: the Inner Feelings; 4. Fleshly and Spiritual Temptations and Comforts and Remedies for them; 5. Confession; 6. Penance; 7. The Pure Heart and the Love of Christ and 8. The Outer Rule.[40]

Chapter 1 identifies in detail the prayers recommended for anchoresses from rising in the morning to going to bed at night. In Chapter 2, the anchoress is urged to avoid bad influences related to the five senses: "sight and hearing, taste and smell and feelings in each part of the body."[41] Chapter 3 presents an analogy between anchorites and birds who leave the earth and fly toward heavenly things,[42] "who spread their wings and make a Cross of themselves as a bird does when it

---

[37] Pamela J.F. Rosof, "The Anchoress in the Twelfth and Thirteen Centuries," in Eds. Lillian T. Shank and John A. Nichols, *Medieval Religious Women: Peaceweavers*, Volume II (Kalamazoo, MI.: Cistercian Publications, 1987), 131.
[38] Sauer, 546.
[39] Ibid.
[40] *Ancrene Wisse: Guide for Anchoresses*, Trans. with an Introduction and Notes by Hugh White (London, U.K.: Penguin Books, 1993), 9-190.
[41] Ibid., 27.
[42] Ibid., 60-85.

flies,"[43] and in Chapter 4 are listed potential temptations, virtues, vices and remedies.[44] Chapters 5 and 6 deal with the topics of Confession and Penance.[45] Chapter 7 speaks of Christ's love which "purifies and brightens the heart,"[46] and Chapter 8 presents guidelines for specific elements of daily life such as diet, work, and visitors.[47]

The *Ancrene Wisse* also used verbal images to describe the small cell, or anchorhold, "in which the anchoress was to enclose herself for life"; some of these include: "a besieged castle," "the city of Jerusalem," "a fox hole," "a nest in a high tree," "Mary's womb," "a grave," and "the Cross."[48]

While her blindness would, of course, have prevented young Margaret from studying guidelines such as those contained in the *Ancrene Wisse*, she may have learned the basics of such spiritual directives from Chaplain Cappellano. As one author commented: "Luckily for Margaret, the Chaplain of the Parish visited her regularly and educated her in the ways of the soul":[49] "He found her mind to be 'luminous' and her patient understanding of life and its problems truly remarkable. He taught her how to accept not only her physical afflictions but also her imprisonment as a special gift from God."[50] The acceptance of physical afflictions was, in fact, addressed in Part 4 of *Ancrene Wisse* which advised the anchoress of the spiritual merit of patiently bearing illness and infirmity:

> Sickness is a hot fire to endure, but…(it) cleanses the soul. Sickness that God sends does these six things: (i) washes away the sins that have been committed before; (ii) guards against those that were on the way; (iii) proves patience; (iv) keeps one in humility; (v) increases the reward; (vi) makes the patient person equal to a martyr. Sickness is thus the soul's healing, medicine for its wounds, a shield to prevent it getting others, as God sees it would, if sickness did not prevent it. Sickness makes a man understand what he is, know himself, and, like a good

---

[43] Mary A. Edsall, "True Anchoresses are Called Birds: Asceticism as Ascent and the Purgative Mysticism of the Ancrene Wisse," *Viator: Medieval and Renaissance Studies* 34:1 (2003): 157-186, 157.
[44] *Ancrene Wisse: Guide for Anchoresses*, 86-138.
[45] Ibid., 139-176.
[46] Ibid., 177.
[47] Ibid., 190-200.
[48] Bob Hassenfratz, "The Anchorhold as Symbolic Space in Ancrene Wisse," *Philological Quarterly* 84:1 (2005): 1-8, 1.
[49] Lucinda Vardey, *Traveling with the Saints in Italy: Contemporary Pilgrimages on Ancient Paths* (Mahwah, N.J.: Hidden Springs, 2005), 151.
[50] Ibid.

master, beats so as to teach well how powerful God is, how worthless the world's bliss is. Sickness is your goldsmith, who gilds your crown in the bliss of heaven.[51]

Finally, we cannot discount the guidance and inspiration of the Holy Spirit who seemed to have taught Blessed Margaret from infancy to death. The decision for "retirement from the world to live a life of prayer and sacrifice was not uncommon in medieval times...it was a lifestyle freely chosen by adults who sought to deepen their spiritual lives. The life of an anchorite, however, was never intended for a child."[52] The cell, or anchorhold, could be "bitterly cold in the winter and stiflingly hot in the summer...(yet) for thirteen years Margaret lived there is solitude with only the birds and the mountain wind for companions."[53]

As author Ivan Innerst observed: "there is no accounting for souls touched by grace. What would appear as an existence so outrageous, so inhuman...as to drive one to madness, failed to alter young Margaret. Those who observed her at this time called her content, even cheerful."[54] Innerst concluded: "That one so young and so scourged by every sort of misfortune should be filled with so great an infusion of grace can only confound the reason. Human logic is found to be wanting when confronted with what it has no means to explain."[55]

Perhaps Blessed Margaret's acceptance of and contentment with her years of enclosure can best be explained by the words of a 20th-century American anchoress, Sister Nazarena of Jesus, who wrote: "The anchoritic life is the one most subject to delusions and to the crafty conspiracy of its two great enemies, the devil and the ego...if one has not been severely tested and has not suffered a great deal, there are reasons to doubt whether one could persevere in solitude for very long."[56] "Little Margaret" had indeed, in her early childhood years, been "severely tested" and "suffered a great deal." That "testing" and "suffering" may have provided the spiritual "glue," which strengthened her resolve to "persevere in solitude" for 13 years.[i]

In order to further comprehend Margaret of Castello's years of anchoritic seclusion, we can briefly explore the experiences of solitude

---

[51] *Ancrene Wisse: Guide for Anchoresses*, 88.
[52] McGrane, 5.
[53] Ibid., 6.
[54] Ivan Innerst, *Saints for Today: Reflections on Lesser Saints* (San Francisco: Ignatius Press, 2000), 80.
[55] Ibid.
[56] Thomas Matus, *Nazarena: An American Anchoress* (Mahwah, N.J.: Paulist Press, 1998), 37-38.

demonstrated in the lives of three exemplary anchoresses (one a temporary anchoress) of history: Margareta Contracta, or Margaret the Lame of Magdeburg (1210-1250); Hildegard of Bingen (apprenticed to an anchoress during her early years, 1098-1179); and Julien of Norwich (1342-1423). These three women were chosen as exemplars of the medieval anchoress vocation as they possessed characteristics reflective of the spiritual journey of Blessed Margaret of Castello. Margareta Contracta, like Blessed Margaret, was rejected by her parents because of lameness. Her mother arranged for an anchoritic cell to be built next to a church; Lame Margaret was enclosed at the young age of twelve. Hildegard of Bingen, as "Little Margaret," lived in an anchorage only during her childhood and adolescence; and Julien of Norwich, perhaps the most familiar of the medieval anchoresses, was greatly admired for her loving heart and her joy of spirit. These were virtues consistently attributed to Blessed Margaret of Castello.

Of the three anchoresses chosen to help elucidate the 13-year anchoress vocation of young Margaret of Castello, Margareta Contracta or Margaret the Lame's, early experience is the one most similar to that of Blessed Margaret. Both "Margarets" began to experience profound spiritual devotion as children partially related to congenital physical afflictions which resulted in each being rejected by their respective families; both turned to prayer and penance, early on, as a way of transforming their suffering into a positive attribute drawing them closer to God. And, both "Margarets" lived, for a significant period of time, within the seclusion of a religious cell or anchorhold. Margaret of Castello did not choose her enclosure but, with God's grace, accepted the solitude and grew to love and appreciate her anchoritic vocation. Margaret the Lame experienced a personal call to live an enclosed religious life but, in distinction to Blessed Margaret of Castello, she also felt called to share her spiritual insights with others in the community; thus, she became an urban recluse having periodic contact with local townspeople.

Margareta Contracta (Margaret the Lame)

Margareta Contracta or Margaret the Lame, sometimes simply referred to as "Lame Margaret," was a thirteenth-century anchoress who lived between 1210-1250. Margareta was disabled from what is believed to have been a congenital deformity resulting in lameness. Because of the physical challenges she was, as Margaret of Castello, rejected by her well-to-do family. When Lame Margaret's mother angrily beat her, she tolerated the abuse patiently: "eventually Margareta conquered her mother by trusting her and obeying her in everything. Inspired by God, the mother then became eager to encourage her poor daughter in her service to God."[57] Margaret of Castello also patiently continued to love and trust her mother and father, despite the emotional abuse she suffered because of their repeated parental rejection.

Seeking solace in religion, Margaret the Lame was frequently seen walking to church with a blind family servant; the two were made fun of by the townspeople.[58] Those observing them "would look at the lame child as if she were a monster, alternately laughing and shouting: 'Look, look, a great miracle! The lame leads the blind!'"[59] Young Lame Margaret found companionship and support primarily from a family servant as did "Little Margaret" of Castello during her first six years living in the family castle.

At twelve years, when she had reached the "age of discernment,"[60] Margaret the Lame "made her choice for an anchoritic existence. Her mother agreed and had a cell arranged for her at St. Alban's Church" in Magdeburg;[61] there she "lived a life of great asceticism and devotion."[62] Despite her embrace of a contemplative lifestyle, "in her childhood, Lame Margaret's faithfulness and compassion for the poor and afflicted were so great that she could not tolerate hearing anyone accuse or reprimand them; she chose the poor as companions."[63] Margaret the Lame's care and concern for the poor brings to mind that of Blessed Margaret of Castello who not only ministered to the sick poor and the outcast but for whom they also became companions during her life with a "family of the streets."

Margaret the Lame had "some reservations about the reclusive state because it would bring her fame and honor, while she sought complete self-effacement for the greater glory of God. But the prospect of devoting herself totally to God outweighed her hesitations."[64] Lame Margaret's life

---

[57] Friar Johannes OP of Magdeburg, *The Vita of Margaret the Lame, a Thirteenth Century Recluse & Mystic* (Trans. with commentary by Gertrud J. Lewis and Tilman Lewis) (Toronto, Ontario: Peregrina Publishing Company, 2001), 14.

[58] Anneke, B. Mulder-Bakker, "Lame Margaret of Magdeburg: The Social Function of a Medieval Recluse," *Journal of Medieval History* 22:2 (1996): 155-169, 157.

[59] Friar Johannes OP, 13.

[60] Ibid.

[61] Anneke B. Mulder-Bakker, "Lame Margaret of Magdeburg and Her Lessons," (pp. 148-263) in Anneke B. Mulder-Bakker, Ed. *Lives of the Anchoresses: The Rise of the Urban Recluse in Medieval Europe* (Trans. Myra Heerspink Scholz) (Phila: University of Pennsylvania Press, 2005), 149.

[62] Mulder-Bakker, 1996, 157.

[63] Friar Johannes OP, 14.

[64] Mulder-Bakker, 2005, 149.

in the anchorhold is described as one of "total renunciation, contrition and self-contempt, all of which entailed extreme suffering. According to one biographer, she did this not in order to win forgiveness of sins or a place in heaven...she simply wanted to give God the glory due Him...she wished to focus solely on the glory of God."[65] This desire to give glory to God is also reminiscent of the ardent wish of Blessed Margaret of Castello to offer her sufferings for the love of God and the salvation of souls.

Margaret the Lame, not only lived a private asceticism, of prayer and penance but also became well-known for her wisdom in counseling others who came to her anchorhold window; she believed that she had personally been taught by Our Lady. As Hildegard of Bingen and other female religious, she may have lacked formal training but she probably did substantial reading in her cell and listened attentively to preachers and visitors. These women called themselves "Indoctae, Illiteratae"; they attributed their knowledge not to themselves but to insights from above."[66] While Margaret of Castello did not teach or counsel others from her cell, she did engage in these activities after becoming a Dominican Tertiary; Blessed Margaret, as Lame Margaret, had not received formal education, other than that of her beloved castle chaplain, Fra Giacomo Cappellano; nevertheless, she was blessed with spiritual wisdom and the ability to teach and advise, directed only by the guidance of the Holy Spirit.

Our knowledge of Lame Margaret comes entirely from the biography written by her confessor, Friar Johannes of Magdeburg, entitled *The Vita of Margaret the Lame: A Thirteenth Century Recluse & Mystic*.[67] The author of the Vita describes himself simply as "Friar Johannes" (Johannes Praedicator). Internal evidence suggests that he lived in Magdeburg and was Margaret's confessor."[68] It appears that Friar

---

[65] Ibid., 149-150.
[66] Anneke B. Mulder-Bakker, "The Reclusorium as an Informal Center of Learning," pp. 245-266, in. Eds. Jan Willem Drijvers and Alasdair A. McDonald, *Centers of Learning: Learning and Location in Pre-Modern Europe and the Near East*, (Leiden, The Neatherlands: E.J. Brill, 1995), 248.
[67] Friar Johannes OP of Magdeburg, *The Vita of Margaret the Lame, a Thirteenth Century Recluse & Mystic*.
[68] Gertrud J. Lewis and Tilman Lewis, "Preface," in Friar Johannes OP of Magdeburg, *The Vita of Margaret the Lame, a Thirteenth Century Recluse & Mystic* (Translated with commentary by Gertrud J. Lewis and Tilman Lewis) (Toronto, Ontario: Peregrina Publishing Company, 2001), 7.

Johannes cannot be further identified "since no name lists of Magdeburg Dominicans of the thirteenth century are extant."[69]

A question has been raised as to whether Margaret the Lame was a real person because "there is no other known document regarding the existence of a thirteenth century recluse in Magdeburg."[70] Was she only "a foil for Friar Johannes own thoughts about matters of theology?"[71] The authors of the preface to Margaret the Lame's *Vita*, Gertrud Lewis and Tilman Lewis, however, argue that a theory of fabrication is "highly unlikely and anachronistic for thirteenth century literature."[72]

Medieval scholar Anneke B. Mulder-Bakker noted that while the *Vita* of Margaret the Lame was "clearly molded in the hagiographic tradition (and) abounds in the stereotypical formulations and conventional images of the genre, (it) simultaneously however...differs in some important ways."[73] "The main departure from the norm," Mulder-Bakker observed, was that the "life does not relate any miracles, concentrating instead almost exclusively on Margareta's inner life."[74] Margaret the Lame's biographer, Friar Johannes, explains his rationale as being "Margareta's own determination not to be associated with any vision, miracle or other charism that would associate her with sainthood."[75]

Margaret of Castello's legend does include the recounting of miracles which occurred through her intervention both prior to and after her death; it is also reported that, even though physically blind, Blessed Margaret saw Our Blessed Lord during the consecration of the Mass. Margaret of Castello would probably never herself have disclosed the visions except when asked to reveal them, under obedience, to her confessor; many additional healing miracles, attributed to the intervention of Blessed Margaret, were recorded after her death.

The *Vita* describing Margaret the Lame's vocation was completed during her lifetime, Friar John's intention being "to record the oral lessons of the anchoress for posterity, lessons for which she herself in

---

[69] Ibid.
[70] Ibid., 9.
[71] Ibid.
[72] Ibid.
[73] "The Life of Margaret the Lame, Anchoress of Magdeburg by Friar Johannes OP of Magdeburg" (pp. 313-395) in Anneke B. Mulder-Bakker, Ed., *Living Saints of the Thirteenth Century: The Lives of Yvette, Anchoress of Huy, Juliana of Cornillon, Author of the Corpus Christi Feast, and Margaret the Lame, Anchoress of Magdeburg* (Translated by Jo Ann McNamara, Barbara Newman and Gertrud E. Lewis and Tilman Lewis) (Turnhout, Belgium: Brepols Publishers, 2011), 306.
[74] Ibid.
[75] Ibid.

her anchorhold formed the living proof."[76] Through her teaching Lame Margaret became well known to the local Christian community; she:

> Summarized her lessons in salient points and handy lists short enough for everyone to memorize easily-the five qualities of a good Christian, the five requirements of a good prayer, the seven torments of hell, the seven preparations for receiving Holy Communion, the ten virtues...point by point summaries that catered to the needs of the illiterate faithful who had grown up in an oral culture. The lists could very quickly be committed to memory.[77]

The concept of "service formed the foundation of Lame Margaret's activities in Magdeburg":[78] "Margareta did not choose the anchorhold out of a penchant for the contemplative life... Her task lay in the community. She had to speak with visitors, even if she lay stiff with pain in her bed or found herself in rapt communion with the Lord. Her 'employment' with God required total service to her fellow human beings."[79] Margareta Contracta was described as "truly the catechizer of the Magdeburg urban community."[80] In her ministry of catechizing, "the anchoress taught and instructed believers; she knew their secret sins and prayed for them. She spoke with fire and conviction. Her lessons were appealing because they contained more than superficial information and touched the hearts of her listeners."[81]

Margaret of Castello also became a well-known servant and spiritual guide in *Citta di Castello* after she was formally accepted as a "Sister of Penance of St. Dominic," and moved about the city wearing the black and white habit of a Dominican *Mantellata*. While Blessed Margaret's primary ministry involved caring for the sick in their homes and for the outcast, incarcerated in the local prison, she also became a religious advisor and teacher in the course of these activities.

While Margaret the Lame's teaching authority was initially questioned by the Magdeburg clergy, "once she had reached the age of the teaching Christ, her authority was uncontested. What the traditional clergy had

---

[76] Mulder-Bakker, 2005, 148.
[77] Ibid., 154.
[78] Ibid., 166.
[79] Ibid., 168.
[80] Ibid., 166.
[81] Ibid., 168-169.

previously declared suspect was now considered heavenly wisdom."[82] Although Lame Margaret's confessor and biographer, Friar Johannes, was her committed spiritual guide, he did, for a period of several years, pay little attention to her thoughts, and "would ridicule her when she displayed great audacity, saying: 'Soon you'll believe yourself very saintly and very great.'"[83] Margareta's reply was, "It is not I who am great, but God who is great in me. Jesus Christ realizes that His love and faithfulness, which I have for your salvation, force me to say these things to you."[84]

Both Margareta Contracta and Margaret of Castello recognized well the Gospel teaching contained in St. Paul's letter to the Corinthians (2 Corinthians 4: 7): "We hold this treasure in earthen vessels, so that it may be made clear that this extraordinary power belongs to God and does not come from us." Neither of the "Margarets" allowed their physical challenges to prevent their serving others with an "extraordinary power," which belonged to God.

In her *vita*, Lame Margaret's "mysticism is (described as) a mysticism of suffering characterized mainly through the triad of suffering, rejection and poverty...(she) accepts her relentless physical suffering as a special gift from God...internalizing her pain, she transforms her suffering into a means of praising God. Giving glory to God is Margareta Contracta's deepest desire."[85] As noted earlier, there are no descriptions of miracles in her *vita*, according to Margaret the Lame's wishes, and "only subdued references to (her) mystical experiences."[86] In sum, "the Dominant theme of this life is Lame Margaret's *imitatio Christi*, which is a typical characteristic of medieval piety, and, specifically, of the anchoritic life."[87]

How similar was Margaret the Lame's wholehearted wish to imitate Christ to that described as the sole desire of Margaret of Castello. It was Blessed Margaret's deeply held longing to imitate her Beloved Christ,

---

[82] Ibid., 169
[83] Friar Johannes, 59.
[84] Ibid.
[85] Anneke Mulder-Bakker, "Introduction" (pp. 305-312) "The Life of Margaret the Lame, Anchoress of Magdeburg by Friar Johannes OP of Magdeburg" (pp. 313-395) in Anneke B. Mulder-Bakker, Ed., *Living Saints of the Thirteenth Century: The Lives of Yvette, Anchoress of Huy, Juliana of Cornillon, Author of the Corpus Christi Feast, and Margaret the Lame, Anchoress of Magdeburg* (Translated by Jo Ann McNamara, Barbara Newman and Gertrud E. Lewis and Tilman Lewis) (Turnhout, Belgium: Brepols Publishers, 2011), 308.
[86] Ibid.
[87] Lewis and Lewis, 10.

that allowed her to accept, with joy and even with gratitude, the physical and emotional suffering with which her young life was continually beset.

Margareta Contracta's enclosure at the age of only 12 years seemed to provide a haven for the young woman, where she could devote herself to prayer and contemplation, as well as providing a solution for the family who were, as Blessed Margaret of Castello's parents, ashamed of their disabled daughter. This is reflected in the fact that Margareta Contracta's own mother "enclosed" her in the cell. At about age 19 or 20, Lame Margaret, also as Blessed Margaret, was forced to move from her anchorhold in the city to a Dominican convent, from which she herself begged to be removed. Ultimately Margaret the Lame was "transferred to a new anchorhold" at Saint Agnes convent.[88]

Margareta Contracta may well be identified as a forerunner of Margaret of Castello because of her disability related family rejection, her early spiritual development, her powerful faith in God and attraction to prayer, the move to an enclosed cell in early life, her love and compassion for the poor and her reputation as a holy woman, counselor and teacher committed to the salvation of souls.

Hildegard of Bingen

Hildegard of Bingen (1098-1179), sometimes referred to as the "Sibyl of the Rhine," was a Benedictine Abbess, mystic, and minister to the ill and infirm. Being born into a noble German family, as the 10th child, Hildegard's parents felt that she should be given to the Church as a "tithe" as a Benedictine oblate. Thus, Hildegard, as a child of only eight years, was given over to the care and tutelage of an anchoress named Jutta von Sponheim who was seeking to locate near a Benedictine monastery. Jutta moved to a small anchorhold near the male Benedictine Monastery at Disibodenburg: she "became a recluse attached to the monastery taking Hildegard...with her."[89]

If the cell was actually "attached to the church of the monastery at Disibodenberg (it's exact location is not certain) Jutta and her youthful companion would have heard the monk's recitation of the Divine Office every day; thus Hildegard from her earliest years would have grown up hearing the monastic chant and prayer. That small cell later became a

---

[88] Mulder-Bakker, 2011, 311.
[89] Hildegard of Bingen, *Selected Writings: Hildegard of Bingen*, Trans. Mark Atherton (N.Y.: Penguin Books, 1956), xiii.

convent, remaining attached to the larger male monastic house at Disibodenburg."[90]

As Jutta had personally adopted a number of ascetic practices, mortifying her body and spirit, it can be assumed that Hildegard may have undertaken similar religious behaviors.

While it is accepted that Hildegard began her formal spiritual journey in her eighth year, there is some confusion in the literature as to whether the journey was initiated at Disibodenburg as oblation or as enclosure.[91] It is suggested, however, that "this apparent discrepancy may be solved by the documentation of the enclosure of Jutta and Hildegard," which is described as "a place that had only a small window, and an entrance which was solidly sealed and cemented."[92] This account fits the general plan of a medieval anchorhold; it appears that Hildegard of Bingen began her lifelong spiritual journey in a manner similar to that of "Little Margaret" of Castello in her cell next to the Chapel of St. Mary of the Fortress of Metola.

Hildegard ultimately became Abbess of a women's monastery at Disibodenburg, but her initial training was that of a recluse under the guidance of Jutta von Sponheim. No specific details remain of her anchoritic spiritual and religious practices, simply the fact that, like Blessed Margaret, she was, as a young child and adolescent, enclosed in a reclusive setting. Ultimately, the anchorage became a monastery with Jutta as Abbess, and at age 15 "Hildegard spoke her vows and assumed the veil of a nun."[93] Some twenty years later, after Jutta died, "the nuns chose Hildegard as her successor."[94]

As an abbess, Hildegard was widely regarded as a healer; she both employed and wrote about a variety of natural remedies for illness. Her diagnoses and treatments were primarily associated with fluctuations in the body's humors: "dry, damp, foamy and cool humors."[95] Hildegard's diagnostic abilities in identifying a variety of diseases and illness

---

[90] Sherri Olson, *Daily Life in a Medieval Monastery* (Santa Barbara, Ca.: Greenwood, 2013), 83.
[91] Emily Sutherland, "Hildegard of Bingen: Entry into Disebodenberg," *Paragon* 27:1 (2010): 53-66, 53.
[92] Ibid.
[93] Hildegard of Bingen, 1956, xiii.
[94] Ibid., xiv.
[95] Hildegard of Bingen, *Hildegard von Bingen's Physica: The Complete English Translation of Her Classic Work on Health and Healing*, Trans. Priscilla Throop (Rochester, Vt.: Healing Arts Press, 1998), 5.

conditions was described as being "a mixture of humoral physiology and Christian moral theology."[96]

Interestingly, in the medieval era when such practices as fasting and bodily mortification were considered worthy religious behaviors, Hildegard placed emphasis on moderation as "the key to good health."[97] In a letter to a Benedictine visionary she wrote: "'Do not lay on more strain than the body can endure. Immoderate straining and abstinence bring nothing useful to the soul.' Hildegard Von Bingen advocated a balanced diet, sufficient rest, alleviation of stress and a wholesome moral life."[98]

Even after she became an abbess, Hildegard maintained her commitment to care for the ill and infirm who sought her advice, as did Blessed Margaret, after becoming a Sister of Penance of St. Dominic, a *Mantellata*, ministering to the sick and to prisoners.

There is a widely retold anecdote about Hildegard's allowing a young man, who had been excommunicated by the Church, but who later confessed and received absolution, to be buried in the holy ground of the Monastery's cemetery. A local prelate demanded the body be removed and when Hildegard refused, as she had promised this burial to his priest, the Abbess and all of her Sisters in the Monastery were place under interdict; this prevented them from chanting the liturgy of the hours and from receiving the sacraments. Hildegard's argument for refusing to remove the young man's corpse was based on her understanding that she had done "nothing wrong in accepting the body of that man, who from the hands of his priest had received everything befitting a Christian and had been buried in our cemetery in the presence of all the inhabitants of Bingen, without any objection being raised."[99]

Hildegard, honored her promise and accepted the penance which lasted for some months until the interdict was removed by the Church. Hildegard's acceptance of the interdict and the suffering related to its imposition reflect a well-known quote in which the abbess asserted that she wished to be "a feather on the breath of God." As the "feather," Hildegard "derives her support from the air that bears her up; in short, the air is the Divine strength on which she draws the breath of

---

[96] Faith Wallis, *Medieval Medicine: A Reader* (Toronto, Canada: University of Toronto Press, 2010), 357.
[97] Hildegard of Bingen, 1998, 6.
[98] Ibid.
[99] Emilie Z. Brunn, *Women Mystics in Medieval Europe* (N.Y.: Paragon House, 1989), 24.

inspiration which she needs for all her ventures into the world of writing and teaching."[100]

As Margaret of Castello, Hildegard lived the reclusive life of an anchoress only temporarily during childhood and early adolescence. Both women were later called by God to the service of others and both seemed to have an affinity for care of the sick; Hildegard through her development of and writing about a variety of therapeutic folk remedies and Blessed Margaret through her visits to the ill and the infirm in their homes and in the prison. Hildegard of Bingen and Margaret of Castello were both strong women, holding to their moral and ethical beliefs and their faith in God despite personal suffering. The example of Hildegard's refusal to remove from blessed ground the body of a man who she believed belonged there in the eyes of God and of the Church might be considered a precursor to Blessed Margaret's refusal to surrender her understanding of the ideals of religious life to a dysfunctional community of nuns even though it meant her expulsion from the community (Margaret's experience with the nuns is discussed in Chapter 4).

Julien of Norwich

The mystic identified as "Julien of Norwich" is probably the best known anchoress of the medieval era. She is believed to have lived between 1342 and 1416, but very little about her life was recorded, even her name. There is no memory of a Christian or family name, but the mystic was accorded the name of "Julien" as it was documented that she lived "the solitary, enclosed life of an anchoress (but with a maidservant to tend her) in a cell adjoining the Parish Church of St. Julien in Conisford at Norwich, opposite the house of the Augustinian Friars."[101]

Although Julien lived as a recluse, her location, attached to the Church of St. Julien, allowed interaction with local citizens: "A main road passed right outside her house and Julien gave spiritual direction and advice to the many people who sought her out."[102] Julien's anchorhold, being so close to the Augustinian Friary, also suggests that "it would have been natural for her to borrow books and engage in conversation with the friars."[103] Julien requested three gifts of God: "to remember Christ's

---

[100] Hildegard of Bingen, 1956, xxvi.
[101] Julien of Norwich, *Showings*, Trans. Edmund Colledge and James Walsh (N.Y.: Paulist Press, 1978), 18.
[102] Julien of Norwich, *All Will Be Well: 30 Days with a Great Spiritual Teacher compiled by Richard Chilson* (Notre Dame, In.: Ave Maria Press, 2008), 2.
[103] Ibid.

passion in a special way," "to suffer from a (mortal) illness" from which she would recover, and "be able to devote herself entirely to the glory of God" and to have three wounds: "the wound of contrition, the wound of compassion and the wound of longing with my will for God."[104] These she received.

In "May of 1373, when Julien was thirty-one, she became sick enough that a priest was called to administer the last rites. While she lay on what she thought as her deathbed, she had a series of intense mystical revelations. She called them 'Showings.'"[105] Julien spoke of her illness repeatedly in "Showings," and "she was granted a vision of Christ's passion that she described vividly and eloquently. The three wounds gave her the grace to share her revelation with others."[106] While Margaret of Castello did not receive a vision of Christ's passion, as Julien, she did admit to witnessing visons of Jesus during the Consecrations of the Masses which she attended. Blessed Margaret's description of what she saw was that of "Infinite Beauty."

In her life as an anchoress, Julien had "plenty of time to ponder the revelations she had received. She wrote first a short text, describing what she had seen on her sickbed, and over the next twenty years, as she further analyzed and meditated on her 'Showings,' she wrote longer text that vividly described all that God had revealed to her."[107]

Theologically, Julien's primary focus was on "three great mysteries, or rather three aspects of the same mystery: God, man and their reconciliation. Furthermore, she sees everything in the light of Christ-the-Servant. It is through Christ that she reaches God."[108] The thinking that Julien was illiterate was fictitious; in fact, she "became such a master of rhetorical art as to merit comparison with Geoffry Chaucer."[109] Blessed Margaret of Castello, perhaps through the instruction of Fra Cappellano, was also considered by local religious scholars to have a profound mastery of theological knowledge.

Julien of Norwich is described as "an example of the healthy soul. For her, love and joy were paramount in the experience of God";[110] this is reflected in her well known and oft quoted words: "All will be well." The anchoress "gives us the gift of joy...God loves us so much that he even

---

[104] Ibid., 3.
[105] Julien of Norwich, *All Shall Be Well: A Modern Language Version of the Revelation of Julien of Norwich* (Vestel, N.Y.: Anamachara Books, 2011), 9.
[106] Julien of Norwich, 2008, 3.
[107] Julien of Norwich, 2011, 11.
[108] Julien of Norwich, 1978, 6.
[109] Ibid., 19
[110] Julien of Norwich, 2008, 4.

stooped to take on human form and die for us...that love oozes out of every moment in all of creation."[111] "Julien," it is pointed out, "may have been an anchoress shut up in a cottage, but that cottage opened upon a walled garden as well as a busy street. The love of creation and human society fills her work ("Showings"/"Revelations of Divine Love"). Her joy is contagious; it overflows."[112]

Blessed Margaret, as Julien, was consistently applauded for her loving heart and her joy of spirit which she openly shared with others:

> In her early years of parental rejection, "Little Margaret" found solace in the servants of the castle who responded to her warm, loving nature...as the years went by the servants saw her loving heart before they saw her limp or her blindness. This was to be a defining characteristic of Margaret of Castello's life: a loving personality that encouraged others to love her for her gifts rather than to reject her for her disabilities.[113]

The Spirituality of Solitude

The spirituality of Christian solitude, which is broadly understood as the desire of an individual to be alone with Christ, has its origins in both the Old and the New Testaments. In the book of Exodus we find Moses leading the Israelites through the desert during a forty year period of solitude and in "New testament's geography, John the Baptist, the 'precursor to Christ,' calls out from the wilderness about Christ's coming ministry; Christ himself withdraws periodically to desert or wilderness to formulate his thoughts and consolidate his resolve; Mary Magdalen will retire to the desert at the end of her life to live as a contemplative and ascetic."[114]

In discussing the "theology of solitude," Clark Gilpin observed that "we encounter this theology in gospel narratives of the wilderness temptation of Jesus" and "in the life of St. Antony and the hermits of the Egyptian desert."[115] The ancient Christian monks, such as Antony, "thought of solitude as a kind of paradise, a place where the full mystery

---

[111] Ibid., 7.
[112] Ibid.
[113] McGrane, 3.
[114] McAvoy, 6.
[115] W. Clark Gilpin, "The Theology of Solitude: Edwards, Emerson, Dickenson," *Spiritus* 1:1 (2001): 31-42, 31.

of God became manifest."[116] They were also aware, however, that it could be a fearful place where "feelings of loneliness and alienation" could be unleashed.[117]

In a discussion of Mechthild of Magdeburg's concept of "flowing in and out of God's presence," it is asserted that solitude is foundational to ministry. Citing the words of Richard Foster, solitude is described as "one of the deepest disciplines of the spiritual life because it crucifies our need for importance and prominence."[118] The concepts of "service and solitude belong together like the ebb and flow of the ocean waves";[119] and it is "only when we maintain that inner intimacy with God can we gain divine perspective on all our disparate activities and contending demands; here we see things from God's vantage point, bringing order to all our misplaced priorities."[120]

Blessed Margaret of Castello's spiritual experiences, as both mystic and minister, might be said to have provided an exemplar for another distinguished Italian Dominican Tertiary who would follow her in living and preaching the Gospel of Jesus, Catherine of Siena.

Saint Catherine of Siena's vocation has been identified as a model for the marriage of solitude and apostolic activity: "While she initially lives a secluded, enclosed life in order to practice a contemplative path, she is inspired by God to practice a charity that requires her to act in the world."[121] After becoming a Dominican Tertiary, Catherine had, for the first three years, lived a life of prayer and penance, enclosed in a small cell in her family home. Then, one day, in contemplation, she heard God calling her to a more active ministry; Catherine begged God not to send her away from the hours of uninterrupted intimacy with Him. But the Lord replied:

> Sweetest daughter, it is necessary for you to fulfill your every duty, so that with my grace you may assist others as well as yourself. I have no intention of cutting you off from me; on the contrary, I wish to bind you more closely to myself, by means of love of the neighbor. You know that the precepts of love are two:

---

[116] Douglas Burton-Christie, "The Work of Loneliness: Solitude, Emptiness and Compassion," *Anglican Theological Review* 88:1 (2006): 25-45, 25.

[117] Ibid., 26

[118] Glenn E. Myers, *Seeking Spiritual Intimacy: Journeying Deeper with Medieval Women of Faith* (Downer's Grove, Il.: IVP Books, 2011),145.

[119] Ibid., 146.

[120] Ibid.

[121] Christopher Roman, "The Dialogue of Catherine of Siena: A Charity Born of Solitude," *Magistra* 21:1 (2015): 110-131,110.

love of me and love of the neighbor; in these, as I have testified, consist the Law and the Prophets. I want you to fulfill these two commandments. On two feet you must walk...and with two wings you must fly to heaven.[122]

After accepting the Lord's call to a more apostolic "love of the neighbor," Catherine replied, "Let Your will be done in all things"; she did, however, express concern about how she, "a frail woman," might minister to her neighbor.[123] The Lord reassured Catherine with the words: "Nothing is impossible to God...am I not He who created the human race and divided it into male and female....In my eyes there is neither male nor female, rich nor poor, but all are equal, for I can do all things with equal ease...It is written of me that I made whatever I willed to make, for nothing is impossible to me (Psalm 113)."[124]

Blessed Margaret of Castello and Saint Catherine of Siena both began their religious lives in solitary interaction with the Lord, Margaret in her anchoritic cell and Catherine, secluded in a small room in her family home. Catherine was directly instructed by God that she must leave her treasured solitude and minister to the needs of her neighbor: "on two feet you must walk." Margaret was led, by the circumstances of her life, to leave, first, the enclosure of her cell, and later the monastic cloister, that she might become a servant of the sick and the outcast.

Neither Catherine nor Margaret were nuns; they were rather Lay Dominicans, Sisters of Penance of St. Dominic, but possessed of a solitude of heart which directed their apostolic activities to care for the needy and the marginalized. In commenting on the topic of "solitude of heart," Cistercian Sister Gail Fitzpatrick observed that enclosure, and resultant solitude, is not restricted to monastics alone. She quotes an anonymous Cistercian nun who wrote: "The real cloister or enclosure is the heart of one dedicated to undivided love of God, not the enclosed space of the cloister."[125] Sister Gail asserted that "the essence of enclosure is the guarding of one's heart. The purpose of guarding one's heart is total availability for God," which is appropriate for the laity as well as for vowed religious.[126]

---

[122] Raymond of Capua, *The Life of Catherine of Siena*, Trans. George Lamb (Charlotte, N.C.: Tan Books, 2011), 89-90.
[123] Ibid., 90.
[124] Ibid.
[125] Ibid.
[126] Ibid., 102.

Blessed Margaret of Castello

The ministries of Blessed Margaret of Castello and Saint Catherine of Siena cannot help but bring to mind the frequently quoted mandate of St. Vincent de Paul when, in the 17th Century, he asked his formerly cloistered Daughters of Charity, to leave their religious houses to minister to the sick and the poor: "Your convent will be the house of the sick; your cell, a hired room; your chapel, the parish church; your cloister, the streets of the city, or the wards of the hospital."[127]

Blessed Margaret of Castello was gifted with the experience of Christian solitude for approximately 14 or 15 years, 13 of those while enclosed in a small cell, initially as a child, and later as an adolescent anchoress. After removal from her anchoritic cell, Margaret was also "enclosed" in an isolated vault in a family palazzo during local warfare (this is discussed in the following chapter). It was, however, Blessed Margaret's anchoritic years, the period of solitary enclosure in her religious cell, which some authors have described as "imprisonment," that became the spiritual catalyst for a future ministry to the sick and the outcast. As noted earlier, "the concepts of service and solitude belong together like the ebb and flow of the ocean waves." Even after being forced to leave the solitude of her small anchorhold, young Margaret sought periods of solitude in local churches, in hidden corners of the homes of the poor, and in a garret space in a residence of the wealthy.

Margaret's times of solitude, spent alone with her Beloved Lord, provided her with the strength, and the compassion and the love to embrace her ministry to the sick and the outcast. It was this solitude that provided the seemingly fragile "Little Margaret" with the courage to respond to a spiritual call to make her way, blind and lame and with curved spine, along the cobblestone streets to the desolate houses of the sick poor and to the hopeless prisons of city, where the ill and the outcasts awaited her tenderness and her caring. It was in solitude that Beata Margherita of *Citta di Castello*, was able to hear the voice of God and to respond with fearless courage: "Here I am Lord, send me!"

The purpose of this chapter has been to explore what reclusive solitude may have been like when lived in the era of the middle ages. As explained earlier, young Margaret did not choose to be enclosed in an anchoritic setting at the age of six years but by the grace of God and the teaching of her priest chaplain, she was able to embrace and even welcome the solitude, not as a punishment but as a gift from the Blessed Lord who, she trusted, only wished to draw her closer to Himself.

---

[127] *Daughters of Charity Vocation Program* (Emmitsburg, Md.: Daughters of Charity, 1993), p. 1.

In the remaining chapters, the many joys and sufferings which accompanied Blessed Margaret's vocation are examined; it was, however, clearly her thirteen years as a religious anchoress which provided the spiritual strength and resilience to cope with the many challenges the blessed was to encounter. Margaret accepted, always with confidence in God's love, whatever difficulties beset her; she embraced painful experiences with a sense of peace and clarity of mind and spirit far beyond her years. In the following chapter, Margaret of Castello's second and third abandonments and her accompanying trust in divine providence are examined.

ENDNOTES for Chapter 2. "The Darkness is Not Dark"

[i] A current internet search documented only 2 contemporary American women listed as "Professed Anchoresses'; one died in January 2016. She had apparently been living as an anchoress since her public profession in an east coast Archdiocese in the year 2000. The other "publicly professed anchoress" is also affiliated with a Roman Catholic Diocese; a website describes the Sister as a "Diocesan Anchoress" and identifies her primary ministry as "prayer and penance…offered for Our Holy Father, all Bishops and clergy, (the Bishop of her Diocese)…the universal Church and every societal culture throughout the world" (www.ourladyoftenderness.com).

Blessed Margaret of Castello

Chapter 3. "He Will Not Break a Bruised Reed"

The Failed Miracle

"He will not break a bruised reed or quench a smoldering wick."
Matthew 12: 20

A Bruised Reed

Rejected anew through human fear,
Bruised and alone this gentle one.
No miracle cure had happened here,
Her only hope the Crucified Son.

She abandoned all to Him alone,
For in the pain her heart was free.
No other love would be ever known,
She would live and serve eternally.

As described in the previous chapter, Blessed Margaret embraced the painful experiences in her life "with a sense of peace and clarity of mind and spirit far beyond her years"; this sense of peace and understanding would, however, be sorely tested now as Margaret was about to encounter a new kind of "solitude"; it was to be a solitude very different from that which she experienced during the 13 years in her small anchorhold.

Before examining this next phase in Blessed Margaret's spiritual journey, it is important to reflect on the history of the Lord's loving care for His precious daughter who trusted implicitly in His guidance and protection. Despite severe physical challenges, as well as the emotional challenge of parental rejection, "Little Margaret" never lost faith in the infinite goodness of God who was the center of her life. It was only that strongly held and unwavering faith in God's protective love and tender care which enabled Margaret to face two additional deeply painful experiences in her young life: the total isolation of an underground vault in the family Palazzo in Mercatello and a failed miracle at the Franciscan Shrine of Fra Giacomo in *Citta di Castello*.

We have already been told by Margaret's biographers that her small body was compromised by lameness, related to one leg being shorter than the other, by a skeletal deformity of the spine which the contemporary medical community would label kyphosis, by congenital blindness, and by very short stature. Any one of these physical challenges might pose a negative spiritual response in a young child; all four could be overwhelming. Yet, "Little Margaret" was consistently described as cheerful, loving and a joy to those she met; it was reported that during her early years she had already developed a serious spiritual life, that she loved God and loved to pray.

According to her biographers, Margaret's father based his decision to enclose his daughter in the cell next to a church because he was told that "Little Margaret" was very devout and liked to spend hours in the chapel praying. While it is, admittedly, difficult for one with a 21st-century mentality to accept that the six-year-old Margaret was "very devout" and liked to "spend hours" in prayer, it must be remembered that childhood, especially childhood spirituality, was perceived very differently in the middle ages. Also, chronological age in the 13th Century cannot be compared to that of the present day as children matured much earlier in that era.[1] In discussing "childhood and adolescence among thirteenth century saints," Michael Goodich observed that "one of the most frequently found images of childhood among the medieval saints is that of a child whose attitudes and behavior before the age of seven are those of an old man or woman."[2] An example Goodich presents is that of "the precocious Margaret of *Citta di Castello* (who) wore a hairshirt and restricted her diet to bread and water" while still a young child.[3]

Such self-chosen penances were not unusual in Blessed Margaret's era; many medieval individuals embraced spiritual practices of suffering, in the absence of martyrdom, in order "to die in small ways for God."[4]

---

[1] Barbara A. Hanawalt, "Medievalists and the Study of Childhood," *Speculum* 77:2 (2002): 440-460.

[2] Michael E. Goodich, *Lives and Miracles of the Saints: Studies in Medieval Latin Hagiography* (Burlington, Vt.: Ashgate Publishing, 2004), 287.

[3] Ibid., 288.

[4] Patricia M. Vinje, *Praying with Catherine of Siena* (Winona, Minn.: Saint Mary's Press, 1990), 18.

Nurse and theologian Judith Allen Shelly has asserted that "stories abound of very young children who made serious and lasting commitments to God."[5] "Little Margaret" of Castello exemplified Shelly's assertion in making a commitment to living a spirit of penance for the salvation of sinners when she was only seven years old.[6]

In exploring the literature on spirituality in childhood one finds a plethora of journal articles focused on such topics as: nurturing a child's spirituality,[7] spirituality and child development,[8] knowing God in childhood,[9] child theology and spirituality,[10] and children as mystics.[11]

While we may tend to think of "Little Margaret" of Castello's childhood spirituality as unique and extraordinary, students of the spirituality of children remind us that the faith of a young child is indeed unique and may, in fact, be extraordinary in a number of cases. The rich inner life of a child's spirituality is an attribute not easily compared to that of an adult. Children are born with a capacity for faith development, but "often their expression of spirituality may be limited by adults' ability to understand them."[12]

As to "Little Margaret"'s desire to pray, even when very young, some understanding is provided by the words of Sofia Cavelleti, author of *The Religious Potential of the Child*: "It is a fact that children have an extraordinary capacity for prayer, as regards duration as well as spontaneity and dignity of expression. Theirs is a prayer of praise and thanksgiving which expresses the nearness and transcendence of God at the same time."[13] Cavaletti asserted: "Children pray with great facility;

---

[5] Judith Allen Shelly, "Jesus and the Children: A Mandate to Care," in *The Spiritual Needs of Children*, Ed. Judith A. Shelly (Downer's Grove, Ill.: Intervarsity Press, 1982), 11-16, 12.

[6] *Blessed Margaret of Castello OP: A Medieval Biography* (Trans. Carolina Accorsi) (Fatima, Portugal: Dominican Nuns of the Perpetual Rosary, 1994), 17.

[7] Rita Pfund, "Nurturing A Child's Spirituality," *Journal of Child Health Care* 4:4 (2000): 143-148.

[8] Joanna Smith, "Spirituality and Child Development: A Concept Analysis," *Journal of Advanced Nursing* 45:3 (2004): 307-315.

[9] Catherine Stonehouse, "Knowing God in Childhood: A Study of Godly Play and the Spirituality of Children," *Christian Education Journal* 5:2 (2001): 27-45.

[10] Vivienne Mountain, "Four Links Between Child Theology and Children's Spirituality," *International Journal of Children's Spirituality* 16 (3): (2011): 261-271.

[11] Joyce A. Mercer, "Children as Mystics, Activists, Sages and Holy Fools: Understanding the Spirituality of Children and It's Significance for Clinical Work," *Pastoral Psychology* 54:5 (2006): 497-515.

[12] Carolyn R. Mueller, "Spirituality in Children: Understanding and Developing Interventions," *Pediatric Nursing* 36:4 (2010): 197-208, 197.

[13] Sofia Cavelleti, *The Religious Potential of the Child*, Trans. Patricia M. Coulter and Julie M. Coulter (Chicago: Liturgy Training Publications, 1992), 44.

we find they are always disposed to prayer, which can be a time of special enchantment for them."[14] For young Margaret, prayer was indeed a time of "enchantment." It was reported that she loved to spend time in communion with God, first in the castle chapel and later during enclosure in her small cell next to the chapel in the forest of Metola.

Some of "Little Margaret"'s spiritual insights, described as emanating from her "luminous" mind, would seem to support the perception of a pediatric chaplain who observed that "children think a lot about faith and have more ability in theological reflection that most adults give them credit for."[15] Margaret of Castello's fervent religious practices also reflect the assertion of spiritual writer Margaret Burkhardt that: "children live in their spirits more than adults," spirituality being the "deepest core of the child's being."[16]

A recent study of the spirituality of children revealed that "a child often asks existential questions related to being aware of powers greater than himself,"[17] and that "children's spirituality is transformational by inspiring others."[18] Children can be viewed as "mystics, activists, sages and holy fools in relation to their spiritual beliefs";[19] child theology considers the aspects of a child's faith as related to "living...in relationships, living in vulnerability, living in creativity and play, living in openness and hope."[20]

Finally, and perhaps most relevant to our interest is Blessed Margaret of Castello, is the perception of the positive relationship between childhood spirituality and resiliency. Spirituality and resiliency in children are believed to "mutually support each other."[21] The attribute of resilience...

> helps us to come to a more complex image of children. Resilience is the potential possessed by people to thrive even after

---

[14] Ibid.

[15] George F. Handzo, "Talking About Faith with Children," *Journal of Christian Nursing* 7:4 (1990): 17-20, 17.

[16] Margaret A. Burkhardt, "Spirituality and Children: Nursing Considerations," *Journal of Holistic Nursing* 9:2 (1991): 31-40, 34.

[17] Joseph M. Cervantes and Alexis V. Arczynski, "Children's Spirituality: Conceptual Understanding of Developmental Transformation," *Spirituality in Clinical Practice* 2: 4(2015): 245-255, 245.

[18] Kathleen I. Harris, "Re-conceptualizing Spirituality in the Light of Educating Young Children," *International Journal of Children's Spirituality* 12:3 (2007): 263-275, 263.

[19] Mercer, 497.

[20] Mountain, 261.

[21] Annemie Dillen, "The Resiliency of Children and Spirituality: A Practical Theological Reflection," *International Journal of Children's Spirituality* 17:1 (2012): 67-75, 61.

experiencing bad conditions. Resilience refers to children's ability to cope with difficult situations and to grow through the experience of these difficulties. Examples often refer to children who have been abused, who live on the streets or in poverty…Children are not only passive victims, destined to suffer endlessly under the bad conditions in which they live, but they may, in some cases, find ways to cope with the difficulties. Resilience can be seen as a specific form of agency possessed by children, although it is at the same time highly influenced by other conditions of the ecological context of children (e.g, family, church, school, society, culture) and, in theological terms, by "grace."[22]

Nurturing spirituality can greatly contribute to and enhance a child's resilience;[23] and supporting spiritual and religious beliefs can help "promote stress resilience in survivors of childhood trauma."[24]

When considering the relationship between spirituality and resilience in children, one cannot help but envision the small Margaret, both in her first six years in the family castle and later as she grew up in the enclosure of an anchoress' cell. Surely no child, either medieval or contemporary, could model more beautifully the concept of resilience following the extreme trauma of parental rejection combined with serious physical challenges; it was indeed "Little Margaret"'s spirituality, manifested by an absolute trust in God and a consistent prayer life, which promoted her resilience in coping with stressors which might well have destroyed another. It must be admitted that Margaret's spirituality and spiritual and religious practices were strongly supported, even in early childhood, by the castle Chaplain Fra Cappellano. The spiritual and religious education and support, provided by her chaplain, no doubt importantly facilitated Blessed Margaret's "stress resilience" following the experience of parental rejection.

The author of a recent article on fostering the spirituality of children with disabilities observed that "the spiritual aspect of life has the potential to affect one's quality of life in terms of the emotional and physical well-being, relationships and social inclusion," and that "spirituality plays an important role in the lives of many people with

---

[22] Ibid., 61-62.
[23] Ibid., 62.
[24] Kathleen Brewer-Smyth and Harold G. Koenig, "Could Spirituality and Religion Promote Stress Resilience in Survivors of Childhood Trauma?" *Issues in Mental Health Nursing* 35:4 (2014): 251-256, 251.

disabilities."[25] Surely Blessed Margaret's legend reflects the fact that spirituality did positively affect her "emotional and physical well-being," as witnessed by her ability to survive and thrive in a variety of stressful environments; spirituality supported her "relationships," in that "Little Margaret" reportedly was loved by all who met her both as a child and later in her adult ministry; and spirituality was central to "social inclusion," reflected in Margaret's loving acceptance by the *Citta di Castello* community, and, more specifically, by the community of Dominican Tertiaries, The Sisters of Penance of St. Dominic.

Thus, it is apparent that, from early childhood, God was preparing His beloved "Little Margaret" to become "Blessed Margaret" in her ministry to the sick and the outcast. Before this ministry of care for the poor could begin, however, Margaret's spirituality was tried, as in a fire, so that her heart would be refined as precious "gold" in the employ of the Master.

Many years ago, in a course on the spirituality of church, our professor reminded his class of enthusiastic "would be" ministers that while we were all filled with excitement and joy at the thought of going forth to serve, and to spread the Gospel message of Jesus, there was a "small matter of a journey to Jerusalem" that went along with the calling. This was the blessed "way of the Cross," which each of us would need to embrace if our service was to be fruitful. Blessed Margaret had already embraced "the way of the Cross" mightily in her young life but the Lord had even greater plans for his daughter.

Margaret may well have learned God's powerful and beautiful scripture promises in her lessons with Fra Cappellano "Come to me, all you that are weary and carrying heavy burdens, and I will give you rest. Take my yoke upon you, and learn from me, for I am gentle and humble of heart and you will find rest for your souls. For my yoke is easy and my burden is light" (Matthew 11: 28-30). Nevertheless, Blessed Margaret's gentle and loving heart would be tried again, and again, in the months to come, and would be cleansed and purified, fit only for the service of a King.

Mercatello
The Palazzo Vault

From the very first days of her enclosure in the small cell or "anchorhold," attached to the church of St. Mary of the Fortress of

---

[25] Kaili D. Zhang, "Fostering the Inner Life of Children with Special Needs," *International Journal of Disability, Development and Education* 60: 3 (2013): 242-252, 242.

Metola, the young Margaret found happiness and comfort in the availability and accessibility of ongoing spiritual support. Because her cell had a window opening into the chancel, Margaret was not only able to hear Mass each day and receive the sacraments of Penance and the Holy Eucharist but she could also pray before Jesus in the Blessed Sacrament as often as she desired. As well as the church liturgies and her private devotions, Blessed Margaret also had the gift of Chaplain Giacomo Cappellano's visits which provided ongoing religious teaching and spiritual guidance. And as, described in the previous chapter, it appears that Margaret's cell had an external window which allowed fresh air and sunlight to enter her room; through the window, also, God sent the songs of her little friends, the thrushes, who sang to her of His companionship and His caring. Margaret may have seemed, to some, to have been a "prisoner" but she was a "prisoner" of love as the Lord sought to draw his precious daughter closer to Himself.

Sadly, however, as Blessed Margaret was reaching later adolescence, the medieval Italian world surrounding her enclosure was in turmoil. We are told by the "Medieval Biographer," by Fr. William Bonniwell and by other authors that, at the time, feelings of anxiety abounded among the Metola Castle residents, including Margaret's parents, and the citizens of the neighboring towns and villages. There was fear that the village of Metola, and the adjacent area of Massa Trabaria, were about to be invaded by hostile armies. This was a valid concern as medieval Italian towns were often "in danger of attack by foreign invaders looking for land and riches, and by neighboring lords and soldiers trying to gain control of the towns from other nobles. These nobles wanted to control the towns so they could collect taxes and tolls from the people who lived there and who visited."[26] Massa Trabaria, the medieval community nearest Castle Metola was particularly at risk as it was a "Papal State," "vulnerable to attack with no guarantee of military defense."[27]

A day ultimately came when it was rumored throughout the local towns and villages that an invasion of Massa Trabaria and Metola, by a military leader named Montefeltro of Urbino, was imminent. This heightened the fears, not only of the local citizens, but especially of young Margaret of Castello. Margaret was not concerned for her own safety; her trust remained in God who had consistently protected her. Blessed Margaret was, however, extremely anxious about the fate of her father who she knew would be leading his army to fight the invaders.

---

[26] Lynne Elliott, *Medieval Towns, Trade and Travel* (N.Y.: Crabtree Publishing, 2004), 6.
[27] Lucinda Vardey, *Traveling with the Saints in Italy: Contemporary Pilgrimages on Ancient Paths* (Mahwah, N.J.: Hidden Springs, 2005),151.

Margaret never lost her love and respect for both parents, despite the repeated rejection of their physically challenged daughter.

It was reported that "in addition to concern for the fate of his estate and the military organization of which he was a competent Captain," the problem of Margherita "reappeared on the horizon for the Lord of Metola."[28] Parisio's priority was to prepare for a military siege but he also wanted to protect his family; one of his greatest fears was that "the identity of Margaret could be discovered."[29] The thought of his enemies finding his physically challenged offspring "terrified him"; he would have become "the laughing stock of his opponents."[30]

Barbara Sartori commented that the author of the *Legenda Maior* "does not dwell on the historical details that made it necessary to move"; it merely "informs us of the fact that, since the wars became more violent, Margherita was forced to walk away from the Church of Santa Maria" (The Church of St. Mary of the Fortress of Metola).[31;i]

Because of the overwhelming fear that his physically compromised daughter might be discovered by an invading hoarde, Margaret's father, Parisio, ordered that she be immediately removed, after 13 years, from her peaceful religious enclosure of the small cell in the forest. The only solution, Parisio determined, was to install Margaret in a vault, located underneath the family palazzo in the nearby town of Mercatello.[32] Thus, Blessed Margaret, now:

> disguised by a veil, traveled by carriage to the palace with her mother. Any hope that Margaret had of reconciliation with her parents was dashed, as she was placed in...a prison, the underground vault of the palace, furnished only with a simple bench and table. She was instructed to remain absolutely quiet, to never call out, and to speak only with the servant who brought her daily meals...there were no visits from the priest and she could not partake of Mass and the sacraments. She had nothing but darkness and total solitude.[33]

---

[28] Barbara Sartori, *Beata Margherita di Citta di Castello* (Milano, Italy: Paoline Editorale Libri, 2011), 29.
[29] Ibid.
[30] Ibid.
[31] Ibid.
[32] *Blessed Margaret of Castello OP*; William R. Bonniwell, *The Life of Blessed Margaret of Castello:1287-1320* (Charlotte, N.C.: Tan Books, 2014).
[33] Vardey, 151.

Father Bonniwell suggests that, "as if to conform to the custom in most jails, (Margaret) was briefed on the regulations of her new prison...Food would be brought to her twice a day; if there was anything she wanted, she was to wait until mealtime to state her wants. Under no circumstances was she to call out; at all times she was to preserve absolute quiet."[34]

After all the rules had been stated, Fr. Bonniwell mused, "the heavy wooden door of the vault was slammed shut, the bolts were shot into their sockets, and Margaret once more found herself alone."[35]

Parisio's rationale for installing Blessed Margaret in the Palazzo vault in Mercatello was different from that of his decision to enclose her in the cell near the forest chapel in Metola. When attempting to convince his wife, Emilia, to support the decision to have a cell or anchorhold built for the the six-year-old "Little Margaret," Parisio rationalized that this would be a safe and secure setting where their afflicted daughter could spend her days in prayer, an activity she had taken to as a young child. In that cell she would have access to the sacraments of the Church and visits from the castle chaplain. Parisio also cited the enclosure of St. Veridiana, who embraced the life of an anchoress at a young age, and continued in the vocation for 34 years. A similar life was envisioned as a potential future for Margaret.

Unfortunately, the move from the peaceful religious setting of her cell to a dark, lonely underground vault was made for a different reason; the fear that, during the ongoing military conflicts in the area, Margaret's anchorhold, and thus her identity, might be discovered and reflect badly on the parentage of Parisio and Emilia. In today's world, Blessed Margaret's imprisonment in the Palazzo vault in Mercatello would be considered parental abuse, both physical and emotional; the young woman was only to interact with servants who delivered her food and must not call out for assistance at any other times. Margaret was, also, in this setting, totally isolated from her religious practices, especially the reception of the sacraments.

In the dank and securely fortified room of the Palazzo vault in Mercatello, Blessed Margaret was now truly "imprisoned." With the exception of those who brought her food, there were no servants from whom to seek information, guidance or even medical assistance if Margaret should become ill. There were no visits from her beloved castle chaplain and no access to the treasured times of prayer before Jesus in the Blessed Sacrament. One cannot help but consider the depth of

---

[34] Bonniwell, 25-26.
[35] Ibid., 26.

loneliness and alienation young Margaret might have been expected to experience in such an isolated environment, devoid of physical, emotional and spiritual support.

But we must also remember that Blessed Margaret had long ago committed her heart to embracing the cross as presented in her life, at whatever time and in whatever way, her Beloved Lord and Savior chose. For Margaret there was no turning back; she had "put her hand to the plough" as a child, and it was this choice which set the direction for her future ministry to the poor, the sick and the outcast.

The lack of attention to Margaret's cruel treatment by her father is explained, to some degree, by the research of scholar of medieval children, Nicholas Orme, who asserted that, in the Middle Ages, "physical abuse in the home, in particular, attracted little attention. Commentators...taught that parents punished their children too lightly, not too much. Courts, whether secular or religious, had small concern with the matter."[36] Thus, even if Margaret's imprisonment in the Mercatello vault was a concern to servants or neighbors it probably would not have been reported to authorities, either civil or ecclesiastical.

This period of enclosure was a time of intense suffering for Margaret because of the isolation from her usual spiritual and religious practices and especially related to the absence of visits from Chaplain Cappellano. Yet, although Blessed Margaret's faith must have been greatly challenged by this experience, she never gave in to despair. The "Medieval Biographer" expressed the opinion that Margaret was being tried by an "envious enemy" (the devil) who sought to "perturb and take advantage of her whom the angel of the Lord prepares and forms in order that he may present her to Jesus Crucified."[37] The early Medieval Biographer asserted that Blessed Margaret, isolated in the palazzo vault at Mercatello, conquered the "enemy" with "patience and humility."[38]

Neither the Medieval Biographer nor Fr. William Bonniwell tell us exactly how long Margaret was forced to remain in the underground palazzo vault, although one author suggests "a couple of years."[39] As it turned out, "the siege of Massa Trabaria" by Montefeltro did not happen.[40] After much negotiation, a peace treaty was signed, and "Emilia

---

[36] Nicholas Orme, *Medieval Children* (New Haven, Ct.: Yale University Press, 2001), 101.
[37] *Blessed Margaret of Castello OP*, 18-19.
[38] Ibid., 20.
[39] Vardey, 152.
[40] Sartori, 31.

and the child were able to return home."[41] This, of course, posed a further dilemma of what to do with Margaret.[ii]

With a new sense of peace in the area, groups of pilgrims were beginning to arrive; this often happened in the middle ages when devout pilgrims travelled some distance "to saints' shrines and other places of religious importance."[42] One group of German pilgrims visiting *Citta di Castello* and the neighboring area captured the attention of the Massa Trabaria townspeople with their stories of miraculous healings of the sick and disabled which had taken place at the tomb of a recently deceased holy Franciscan, Fra Giacomo of Castello; it was reported that many miracles had occurred through his intervention.[43] The pilgrims' stories eventually reached the ears of Margaret's mother, Emilia, who was captivated by the accounts of healings; she immediately envisioned a possible solution to the dilemma of coping with her daughter's physical challenges. Margaret could be cured!

The concept of a healing pilgrimage for young Margaret was not unheard of in the era of the middle ages. Nicholas Orme, in his writing on medieval children, observed that for an ill or disabled child often "a personal pilgrimage was needed before a cure was received."[44] As examples he identified three cases of healings: one, a boy with a stone lodged in his ear which, it was believed, could not be removed until he visited a shrine; the healing of a crippled girl who had "needed a staff to support her" walking; and, a seven year old girl who had such badly crippled fingers that she could not feed herself. All three were cured after visiting a saint's tomb.[45]

Margaret's mother, Emilia, desperately sought a healing miracle for her daughter. This was not solely for Margaret's sake but was particularly important for the image and status of Emilia and Parisio as noble parents. Sadly, a medieval child born with disfigurements, missing limbs, short stature, could be blamed on the parent's inadequacies; it was believed that the "parents might physically generate too much or too little material to form a perfect child."[46] Any affliction, or "disablement," "might also be traced to parents thoughts or actions...during pregnancy which were then transferred to their

---

[41] Ibid., 33.
[42] Elliott, 27.
[43] Sartori, 31.
[44] Orme, 111.
[45] Ibid.
[46] Orme, 96.

offspring."[47] And, shockingly, "badly disabled children also invited questions about their identity; were they human?"[48] One can understand, in some sense, then, why Margaret's parents, Parisio and Emilia, were so distraught at having conceived and given birth to a severely physically challenged child; and, why they were so fearful of anyone outside of their immediate castle environment learning of Margaret's afflictions.

It is, however, also important to point out that, in the Middle Ages, "deformity" also aroused compassion: "Some such children were loved and nurtured as dearly as the fully formed."[49] Orme gives an example of remains found in "the graves of disabled adults, one with a congenitally absent left arm and the second with an imperfectly grown right leg...both implied survival, thanks to the care and support of others."[50] Had "Little Margaret"'s parents not been so concerned for the reputation of their noble family, a different path might have been chosen for their daughter.

While it took some persuasion to convince Parisio of the possibility of a healing miracle occurring for Margaret, he finally agreed to a family visit to the tomb of Fra Giacomo in *Citta di Castello*. Thus:

> After two years in solitary confinement in the vault in her family's home, Margaret, who was now almost twenty, was led out in a party, including both her parents. They left early on a foggy morning...arriving in *Citta di Castello* to stay at an inn for the night. The family attended early morning Mass the next day at the Church of St. Francis, and then prayed at Fra. Giacomo's tomb for a miracle cure.[51]

The miracle, Parisio and Emilia believed, "was to be their salvation: a daughter whose sight was restored and her body made whole."[52] The parents believed that surely the Lord would not withhold a miraculous cure from such a noble family. Margaret also embraced the hope that a healing miracle could finally relieve her parents of the burden her afflictions had placed on them from the time of her birth. Blessed

---

[47] Ibid., 96-97.
[48] Ibid., 97
[49] Ibid.
[50] Ibid.
[51] Lucinda Vardey, *Traveling with the Saints in Italy: Contemporary Pilgrimages on Ancient Paths* (Mahwah, N.J.: Hidden Springs, 2005), 152.
[52] Ivan Innerst, *Saints for Today: Reflections on Lesser Saints* (San Francisco: Ignatius Press, 2000), 81.

Margaret, as usual, always thought of the needs and concerns of others before herself.

Citta di Castello
The Failed Miracle

After morning Mass and prayers at the tomb of Fra Giacomo, Margaret's parents left her with instructions to pray as hard as possible for a cure from all of her infirmities. Margaret obeyed her parents in praying for a cure but, with a faith and love born of many years of intimacy with the Lord, she also prayed "not my will but thine be done"; young Margaret remained in prayer of both petition and acceptance. "If God wanted her healed, she would accept it, but if He wanted her to remain in her present physical condition, she would accept that too. She passed the entire day at the Shrine and enjoyed being in a new environment, especially one as holy as this."[53]

During her time at the Shrine, Margaret must have become fatigued from the long journey which had, the day before, preceded her visit yet she is described as having remained deeply in prayer for many hours; such was Blessed Margaret's love for and devotion to God and so powerful was her trust in His care and compassion. He would take care of her, in His own way, Margaret had no doubt.

At the day's end Parisio and Emilia returned to the church fully expecting the anticipated miracle of healing and wholeness for Margaret; they felt that, being a distinguished family, God could not possibly refuse a request for healing which, they had been told, had been granted to other pilgrims, less important than themselves. But it was not to be. They saw Margaret rapt in prayer but recognized immediately that the wished for miracle had not taken place. They were sorely distressed. Parisio and Emilia's blind daughter remained blind and afflicted: "God had tricked them, had made fun of them. So the parents, 'reports the *Legenda Maior*,' are overwhelmed by this grief because they see their daughter denied of sight, and ruthless as they are," they leave Margaret alone in *Citta di Castello* "without any human help."[54]

The Medieval Biographer provided a spiritual understanding of the Lord's failure to heal Margaret's blindness: "The Lord has made her blind, for fear that through sight of lands, she be deprived of the celestial vision by which He was enlightening her mind through contemplation."[55]

---

[53] James Heater and Coleen Heater, *The Pilgrim's Italy: A Travel Guide to the Saints* (Nevada City, Ca.: Inner Travel Books, 2008), 208.
[54] Sartori, 36.
[55] *Blessed Margaret of Castello OP*, 20-21.

Another interpretation of the "failed miracle" was offered by Ivan Innerst:

> (The cure) was not to happen as (the parents) hoped, and we are left once more to reflect on the ways of providence. For there were, as has been said, miraculous cures reported at this shrine. Could it be that in the eyes of God she (Margaret) was in no need of a cure, without blemish? Could this blind and lame young woman be just as He intended she be, so there was nothing whatever He meant to have changed? Perhaps she was for the edification of us all?[56]

Innerst continued: "The wishes of the couple from the castle were not, in any case, granted. Nothing about their daughter was altered or in any manner transformed, and they responded in a fashion wholly typical for them. They left her, who was in their lives so great a burden, to fend for herself in the streets of a strange city."[57] In the words of the Medieval Biographer: "after their daughter had been denied restitution of her vision, her parents were overcome by fatigue (and, he added) because they loathed her, the impious ones left her alone, away from all human aid."[58]

As soon as the realization hit Margaret's parents that their daughter had not been cured of her physical challenges, and probably never would be, they sought to return with haste to the peace and safety of their castle:

> God's refusal to meet their demand was the last straw. Once certain there would be no miracle, they (the parents) left their daughter exactly where she was, praying at the tomb of Fra Giocoso (sic). They abandoned her to the streets of Castello and returned to their castle, never to be threatened again by the "shame" of a severely disabled daughter. They never saw Margaret again.[59]

Meanwhile, young Margaret, remained in prayer and anticipation of her parents return; she could not, at first, believe that they had deserted

---

[56] Innerst, 81.
[57] Ibid.
[58] *Blessed Margaret of Castello OP*, 21.
[59] Janice McGrane, *Saints to Lean On: Spiritual Companions for Illness and Disability* (Cincinnati, Ohio: St. Anthony Messenger Press, 2006), 7.

her. As evening approached, she was told, kindly but firmly, by a Franciscan lay Brother, that she must leave the church so the door could be locked for the night. Thus, Margaret "found herself cold, hungry and lost on the steps of a church in a town she didn't know."[60;iii]

As the Church door was now locked, and Margaret had no money or acquaintances in *Citta di Castello*, her only recourse was to remain huddled on the Chiesa di San Francesco steps while continuing to hope that Parisio and Emilia would come for her. As the hours passed, however, we can only imagine what Margaret must have experienced, alone, frightened, tired and wondering what she would do if her parents did not return. The abandonment would have been devastating for any young woman; Blessed Margaret's physical challenges, being blind and lame especially, surely must have added to her anxiety and her suffering.

Trust in God's Providence

Despite the abandoned state in which Margaret found herself in *Citta di Castello*, she never lost trust in God's providence. Author Ubaldo Valentini observed that "Blessed Margaret reminds us that life is worth living and just as we were given…Margaret chose eternity, while having reasonable grounds to rebel against man and God. Not only did she not, but she accepted God with enthusiasm and loved her neighbor as herself".[61] "Here," Valentini added "is her greatness and her eternity."[62]

One wonders how Blessed Margaret, as a young woman suddenly alone as never before, as the result of a second rejection by her parents, could possibly continue to trust in God, to trust in His Divine providence? To attempt to comprehend her faith we must remember that as a child, when she was indeed "Little Margaret," the blessed "lived at the school of the Cross."[63] The "life of Blessed Margaret," Valentini reminds us, was "closely tied to the Cross of Christ and all of (His) pain and suffering."[64] Margaret "embraces the Cross for love and thus becomes capable of loving brothers as did Francis of Assisi with the leper or Dominic de Guzman with crowds deceived by heretics."[65] To Margaret, trust in God's providence for her life, was her life.

---

[60] Vardey, 152.
[61] Ubaldo Valentini, *Beata Margherita De La Metola Una Sfida Alla Emarginazione* (Perugia, Italy: Petruzzi Editore, 1988), 15.
[62] Ibid.
[63] Valentini, 63.
[64] Ibid., 8.
[65] Sartori, 11.

Divine providence is defined broadly as "the way God has chosen to relate to us and provide for our well-being";[66] put more simply, providence is the way God cares for us. There are witnesses to God's providence in both the Old and the New Testaments: Adam and Eve's provisions in the Garden of Eden; God's plan for the Jewish people's exodus from Egypt; Jesus' teachings: in Matthew 10:29, that the hairs on our heads are numbered; and the Lord's promise in Matthew 7:7: "Ask and it will be given, seek and you will find."[67] God's providence is a "central article of the Christian faith. If the doctrines of creation and redemption are to be properly related, then some account must be given of how the work of the Creator is extended beyond an initial act of making the universe from out of nothing."[68]

There are times when many of us may question the way God has chosen to provide for our well-being; Margaret never did. She simply accepted that His love would never fail!

Frustration sometimes emerges when the response to those things which "we seek" from God do not seem to be forthcoming, at least not in the way or according to the timing which we desire. Blessed Margaret's request for healing, prayed at Fra Giacomo's tomb, provides the spiritual guidance: "Not my will, but Thine be done." For Margaret, the understanding of God's providence was simple: "If God wanted her to be healed she would accept it; but if He wanted her to remain in her present physical condition, she would accept that too."

Discussing the issue of God's providence and the suffering world, Rev. John Vissers observed: "The Christian doctrine of providence teaches that God not only created the world but also guides and guards it with a purpose."[69] Vissers admits, however, that "the Bible provides no ultimate theoretical answer to the problem of evil and suffering. Rather, Christian faith clings to Christ in the midst of it all."[70] Margaret of Castello's life is the example, par excellence, of this Christian faith.

As asserted by David Fergusson, in discussing the "theology" of Providence:

---

[66] John Sanders, *The God Who Risks: A Theology of Divine Providence* (Downer's Grove, Il.: IVP Academics, 2007), 12.

[67] Haydn J. McLean, "Thinking Out Loud: Pondering the Providence of God," *The Journal of Pastoral Care & Counseling* 62:3 (2008): 303-307, 303-304.

[68] David Fergusson, "The Theology of Providence," *Theology Today* 67:1 (2010): 261-278, 261.

[69] John Vissers, "God's Crucified Messiah: Providence, Incarnation and the Suffering World," *The Presbyterian Record* 133: 4 (2009): 31-32, 31.

[70] Ibid., 32.

God's providence in our lives is most evidently displayed not in material success, health, or other forms of prosperity. It is best evidenced in the knowledge of the forgiveness of sins and in the power of the sanctifying spirit. Providence is evident less in what happens to us than in how we live amidst the changes and chances of this mortal life. Its center is in the church's life of praise, confession, supplication, and obedience. From there, we can understand the course of our lives and our world as governed by God's good providence. But this must remain an expression of faith rather than a psychological insight, a cosmic vision or a political philosophy.[71]

Fergusson concludes that our understanding of providence must proceed "outward from the center of a faith grounded in the 'foolishness' of the Cross."[72] Margaret's entire life, albeit brief in today's understanding of mortality, was unequivocally centered in faith and in embracing the Cross. Her consistent and unfailing trust in God's desire for her well-being provided the bed-rock for the unequivocal faith that was demonstrated in the life of Blessed Margaret of Castello.

Despite the multiple physical challenges described earlier and myriad painful experiences of parental rejection and abandonment, Margaret's faith in the love and care of God never faltered. This was evident in all of the accounts of the blessed's spiritual journey. Margaret did not focus her desires on "material success, health or prosperity"; she believed that her life was "governed by God's good providence." Her understanding of God's care indeed "proceeded outward from the center of a faith grounded in the "foolishness of the Cross."

The Medieval Biographer tells us that, even though abandoned at the church in *Citta di Castello*, Blessed Margaret "was grateful to her Creator...she grew closer to Christ...(and) was received by God and began to radiate everlasting light."[73] The biographer explained: "(Margaret) was separated from the world so that her mind would enter eternal meditation more freely."[74]

Although they left her alone in the church in *Citta di Castello*, Margaret could not, initially, believe that her parents had deserted her; rather, she worried that some terrible evil had befallen Parisio and Emilia, her dear father and mother. One cannot help but be amazed at

---

[71] Fergusson, 275.
[72] Ibid.
[73] *Blessed Margaret of Castello OP*, 21-22.
[74] Ibid., 22.

this gentle young woman's humility and refusal to think ill of her parents despite the persistent lack of caring and compassion for their fragile daughter.

In today's world, the behavior of Blessed Margaret's parents would be condemned as criminal child abandonment; Parisio and Emilia would most likely be the ones imprisoned, not their physically challenged daughter. Current studies of parental abandonment have revealed that such behavior often results in a variety of negative mental health attitudes and behaviors on part of the abandoned child including anxiety, insecurity, anger, depression, aggression, and negative self-image.[75]

While the young Margaret may, of course, have experienced insecurity and anxiety when left by her parents in *Citta di Castello*, she never expressed thoughts of anger, depression, or aggression; her spirituality, demonstrated by faith and trust in God, overcame the destructive mental health deficits which might otherwise have overwhelmed her. Margaret was consistently forgiving in her judgement of her parents, Parisio and Emilia.

Forgiveness

Perhaps one of the most difficult virtues for many of us in that of forgiveness; forgiveness especially when we feel that we have been wounded unjustly. And, yet, Margaret, who was so many times wounded and so many times made to suffer unjustly, is the consummate model of Christian love and forgiveness. Margaret, through the example of her short time on earth, speaks to us of "a style of Christian life which is not only possible to look at, but which (we) are invited to share."[76] Barbara Sartori notes that Margaret can speak to the "disabled" and the "non-disabled"; to offer "an invitation not to be daunted by human misery, our

---

[75] Ronald Rohner, "The Parental 'Acceptance-Rejection' Syndrome: Universal Correlates of Perceived Rejection," *American Psychologist* 59:8 (2004): 830-840; Charles R. McAdams, John A. Dewell and Angela R. Holman, "Children and Chronic Sorrow: Reconceptualizing the Emotional Impact of Parental Rejection and Its Treatment," *Journal of Humanistic Counseling* 50:1 (2011): 27-41; Cheryl A. Boyce and Valerie Maholmes, "Attention to the Neglected: Prospects for Research on Child Neglect for the Next Decade," *Child Maltreatment* 18:1 (2013): 65-68; Joyce Akse, William Hale, Rutger Engels, Quinten Raaijmakers and Wim. Mseus, "Personality, Perceived Parental Rejection and Problem Behavior in Adolescence," *Social Psychiatry and Psychiatric Epidemiology* 39: 1 (2004): 980-988.

[76] Sartori, 10.

own or others'; to accept the challenge of relationships...and...to be fully men and women born from love and, therefore, called to love."[77]

Recently, "the study of forgiveness has flourished";[78] forgiveness is "considered a virtue in a diverse array of spiritual and religious traditions."[79] Forgiveness can be described as "a victim's reduction of negative (and usually increase in positive) thoughts, emotions, motivations and behaviors toward an offender";[80] the concept may be "sanctified" by "imbuing forgiveness with sacred meaning";[81] and is "closely related to religiousness and spirituality."[82] For Margaret of Castello, forgiveness was an imperative as she sought to imitate her Beloved Savior who surrendered his life asking: "Father, forgive them for they know not what they do!"

Forgiveness is also defined as a "freely made choice to give up revenge and resentment toward a person who caused a hurt and to strive to respond with generosity, compassion and kindness toward that person."[83] With forgiveness, "internal negative thoughts, behaviors, and feelings have been found to decrease, while positive thoughts, behaviors and feelings increase s one forgives another";[84] "in fact, increased mental and physical health is associated with forgiveness."[85]

This latter benefit of forgiveness is surely why our Blessed Margaret was able, despite a history of myriad physical and emotional challenges, to spend the final years of her life serving the sick and the outcast. She was lame, and yet she walked the streets of *Citta di Castello* seeking out

---

[77] Ibid. 118.
[78] D.E. Davis, J.N. Hook, E.L. Worthington, D.R. Van Tongren, A.L. Gartner and D.J. Jennings, "Relational Spirituality and Forgiveness: Development of the Spiritual Humility Scale," *Journal of Psychology and Theology* 38:1 (2010): 91-100, 91.
[79] Steven J. Sandage and Ian T. Williamson, "Relational Spirituality of Dispositional Forgiveness," *Journal of Psychology and Theology* 38:1 (2010): 255-266, 255.
[80] D.E. Davis, J.N. Hook, D.R. Van Tongren and E.L Worthington, "Sanctification of Forgiveness," *Psychology of Religion and Spirituality* 4 (2012): 31-39, 31.
[81] Ibid.
[82] Loren L. Toussaint, David R. Williams, Marc A. Musick and Susan A. Everson, "Forgiveness and Health: Age Differences in a U.S. Probability Sample," *Journal of Adult Development* 8:4 (2001): 249-257, 249.
[83] Inez Tuck and Lorraine Anderson, "Forgiveness, Flourishing and Resilience: The Influences of Expressions of Spirituality on Mental Health Recovery," *Mental Health Nursing* 35:4 (2014): 277-282, 278.
[84] Sarah L. Vasiliaukas and Mark R. McMinn, "The Effects of Prayer Intervention on the Process of Forgiveness," *Psychology of Religion and Spirituality* 5:1 (2013): 23-33, 23.
[85] L. Chang Hafnidar, "The Relationship among Five Factor Model of Personality, Spirituality and Forgiveness," *International Journal of Social Science and Humanity* 3:2 (2013), 167-176, 167.

the sick poor in need of her care and her compassion; she was blind, and yet she saw clearly the pain and suffering of incarcerated prisoners who needed her tenderness and her prayerful support; she was small of stature, with a curved spine, yet, spiritually, she stood straight and tall, a beacon of love and inspiration for all she met.

Forgiveness may sometimes involve a lengthy process; an individual's personal faith beliefs may, however, significantly facilitate closure. Three "negative spiritual appraisals" were identified which might hinder forgiveness; these included: "being angry toward God, viewing the transgression as a desecration or viewing the offender as evil."[86] Blessed Margaret never expressed anger toward God, never viewed transgressions against her as desecration and never considered her offending parents as evil; in fact, she used every kind consideration imaginable to excuse the behavior of those who had hurt or humiliated her.

One of the most important lessons Margaret has to share with us, by the example of her short but blessed life, is the importance of forgiveness. Over and over, Blessed Margaret was called upon to forgive and, over and over again, she did; and she did it with love and understanding. As soon as "Little Margaret" became aware that she was not really loved or accepted by Parisio and Emilia, she sought to forgive them; she accepted, as reality, the fact that, because her physical challenges prevented these noble parents from accepting her, they might be absolved from their shame.

When she was suddenly "enclosed" in a small cell with little explanation, Margaret again forgave her parents and trusted that God had provided a gift to bring her closer to Himself. While the move from her cell to the Palazzo vault was devastating in its isolation from spiritual support and religious practice, again, Margaret trusted that her parents were only trying to protect their daughter in not allowing her to be seen in public; they must be forgiven. After joyful anticipation of a family trip to the Franciscan shrine at *Citta di Castello*, Margaret forgave Parisio and Emilia for deserting her, believing that she had been a burden all of her life and thus their abandonment could be understood and accepted in the aftermath of the failed miracle of healing; Margaret even forgave God for not bringing about the miracle for which she had prayed, confident that His will was to be trusted and not hers.

---

[86] Don E. Davis, Joshua N. Hook, Everett L. Worthington, Daryl R. Van Tongeren, Edward B. Davis, and Stephanie Foxman, "Relational Spirituality and Forgiveness: Appraisals that May Hinder Forgiveness," *Psychology of Religion and Spirituality* 6:2 (2014): 102-112.

And, as is described in Chapter Four of this book, Margaret forgave a community of nuns who expelled her from their monastery for her valiant efforts to be obedient to the religious rules governing the monastic vocation. Blessed Margaret's extraordinary ability to forgive would put most of us to shame when we consider our own spiritual journeys. Her spirituality of forgiveness is one which we can only emulate and prayerfully hope to imitate with the grace we are given by God.

The examples from Blessed Margaret's legend included in this chapter have provided a beautiful lesson on forgiveness: from Margaret's initial unexpected enclosure in a cell at age six, to a forced move to the underground vault in the family palazzo in Mercatello, and finally to her abandonment at *Citta di Castello*. In the following chapter Blessed Margaret's virtue of gentle forgiveness continues to be reflected in the interactions with her "family of the streets," in an understanding of the nuns who rejected her and those who misjudged the reason for her monastic departure, and in the myriad ongoing difficulties imposed on her young life because of physical afflictions.

How blest we are to have Margaret of Castello, a consummate model of forgiveness, to whom we can look for inspiration and for guidance.

ENDNOTES – Chapter 3. "He Will Not Break a Bruised Reed"

[i] Barbara Sartori adds that the "tolling of the alarm bells" and "escape to Mercatello" could not have failed to arouse "a huge scare" in "a child of seven" (p. 29). The identification of Margherita as "a child of seven" is in stark contrast to the biography of William Bonniwell who noted that Margaret's move to the prison in Mercatello occurred after "13 years" in the cell next to the Church of St. Mary of the Fortress of Metola (Bonniwell, 1983, p. 25). As Bonniwell identified Margaret's age as six years, when the decision was made to enclose her in the cell (Bonniwell, 1983, p. 9), that would have made the young Margaret 18 or 19 years of age, rather than seven, when her parents moved her to the underground vault in Mercatello. Bonniwell validates Margaret's age on the move from Mercatello to *Citta di Castello* in an imagined conversation between Margaret and a Franciscan Brother at the Shrine of Fra Giacomo. The Brother called Margaret "Little Girl" and then asked "How old are you"? Margaret's response was: "I am 20 years old...I suppose my size misled you" (Bonn., p. 39). A number of dates and ages related to events in Margaret's legend vary in the literature. Based on Fr. William Bonniwell's two years of extensive research, some conducted in Rome, France, Metola and *Citta di Castello*, one aim of which was to validate the specific dates of important events in Margaret's life, I have chosen to use his timing for the present work (see documentation of sources in Chapter 1).

[ii] Biographer Barbara Sartori notes that in regard to these events in Blessed Margaret's life, the *Legendae* "does not bother to provide accurate time references" (p. 31).

[iii] Barbara Sartori again points out that the *Legendae* does not provide any useful information to reconstruct with certainty the date of the "pilgrimage of hope from Metola to the tomb of Fra Giacomo" (p. 39).

Chapter 4. "The Strength that God Supplies"

A Saint of the Streets

"Whoever serves must do so with the strength that God supplies, so that God may be glorified in all things through Jesus Christ."

1 Peter 4: 11

God's Strength

> The strength that He gave was beyond all ends,
> For the Lord had plans for His Margaret blest.
> Surrounded by loving, caring friends,
> God held her close to His loving breast.
>
> Indeed, in this time of lonely fear,
> Margaret trusted solely in God Alone
> This Child of God was ever dear,
> To the only spouse her Heart had known.

Blessed Margaret spent her first night alone in *Citta di Castello*, huddled for warmth and shelter, on the steps of La Chiesa di San Francesco. She still hoped that her parents, perhaps unavoidably delayed by some ill-fated incident, would return for her. The generous hearted young Margaret could not believe that she had been deserted. Her greatest fear was that some evil had befallen Parisio and Emilia; that they had been attacked by enemies and either killed or imprisoned. If that were the case, however, Margaret realized that she might truly now be completely alone and homeless in a city where she knew no one.

As morning broke, Blessed Margaret was discovered by two street beggars who had come to the church doorway seeking alms. The beggars, a young man and young woman, saw "Little Margaret," "resembling a small girl, who told them she was waiting for her parents to come for her. Moved by compassion, the beggars made inquiries on her behalf, among the townsfolk, only to discover that Margaret's parents had left town the previous day."[1] Thus, suddenly and unexpectedly, Blessed Margaret, "blind and short of stature, became a homeless person. Totally alone and totally unprepared, she was now to fend for herself on the streets of Castello."[2]

Homelessness

We can only guess what fears and anxieties this initial state of homelessness might have caused for young Margaret. There are only sketchy descriptions of "street life" for those forced to live "homeless" in the medieval era of Blessed Margaret's day. A brief examination of the concept of "homelessness" in today's society provides some hints as to what Margaret of Castello experienced in the early 14th Century.

Homelessness is generally understood as the absence of any fixed address or regular nighttime residence;[3] it is usually a traumatic event which puts individuals "in a heightened emotional state and is detrimental to (their) well-being."[4] While homelessness can sometimes involve a separation from God, alternately, "spirituality may have a profound effect on one's ability to cope with and to transcend the homeless circumstance."[5] Spiritual support from a religious figure is an "important component in the lives of persons who are homeless";[6] and "personal prayer can help the homeless person articulate his or her burdens" and thus alleviate to some degree the toll they take on both mental and physical health.[7]

---

[1] Lucinda Vardey, *Traveling with the Saints in Italy: Contemporary Pilgrimages on Ancient Paths* (Mahwah, N.J.: Hidden Springs, 2005), 152.

[2] Janice McGrane, *Saints to Lean On: Spiritual Companions for Illness and Disability* (Cincinnati, Ohio: St. Anthony Messenger Press, 2006), 7.

[3] Linda Grabbe, Scott Nguy and Melinda Higgins, "Spiritual Development for Homeless Youth: A Mindfulness Meditation," *Journal of Childhood Family Studies* 21;6 (2012): 925-937, 925.

[4] Stephanie Pergantis, Liz Tolliver and Jennifer Bishop, "A Holistic View of Homelessness," *Career Planning and Adult Development Journal* 32:1 (2016): 179-187, 182.

[5] Jill Snodgrass, "Spirituality and Homelessness: Implications for Pastoral Counseling," *Pastoral Psychology* 63: 2 (2014): 307-317, 308.

[6] Ann Connor and Monica L. Donohue, "Integrating Faith and Health in the Care of Persons Experiencing Homelessness," *Family & Community Health* 33:2 (2010) 123-132, 125.

[7] David P. Moxley, Olivia G. Washington and Joe McElhaney, "I Don't Have a Home: Helping Homeless People Through Faith, Spirituality and Compassionate Service," *Journal of Religion and Health* 51:2 (2012): 431-449, 441.

Although Margaret, now distanced from her dear Fra Cappellano, no longer had the support of a "religious figure," she did have the blessing of a profound personal spirituality. We can trust that she continued to pray mightily during those early days of homelessness in *Citta di Castello*.

Unfortunately, homeless people have been in the past, and are still today, sometimes cruelly looked upon as "derelicts of society."[8] And yet, the Christian gospel tells us that Jesus, Himself, was homeless. For, when one of his would-be disciples asserted: "'I will follow you wherever you go,' Jesus said to him: 'Foxes have holes, and birds of the air have nests; but the Son of Man has nowhere to lay his head'" (Luke 9: 57-58). Commenting on this passage in the Gospel of St. Luke, biblical scholar Jerome Kodell, O.S.B., explained that Jesus was trying to dispel the illusions of His disciples: "The person who offered himself with absolute availability (V. 57) is told the cost: you will be less secure than the foxes and the birds."[9]

As painful as her experience of homelessness must have been for Blessed Margaret, no doubt she embraced the Cross in identification with the suffering Jesus whom she had so often sought to imitate in the past. If her dearest Lord had "nowhere to lay His head," how could she, His humble servant, not desire to live the same way?

The Christian spirituality of homelessness is reflected in a "Parable of the Homeless Patient" as envisioned in the imagination of a contemporary emergency department (ED) nurse employed in an urban hospital. The "parable" begins by the nurse musing that she had, one evening, approached an ED admissions clerk to determine where she was needed; the clerk replied:

> "Well, there's this homeless man in room 3. I mean, I guess he's homeless; he certainly looks it. You know, ragged clothes, long hair and beard, kind of like a sixties hippie. I didn't really get much out of him." "But," she added, "somebody definitely beat him up. The police found him falling down in the street and brought him in. Maybe you could check him out, and," she concluded, raising a skeptical eyebrow, "find out if he really belongs here!"

The Nurse recalled:

---

[8] Mary Elizabeth O'Brien, *Spirituality in Nursing: Standing On Holy Ground* (Sudbury, MA.: Jones and Bartlett Publishers, 2011), 218.

[9] Jerome Kodell, "Luke" (pp. 936-980) In Robert J. Karris, Ed. *The Collegeville Bible Commentary, New Testament* (Collegeville, Minn.: The Liturgical Press, 1992), 956.

As I drew back the curtain in room 3, I saw that the clerk had accurately described our latest admission. He was stretched out on a gurney dressed in worn sandals, faded jeans and a threadbare sweatshirt; his hands were tucked monk-like, into the front pockets of his pullover. His hair was held in place by a frayed bandana wrapped around his forehead and tied in the back.

The patient opened his eyes and smiled weakly as I approached the bed. I tried a barrage of questions: "Sir, could you tell me your name? Do you know where you are? Can you remember what happened to you?" He simply nodded serenely and said: "They beat me; they didn't know what they were doing." "Are you in pain?" I asked anxiously. "I'm thirsty," he replied. I brought him a large glass of juice which he eagerly gulped through the straw I held for him. He kept his hands hidden; *probably doesn't want me to see the needle tracks that would identify him as an addict*, I guessed.

His vital signs were stable, and his color improved markedly after downing both a second and a third glass of juice. He sat up slowly and said: "I think I can leave now; I'm feeling better. I'm just so very tired." "I wish I could let you sleep here," I responded sadly, "but we're really busy." I hastily added: "I'm sure the shelter down the street will put you up for the night." "I understand," he replied, kindly.

I put my arm around his shoulders and carefully helped him off the gurney. As he stood up, he gazed at me with the most piercing and the most tender look I had ever seen, and said: 'I'll always remember how you cared for me'. As he spoke the words, he removed his hands from the sweatshirt and gently grasped my own between them.

That's when I saw his scars; not the needle marks I had almost expected but the nail holes I had almost missed. My Lord and my God![10]

Blessed Margaret of Castello, bearing her own spiritual "nail holes" of Christ, had now joined the ranks of God's beloved "homeless"; this experience prepared her well so that later, when ministering to the homeless and the outcast, she would also recognize the scars of Christ in the afflictions of the sick and the poor.

---

[10] Mary Elizabeth O'Brien, *Prayer in Nursing: The Spirituality of Compassionate Caregiving* (Sudbury, MA.: Jones and Bartlett Publishers, 2003), 3-4.

Despite myriad trials related to past living experiences, in the Metola castle, in the religious cell and in the palazzo vault, Margaret had never before been "homeless." She had always had a place to call "home," be it an isolated room in the family castle, a small cell next to a church in the forest, or an underground chamber in a palace. And Margaret had never been totally alone, left to depend only on herself for survival; always there was support, even if sporadic, from caregivers such as the castle chaplain and her parents' servants. Now Blessed Margaret was truly on her own, without "kith or kin" for protection and care.

This might have been a terrifying condition for one inexperienced in poverty and homelessness, to say nothing of having to cope with such a drastic life change accompanied by a variety of physical afflictions. Yet, we are told that Blessed Margaret embraced and even welcomed this new challenge as another gift from God that He had chosen for His beloved daughter; a gift that would draw her closer to His Divine Son who also "had nowhere to lay His head." In her suffering, Margaret "besought God that she might more perfectly devote herself to Him, her heavenly Father, now that she no longer had an earthly father."[11]

A Family of the Streets

With acceptance of the news that her parents had left the town to return to the castle without her, Blessed Margaret resigned herself to begging for survival. Her newly acquired homeless friends "taught Margaret the streets of *Citta di Castello* so she could locate fountains for drinking and washing, and the sheltered doorways where she could spend her nights."[12] Margaret became, overnight, "what she could hardly avoid becoming, a homeless beggar who slept in doorways and drank from public fountains."[13] Because of her humble and gentle manner, young Margaret now found among the city's poor beggars a compassionate and caring "family of the streets":

> Her new companions, the outcasts of the city, taught Margaret the streets of the town, leading her over them again and again until she had memorized them well enough to make her way alone. It was the human derelicts who showed the location of the fountains where she might wash and slake her thirst, and the

---

[11] William R. Bonniwell, *The Life of Blessed Margaret of Castello:1287-1320* (Charlotte, N.C.: Tan Books, 2014), 46.
[12] Vardey, 152.
[13] Ivan Innerst, *Saints for Today: Reflections on Lesser Saints* (San Francisco: Ignatius Press, 2000), 81.

most sheltered doorways where she might sleep at night without being driven away by the suspicious night patrol.[14]

This new "family of the streets" also told Margaret that they would show her "a good place to station" herself to beg for alms and added: "If things get too bad for you, the other beggars will try to help you: that's our rule."[15]

Admittedly, it is reported that:

> living on the streets of a medieval town was daunting. The streets were unpaved and unsanitary, with garbage (and other trash) everywhere. The streets were also dangerous: thieves, beggars, and bands of unsavory characters roamed about unchallenged. Women were vulnerable to sexual predators. And, of course, there were no soup kitchens, shelters or programs to assist homeless people. For Margaret, these dangers were aggravated by her lack of sight and other disabilities. She had to learn the streets and byways of Castello...and how to eke out a living by begging for alms.[16]

Nevertheless, it has been observed that Margaret also had many gifts, which supported her transition to the condition of homelessness:

> While Margaret certainly had much against her, she also had a great deal working for her...she had an innate intelligence that helped her cope with her various disabilities. Her warm, loving nature tended to draw people toward her. But her greatest asset in coping with life on the streets was the profound depth of her relationship with God...Margaret, as other mystics before and after have done, recognized the spiritual gold in the human hardship of her life. She had been well schooled in the Gospels by Padre Cappellano and no doubt recognized the opportunity to model the suffering in her life on the life and suffering of Jesus.[17]

As explained by Blessed Margaret's earliest biographer, as well as by others, Margaret now wandered the streets and byways of *Citta di Castello*, following in the steps of her Blessed Lord who also "had

---

[14] Bonniwell, 47.
[15] Ibid.
[16] McGrane, 7.
[17] Ibid., 7-8.

nowhere to lay his head" (Luke 9:58); she placed her hope in God alone and trusted in the Gospel message that He would always care for her. Although, Margaret's blindness prevented reading the Holy Scriptures, we are told that she learned many passages by heart from listening to sermons at Mass and through the instruction of Fra Cappellano. One might then imagine that another consoling scripture for Margaret, at this point in her spiritual journey, might have been the promise given by God to the Prophet Jeremiah:

> For surely I know the plans I have for you says the Lord, plans for your welfare and not for harm, to give you a future with hope. Then when you call upon me and come and pray to me, I will hear you. When you search for me, you will find me; if you seek me with all your heart, I will let you find me says the Lord, and I will restore your fortunes and gather you from all nations and all the places where I have driven you, says the Lord, and I will bring you back to the place from which I sent you into exile (Jeremiah, 29: 11-14).

Truly, this message would have provided great consolation and joy to the heart of "Little Margaret" who had already been sent into "exile" on so many occasions in her short life. Margaret may also have received consolation in the present exile because of the support of her new membership in a family of the streets.

Contemporary literature on the importance of "street families" in ameliorating the stress and loneliness of the homeless can give us a window into Blessed Margaret's medieval experience and adaptation during her early days of homelessness in *Citta di Castello*. The author of a 21st-century article, entitled "Searching for Kinship," asserts that "street families" play a critical role in the daily survival of one living in the streets by "helping fulfill the need for emotional and material support and companionship, by combatting feelings of alienation and loneliness, and by helping mitigate the continuing demands of the streets."[18] As street life can be "marked by both wrenching solitude and intense solidarity," it is important to cultivate familial type relationships, as "learning of the new street lifestyle comes from others on the streets."[19]

For Margaret, both blind and lame, a "street family" did indeed play a critical role in her survival. Without the advice and guidance of her

---

[18] Hilary Smith, "Searching for Kinship: The Creation of Street Families Among Homeless Youth," *American Behavioral Scientist* 51:6 (2008): 756-771, 769.
[19] Ibid., 762.

caring and protective friends from the streets, Blessed Margaret would never have been able to locate such needed resources as water fountains for drinking and washing and quiet corners for sleeping where she would be safe.

In general, family "serves a variety of purposes including survival, socialization, a sense of belonging, access to resources and feeling of love, support and security";[20] however, "street friendships can augment or replace the intimacy, support and other resources characteristically provided by families."[21] For young Margaret such "street friendships" now substituted for the family support so needed at this time in her life. These new friends had little in the way of material resources but what they had they willingly shared with the small, fragile woman who had been so abruptly forced to enter their world. The sharing of resources tends to be done generously by street families even when their "only possessions" consist of a few clothes and "they do not even know where their next meal will come from; sometimes it might be scavenged from a bin, or it might mean begging" and they can be found "sleeping on a sidewalk or in a doorway and survive on their wits."[22]

Blessed Margaret no longer had a nuclear family available to provide her with "feelings of love" and "support and security"; thus, it was her "family of the streets," the poor beggars of *Citta di Castello*, who now became true "family." Margaret's "family of the streets" might be said to be the first "real family" the young woman had ever known.

In an experiment of living on the streets for ten weeks, author Harlan Ellison wrote that the experience reflected "ten weeks in hell" because of the violence and dysfunction of the environment."[23] Young Margaret must also have faced "violence and dysfunction" in the 14th-century environment of the streets; she, however, came to view her new home, not as a "hell" but as a precious means to draw closer to Christ, ultimately through service to the "least of His brothers and sisters," the sick poor and the outcasts.

As observed earlier, loneliness is one of the most painful dimensions of living on the streets. Loneliness, which has been defined as "a subjective feeling that can be debilitating, frightening and undesirable,"

---

[20] Ibid.

[21] Bill McCarthy, John Hagan and Monica J. Martin, "In and Out of Harm's Way: Violent Victimization and the Social Capitol of Fictive Street Families," *Criminology* 40:4 (2002): 831-865, 831.

[22] Veli Duyan, "Relationships Between the Sociodemographic and Family Characteristics, Street Life Experiences, and Hopelessness of Street Children," *Childhood* 12: 4 (2005): 445-459, 446.

[23] Harlan Ellison, *Children of the Streets* (N.Y.: Open Road Media, 1961 and 2011), 2-20.

may be "a key risk factor in a range of negative health outcomes";[24] "being alone and being lonely are not synonymous but a lack of social contact and support are key antecedents that can lead to loneliness."[25] For the physically challenged, such as Margaret of Castello, loneliness "has been found to be a frequent companion."[26]

Such loneliness was, however, greatly alleviated for Blessed Margaret by her treasured new companions; they were poor, they were beggars, but they were caring and loving and attentive to the needs of their "Little Margaret," this beloved group of friends, her "family of the streets."

It is difficult for anyone to know how best to handle loneliness from a spiritual perspective but through personal experiences of two distinguished Catholic laywomen, Catherine Doherty and Caryll Houselander, provided for us:

> A theology of solitude that pointed to the Divine loneliness of Christ. Each in her own way offers the Incarnate Christ as the only one who can slake every human thirst. Each woman knew from experience that only in the healing humanity of Christ can every human ache be comforted. For only when we empty ourselves in Christ's own kenosis (emptying), are we able to embrace our own loneliness in His. When this happens, that place of solitude and wonder within becomes the very field where God can begin to cultivate His Own Divine life within each of us.[27]

As the holy women described above, Blessed Margaret placed the loneliness she must have felt in the "healing humanity of Christ" to whom she had committed her life. Although Margaret had been gifted by her new "family of the streets," she may, at times, have experienced loneliness: loneliness for the parents she never really knew but loved

---

[24] Vasiliki Tzouvara, Chris Papodopoulos and Gurch Randhawa, "A Narrative Review of the Theoretical Foundations of Loneliness," *International Journal of Social Psychiatry* 20:7 (2015):329-334, 329.

[25] M. Nicholaisen and K. Thorsen, "Who are lonely? Loneliness in Different Age Groups (18-81) Using Two Measures of Loneliness," *International Journal of Aging and Human Development* 78:3 (2014): 229-257, 231.

[26] Ami Rokach, "Loneliness of People with Physical Disabilities," *Social Behavior and Personality: An International Journal* 34:6 (2006): 681-700, 691.

[27] David V. Meconi, "Two Apostles of Loneliness: Caryll Houselander and Catherine Doherty on the Mystical Body of Christ," *Logos: A Journal of Catholic Thought and Culture* 17:2 (2014): 58-76.

nonetheless; loneliness for the kindly castle servant who cared for her until the age of six; loneliness for her dear chaplain and teacher, Fra Cappellano; and even loneliness for her small cell attached to the chapel in the forest which had provided the blessing of access to daily Mass, reception of Penance and the Holy Eucharist and her daily hours of prayer before Jesus in the Blessed Sacrament for thirteen years. Despite such personal loneliness, Margaret caringly reached out to her neighbors in *Citta di Castello* and "was soon known throughout the city for her cheerfulness, kindness and patience."[28]

The Medieval Biographer tells us that since "God is not far from the person whom He chooses...God moved the hearts of different people" to care for Blessed Margaret.[29] And while many of those who sought to help Margaret were themselves poor, they did what they could to support and even to house her. As well as her "street friends," individual poor families began to invite Margaret to stay with them for a time. While each family welcomed Margaret for a brief period, she was forced to move from one home to another; this was to prevent too heavy a burden being imposed on any one household.

As Fr. Bonniwell observed:

> It was a surprising situation, a homeless beggar being practically adopted by the poor of a city; we know of no similar instance in the annals of history, Margaret had indeed lost her family home, but she had acquired a large number of homes in exchange... And it was in the homes of the poor that the blind girl experienced for the first time what her heart had hungered for during her life, and what her own parents had denied her: a warm welcome, sincere affection and unselfish love.[30]

The people, both the poor of the streets and the impoverished families of *Citta di Castello*, were drawn to help Margaret as one of their own because, as the Medieval Biographer reported, "Her holy life shone. Her virtues and examples poured forth, causing her reputation to increase" far and wide in the small town.[31]

Margaret's "family of the streets" and the poor families of the city were, however, not the only ones who recognized her holiness. Other

---

[28] Innerst, 82.
[29] *Blessed Margaret of Castello OP*, 23.
[30] Bonniwell, 50-51.
[31] *Blessed Margaret of Castello OP*, 23.

citizens began to notice "the dignity with which Margaret lived her beggar condition, the sweetness with which she approached people, the fidelity to prayer that led her to spend much of her day meditating in church."[32] Many people were amazed at the resilience of this "small blind girl"; the "providence in which Margaret trusted...moved the hearts of different people, chosen by God...(who) began caring for the child, guaranteeing board and lodging...devoted ladies who began to give her hospitality."[33]

Sister Janice McGrane commented that:

> As so often happens with people whom societies marginalize, they come together to help one another. Margaret's remarkable grace in the midst of harrowing life circumstances, plus her obvious spiritual gifts and loving nature, began to draw people, both like and unlike herself, near to her. A consensus grew among them that Margaret should enter the local convent, ironically called the Convent of St. Margaret. There she would be able to live her spiritual life and be safe from the vagaries and hazards of life on the streets.[34]

As noted by author Barbara Sartori, Margaret's "fame spread beyond the secular environments, reaching beyond monastery gratings; thus, it was, that a community of nuns decided to open the doors to this bright jewel of holiness. It was a small monastery dedicated to St. Margaret, virgin and martyr" probably founded by Benedictines.[35]

Monastero di Santa Margherita

The monastery dedicated to St. Margaret, located in *Citta di Castello*, in the late 13th and early 14th Centuries was named "Monastero di Santa Margherita": "While male monasteries had the highest profile in medieval society, monasteries for women were also an important feature of the medieval world...the nuns themselves were recruited from the upper levels of society; in fact, nunneries tended to be more socially exclusive than monasteries" although they might include lay sisters.[36]

---

[32] Barbara Sartori, *Beata Margherita di Citta di Castello* (Milano, Italy: Paoline Editorale Libri, 2011), 47.

[33] Ibid.

[34] McGrane, 8

[35] Sartori, 47.

[36] Jeffrey L. Singman, *The Middle Ages: Everyday Life in Medieval Europe* (N.Y.: Sterling, 2013), 195.

Because of the requirement of a dowry, "poor women were more likely to be numbered among the lay sisters who did much of the manual work, than among the nuns."[37]

The monastery's "daily cycle was built around the Divine Office, and the nun's work often featured reading and writing…(and) needlework to furnish richly embroidered cloths for liturgical use."[38] Because "the honor of women was bound up with their chastity, canon law proposed a general ideal for nuns of strict enclosure within convent walls."[39]

The daily lives "of nuns across Christendom displayed both uniformity and variety (related to) the types of women recruited and the standard's maintained."[40] Significant changing ideas about religious life were introduced in the 12th and 13th Centuries[41] with "different interpretations of the rules."[42] Medieval historians suggest that during the Middle Ages there was a period of relaxed standards among some religious communities, especially in such areas as the ownership of property and the vow of chastity.

There occurred in certain orders "a breakdown in community life and some nuns were allowed to make family visits and go out on business. References in nun's wills to furs and jewels point to the existence of private property," and relationships sometimes developed between nuns and clergy.[43] In one example given of a women's monastery, there appeared to be "a complete breakdown of monastic life and obedience. The rule was not observed, nor was the Opus Dei celebrated at the proper times."[44]

Another notable problem for nunneries in the 13th and 14th Century was the fact that male monastics were often hesitant to undertake spiritual guidance of women's monasteries and/or to provide access to liturgy and the sacraments; "religious leaders showed little concern for encouraging women's religiosity."[45]

Nevertheless, as Blessed Margaret's friends observed her gentle and holy way of living and interacting with those around her, they became concerned about her having to move frequently from one home to

---

[37] J. Ward, *Women in Medieval Europe: 1200-1500* (London: Longmans, 2002), 161.
[38] Singman, 196.
[39] Joseph Lynch, *The Medieval Church: A Brief History* (London: Longman, 1992), 213.
[40] Ward, 160.
[41] Ibid., 161.
[42] Lynch, 215.
[43] Ward, 168.
[44] Ibid., 169.
[45] Caroline W. Bynum, *Holy Feast and Holy Fast: The Religious Significance of Food to Medieval Women* (Berkely, Ca.: University of California Press, 1987), 14.

another so as not to become a burden on a particular family. These friends also became more and more aware of Margaret's spiritual gifts and loving nature which, in turn, led them to the final conclusion: that Margaret should indeed enter the local convent of nuns, the Monastero di Santa Margherita.

As the nuns of the Monastero di Santa Margherita knew nothing of Blessed Margaret's background, they found it necessary to enter into a period of discernment before accepting her into their community; there were also a variety of canonical requirements to be clarified for her to enter the monastery as a novice. The monastery nuns worried about Margaret's physical condition, especially whether she "would be able to faithfully follow the commitments of prayer and penance imposed by the Rule."[46] Margaret's disability was seen as a possible hindrance to community life.

After an examination and approval by the local Bishop, however, which significantly alleviated the worries of the Abbess, the nuns of Monastero di Santa Margherita "invited Margaret to join their community...and the blind girl accepted the invitation with joy. No longer would she be a burden on the poor who has so lovingly supported her....In addition she could now devote herself to a life of prayer and work, and make excellent use of the convent's quiet solitude."[47] For Margaret, who had always lived like a contemplative without official recognition, "it was like a dream come true...now she had a new home, a new family, and what's more, she could devote herself to God."[48]

Although the nuns at Monastero di Santa Margherita believed, because of her physical challenges, that they would have to care for Margaret, they were mistaken. Margaret was very capable of making her way around the convent as she had been in the streets of the city; "accustomed as she was to maneuvering through the narrow streets of *Citta di Castello*, she learned quickly to move in the convent."[49] Margaret could not only take care of herself but she could assist with a variety of household duties such as cooking, cleaning, washing of dishes and kitchen utensils and other small tasks needed for the upkeep of the monastery.

---

[46] Sartori, 47.
[47] Ibid., 49.
[48] McGrane, 8.
[49] Sartori, 49.

Monastic Rejection

At first, the Medieval Biographer asserted, the nuns at the Monastery received Margaret "among them and cherished her very much and directed her. But, inflamed with charity and with continuous Divine fervor, she gently warned them and chided and urged the weak by words and examples."[50] The nuns, Margaret had discovered, "largely ignored the strict 'Rule' established for their convent. They broke the vow of silence imposed on them at certain times throughout the day. They accepted gifts from others. They entertained guests, family and friends in the parlor."[51]

For Margaret, who had embraced the "Rule" as a guide to holy obedience upon entering the monastery, the behavior of the nuns was very painful. And, on their part, the nuns, especially the Prioress, were distressed that Margaret could not accept the fact that the "Rule" had been relaxed; many of its prescriptions were now considered outdated by the community. The nuns felt that Margaret was being critical of their lifestyle in her attempt to be faithful to a "Rule," which, most of them believed, needed to be significantly modified, and thus, to which they no longer adhered.

As a result, there were complaints to the Prioress about the young novice, Margaret's, failure to adapt to community life; the Medieval Biographer explains these complaints as related to envy among the nuns: "They harboured pride and anger. The nuns despised Margaret's corrections to their sanctity, and were unable to bear her humble acts of charity. The more virtue shone in Margaret, the more the nuns were kindled with wrath."[52] Ultimately, the Monastery Prioress cautioned the novice to change her behavior immediately if she wished to remain in the community.

Father Bonniwell described Margaret's dilemma:

> Desperately as she wanted peace and harmony with her Sister religious, her inherent honesty would not permit her to evade the real issue. As a mere child she had determined to serve God with her whole heart, her whole mind, her whole soul, and ever since she had faithfully striven to do so. She could not find it in her heart to begin now to give God lukewarm service. Cost what it might, she had to follow the voice of her conscience.[53]

---

[50] *Blessed Margaret of Castello OP*, 23.
[51] Innerst, 82.
[52] *Blessed Margaret of Castello OP*, 24.
[53] Bonniwell, 59.

Sadly, Sister Margaret's continued desire to live completely the "Rule" of her new community was considered a failure in obedience; she was ultimately forced to leave the monastery.

Thus, we learn that "once again Margaret of Castello experienced extreme rejection. It must have cut into her soul to be cast out again on the streets, this time not because of her disabilities but because of her convictions. Was she tempted to give up, to despair, to turn against God? If so, her despair probably did not last long."[54] Margaret, as during so many trials in the past, turned to God as her protector and guide in whom she placed all of her hope and her trust. But,

> Life on the streets was not the same as before. Cast out of the convent, Margaret was now perceived as a victim of shame, and gossip about her spread. She was called all sorts of insulting names, and children ridiculed her, calling her 'the saint'; but Margaret never spoke unkindly about the nuns or her time in the convent, only remorse that she had disappointed them. She never answered or defended the accusations against her. In humility and love she carried on, spending much of her time praying in the local Dominican Church which became her favorite, La Chiesa della Carita (the Church of Charity).[55]

Blessed Margaret was initially beset by heartbreak and anxiety brought about by her fear that it may not have been the nuns "but God who had rejected her; that it was God who was chastising her."[56] After struggling prayerfully with a period of hopelessness and discouragement, however, Margaret was blessed with the grace to recall how "long ago she had offered herself to God; she had asked Him to do with her what He wished...it was as if the dying Savior said to her from the Cross: 'Margaret, will you, too, leave me?' (and) instantly the battle was over...she still wanted God, at any cost, at any price."[57]

Blessed Margaret's struggle cannot help but bring to mind a similar trial experienced by the protagonist "Much Afraid" in the classic allegory "Hinds Feet on High Places." Near the end of the allegory, "Much Afraid" pledges her love for the "Shepherd," asserting the confidence that He, of all people, could never deceive her. But the "Shepherd" replied: "Would you be willing to trust me even if everything in the wide world seemed

---

[54] McGrane, 9.
[55] Vardey, 154.
[56] Bonniwell, 60.
[57] Ibid., 60-61.

to say that I was deceiving you; indeed that I had deceived you all along?"[58] "Much Afraid" affirmed her belief that it was "impossible" that the "Shepherd" should deceive her. Then the "Shepherd" responded with a more pointed question: "'Much Afraid,' supposing I really did deceive you? What then?"[59] "Much Afraid," after searching her heart, responded: "My Lord, if you can deceive me, you may. It can make no difference. I must love you as long as I continue to exist. I cannot live without loving you."[60]

And so, after yet another initially joy-filled attempt to consecrate her life to the Lord, Margaret was once again homeless, poor and living on the streets. One cannot help but wonder what allowed her any peace after yet another rejection but it is reported that Margaret was "steeped in the Gospels"; she was "acutely aware that suffering, especially the suffering of rejection, was experienced by Christ. And she had decided long ago to take up her cross and follow Him."[61] Like "Much Afraid," Blessed Margaret could not "live without loving" her "Shepherd."

Seeds of Ministry to the Sick and the Outcast

While some of Margaret's friends understood why she could not adjust to the relaxed standards of community life, as lived in Monastero di Santa Margherita, other residents of *Citta di Castello*, who did not know Blessed Margaret well, did not. There was, initially, gossip and criticism from some in the town who had previously admired her; cruel comments were made about Margaret's failure in the monastic novitiate of Monastero di Santa Margherita. Margaret had not only experienced a "failed" miracle; she was now a "failed" nun. While the derision and contempt would eventually pass, it was during this time that Blessed Margaret truly came to understand the meaning of being an "outcast"; an understanding that was to provide the catalyst for her future ministry to prisoners.

Margaret had, from childhood, been forced to deal with what some might have considered a "stigma" related to her severe physical challenges. However, she had never experienced the stigma of being considered an "outcast" for a personal failure such as she now understood as an "outcast" from religious life; as one cast out by an ostensibly holy community of nuns who occupied the Monastero di

---

[58] Hannah Hurnard, *Hinds Feet on High Places* (Wheaton, Ill.: Tyndale House, 1975), p. 190.
[59] Ibid.
[60] Ibid.
[61] McGrane, 9.

Santa Margherita. During the "lived experience" of being herself an "outcast," Margaret's heart was taught not only care and concern for those who lived with the stigma of physical affliction, but especially love for those who lived with the stigma of being considered outcasts.

The term "stigma" has had a variety of meanings over time; it generally refers to "a personal attribute which marks a person as different from 'normal people,' that is, 'abnormal' with all its negative connotations, namely exclusion from 'normal' society. Studies have supported the idea that illnesses are stigmatized because of the limitation they entail and the negative social attitudes they generate."[62] From the time of her birth, Blessed Margaret was considered by her parents to bear a stigma, because of physical challenges; they, as parents, also felt stigmatized for having given birth to a less than perfect offspring.

When one has a health condition or disability with a "publicly recognizable aspect," such stigma may be "more difficult to cope with than the disability or health condition itself."[63] While the parents, Parisio and Emila, were not able to cope with the stigma of their "Little Margaret"'s publicly recognizable afflictions, she herself seemed to handle her physical challenges with grace and dignity. In regard to her afflictions, we have no record of Margaret ever asking the question of her parents or of her God: "Why has this happened to me?"

Stigma associated with a physical disability can cause significant harm "through social rejection and discrimination."[64] Margaret of Castello having been, from birth, rejected by her parents, thus understood the pain associated with such stigma. She was not, however, rejected by her nurse who named her "Margherita," her chaplain and teacher, Fra Cappellano, who loved "Little Margaret" and ministered to her, and her "family of the streets" in *Citta di Castello* who embraced Margaret as one of their own. Blessed Margaret knew the pain and suffering of rejection; she alternately knew the blessing and joy of acceptance. These experiences provided the "seeds" for her future

---

[62] Mimi Lusli, Marjolein Zweskhorst, Beatriz Miranda-Galarza, Ruth Peters, Sarah Cummings, Francisia Seda, Joske Bunders and Irwanto, "Dealing with Stigma: Experiences of Persons with Disabilities and Leprosy," *BioM+ed Research International* 1 (2015): 1-9, 1.

[63] Cheryl B. Gartley and Mary R. Klein, "Stigma and Health Conditions, Part I," *Exceptional Parent Magazine* 45:11 (2015): 44-46, 44.

[64] Amy C. Watson and Jonathon E. Larson, "Personal Responses to Disability Stigma: From Self-Stigma to Empowerment," *Rehabilitation Education* 20:4 (2006): 235-246, 235.

ministry to those who were sick and poor and to those who were considered outcasts, incarcerated in a local prison.

The Spirituality of Disability

In writing about Blessed Margaret, I have been loath to describe her physical challenges in terms of "disability." That is because I don't believe that Margaret was, in fact, "disabled." Surely her "legend" does not reveal what might be considered "disability." Margaret was blind, but able to quickly adapt to new living situations in which she needed to provide for her own basic needs; she was lame, but as described in later chapters, was able to make her way around the town of *Citta di Castello* to minister to the sick in their homes and to those in the local prison; she had a severe curvature of the spine but worshipped at Mass whenever the opportunity presented itself and she cared for others who were ill or infirm in the final years of her life.

Current literature on "disability" admits to some controversy over use of the term; that is, some individuals with physical challenges prefer the label "differently abled" while others choose to call themselves "disabled," believing that the word explains why they may not be able to accomplish certain activities open to those with no health challenges. Thus, I have more often described Blessed Margaret as physically challenged rather than disabled.

The extant literature suggests that whether "disability" or physical or cognitive challenge "encourages or limits spiritual growth" is not fully understood[65]; some studies have concluded that there is a "reciprocal relationship" between disability and spirituality, that "the interaction between disability and spirituality is an on-going process of re-envisioning of both disability and spirituality."[66]

A variety of conclusions have been generated through research on the spirituality of disability, for example, disability may be "a vehicle to discover God's purpose" or "a catalyst for spiritual awakening;"[67] spirituality can be viewed as a "resource" for dealing with disability and illness;[68] spirituality may be a "personal source of comfort and strength"

---

[65] Boni Boswell, Michael Hamer, Sharon Knight, Mary Glacoff and Jon McChesney, "Dance of Disability and Spirituality," *Journal of Rehabilitation* 73:4 (2007): 33-40, 33.

[66] Boni Boswell, Sharon Knight and Michael Hamer, "Disability and Spirituality: A Reciprocal Relationship with Implications for the Rehabilitation Process," *Journal of Rehabilitation* 67:4 (2001): 20-25, 20.

[67] Emily K. Schultz, "The Meaning of Spirituality for Individuals with Disabilities," *Disability and Rehabilitation* 27:21 (2005): 1283-1295, 1283.

[68] Judy Kaye and Senthil K. Raghavan, "Spirituality in Disability and Illness," *Journal of Religion and Health* 41:3 (2002): 231-242, 231.

in those with disabilities;[69] and spirituality can be a determinant of health for persons with physical disabilities.[70]

Blessed Margaret of Castello's physical challenges did not "limit" her spiritual growth; they rather enhanced spiritual development as she sought to embrace suffering in imitation of the suffering of Christ, her beloved Lord and Master.

Blessed Margaret was forced to cope with the physical afflictions of a severe curvature of the spine (some authors labeled her a "hunchback"), the shortening of one leg resulting in lameness, and what was described as very short stature. Despite the sometimes limiting effects of these conditions, perhaps the most significant physical challenge was that of Margaret's congenital blindness. No discussions of the impact of such blindness were found in the medieval medical literature descriptive of Blessed Margaret's era. In current professional journals, however, one finds a plethora of articles exploring the impact of congenital blindness on a child; from these writings we can gain some understanding of the impact "Little Margaret"'s lack of vision may have had on her early life, especially within the castle fortress environment.

The term "blindness" is "defined as the inability to see or the loss or absence of perception of visual stimuli."[71] Blindness is further defined by the World Health Organization "as having visual acuity of less than 3/60 to no perception of light."[72] (We assume that Blessed Margaret experienced a total "inability to see" from birth, as her early biographers did not provide any modifiers when describing her as "blind.")

It is suggested that severe congenital blindness may put children "at risk of suffering from psychological disorders, vision being an important sensory channel that facilitates interactions between a child and the outer world":[73]

---

[69] Patricia Baldwin, Jan Evans, Nicole Etherington, Megan Nichols, Virginia Wright and Janette McDougall, "Youth with Disabilities Talk About Spirituality: A Qualitative Descriptive Study," *The Qualitative Report* 20:7 (2015): 941-958, 941.

[70] K. Faull, M.D. Hills, G. Cochrane, J. Gray, M. Hunt, C. McKenzie and L. Winter, "Investigation of Health Perspectives of Those with Physical Disabilities: The Role of Spirituality as a Determinant of Health," *Disability and Rehabilitation* 26:3 (2004): 129-144, 129.

[71] Turkay Demir, Nurullah Bolat, Mesut Yavuz, Gul Karacetin, Burak Dogangun and Levent Kayaalp, "Attachment Characteristics and Behavioral Problems in Children and Adolescents with Congenital Blindness," *Archives of Neuropsychiatry* 51:1 (2014): 116-121, 117.

[72] C. Gilbert and H. Awan, "Blindness in Children," *British Medical Journal* 327:1 (2003): 760-761, 760.

[73] Demir et al., 117.

Eye to eye contact, for example, provides a unifying mechanism through which children share their opinions, develop joint attention, and gain the ability to impute mental states to themselves and others. Moreover, eye to eye contact is crucial for children to express and convey their emotions to their mothers, so that she can understand the clues given by the child; in this way, the attachment system is activated.[74]

The importance of the concept of maternal attachment is particularly noted as children need to "seek the proximity of a reference figure that can provide protection and care when they require it."[75] This "emotional availability," which may be missing for blind children, is considered an "essential part of the interactions between parents and children in which their responsiveness to each other's feelings is expressed through eye contact, gestures and words."[76]

Some other significant problems frequently identified for a blind child include limitations in social interactions and problems in learning because of lack of adequate reading/listening materials. Associated with the difficulty in making friends, many blind children suffer from loneliness. Loneliness, defined as "the absence or perceived absence of satisfying social relationships,"[77] was found to be greater in a study of blind students compared to their sighted peers; "students with blindness reported significantly higher degrees of loneliness than sighted students."[78]

While the above comments and study findings represent 21st-century data, they can help us understand, to some degree, the challenges presented and the courage needed to face those challenges, in the life of a 14th-century child such as "Little Margaret" of Castello. In terms of the potential "psychological disorders," which a blind child is thought to be subject to, the "eye to eye" contact described is generally envisioned as occurring between an infant and mother; this is related to the concept of maternal attachment. As we have learned from the early biographers, "Little Margaret"'s care was provided not by her mother, Emelia, but was

---

[74] Ibid.
[75] Ibid.
[76] Julie Campbell and Christine Johnston, "Emotional Availability in Parent-Child Dyads Where Children Are Blind," *Parenting: Science and Practice* 9: 3/4 (2009): 216-227, 216.
[77] Muna S. Hadidi and Jamal M. Alkhateeb, "Loneliness Among Students with Blindness and Sighted Students in Jordan: A Brief Report," *International Journal of Disability, Development and Education* 60:2 (2013): 167-172, 167.
[78] Ibid.

rather given over to that of a trusted castle nursemaid. In recalling that it was indeed that same nursemaid who arranged for Margaret's baptism and for her receiving a beautiful name meaning "pearl," we might trust that "Little Margaret" did have a surrogate maternal attachment with her castle nurse. This nursemaid would have then become the woman to whom Margaret looked and from whom she received, "protection and care." "Little Margaret" surely must have been loved and valued by the nurse who caringly named her Margherita.

Another important figure in the early life of Blessed Margaret was the kindly castle chaplain, Fra Giacomo Cappellano. As Fra Giacomo, early on, described Margaret's mind as "luminous" and portrayed her as highly intelligent, it would appear that he also had become a trusted figure of "protection and care" for his small student, despite her lack of physical vision.

Did Margaret suffer from blindness-related loneliness? It would seem, because of the descriptions of "Little Margaret" as a joyful child, that the love and support of Fra Cappellano, and the castle servants prevented loneliness during her early development; Margaret's profound spirituality, encompassing a deep love of and trust in God, while still a young child also significantly ameliorated the sense of material or physical loneliness which might have resulted from her blindness.

As noted earlier, I do not consider Blessed Margaret of Castello "disabled"; she was, however, burdened with multiple physical challenges. Findings revealed in studies of the relationship between spirituality and disability might be translated, in Margaret's case, to the "relationship between spirituality and living with physical challenges". Thus, Blessed Margaret provides a beautiful model for others experiencing such challenges. For Margaret, the physical challenges were indeed "a vehicle for finding God's purpose in her life"; they provided a "resource for dealing with her afflictions"; because she viewed her challenges as a gift from God, to draw her closer to Himself, they became a "personal source of comfort and strength" and they served as "a determinant of health" to support Margaret's activities of daily living and, ultimately her ministry to others, especially the sick and the outcast.

In several works on the life of Blessed Margaret, especially that of the Medieval Biographer, it is pointed out that even as a young child, both in the castle and while enclosed in the religious cell or anchorhold for thirteen years, Margaret embraced the concept of "fasting," as a dimension of her religious devotions; she undertook this bodily mortification even though already beset by the above noted multiple physical "afflictions" with which she was born.

Although fasting for spiritual reasons is surely not considered a "disability," mortification, such as significantly limiting one's nutritional intake, may result in physiologically and/or emotionally challenging symptoms. One might surely wonder why a young woman, already coping with blindness, curvature of the spine, lameness and very small stature would attempt to take on yet another physical challenge. "Fasting" was, however, considered a truly valued spiritual practice for the devout of the Middle Ages.

In the introduction to her classic work, *Holy Feast and Holy Fast: The Religious Significance of Food to Medieval Women*, Caroline Walker Bynum explains the meaning of fasting to religious women of Blessed Margaret's era: "In the Europe of the later thirteenth and fourteenth centuries famine was on the increase again, after several centuries of agricultural growth and relative plenty."[79] Thus,

> sharing of one's own meager food with a stranger (who might turn out to be an angel, a fairy, a god or Christ himself) was in hagiography and folk tale alike, a standard indication of heroic or saintly generosity. Small wonder, too, that self-starvation, the deliberate and extreme renunciation of food and drink, seemed to medieval people the most basic asceticism, requiring the kind of courage and holy foolishness that marked the saints. To repress eating and hunger was to control the body in a discipline far more basic than any achieved by shedding the less frequent gratifications of sex or money. As Christ supposedly said in a vision granted to Margaret of Cortona (d.1297): "In this life, Christians cannot be perfect unless they restrain their appetites from vices, for without abstinence from food and drink the war of the flesh will never end; and they feel and suffer most from the rebellion of the flesh who refuse this saving remedy."[80]

Caroline Bynum also cited the words of a Cistercian historian who wrote, around the year 1200: "Fasting is useful for expelling demons, excluding evil thoughts, remitting sins, mortifying vices, giving certain hope of future goods and a foretaste of celestial joys."[81] It is understandable, then, given the perception of the importance and

---

[79] Bynum, 2.
[80] Ibid.
[81] Ibid., 2-3.

positive spiritual benefits of fasting, that Margaret of Castello would have undertaken the practice with enthusiasm during her early contemplative days and probably continued it, to some degree, while engaged in the active apostolate of ministry to the sick and the outcast.

The present chapter has explored a variety of both negative and positive spiritual experiences in the life of Margaret of Castello. The unexpected occurrence of homelessness, which may have been initially devastating for young Margaret, was quickly ameliorated by the encountering of a caring "family of the streets" who lovingly provided their support and guidance. Margaret was painfully rejected by a community of nuns, after only a brief period of novitiate, but was soon embraced by townspeople who again offered her hospitality. And, most importantly, Blessed Margaret found in these experiences a renewed trust in God, as well as the seeds of her future ministry to the sick poor and the outcast.

In the following chapter, Blessed Margaret's "holy calling" is explored: a calling to minister to the impoverished ill and infirm in their homes and to the poor outcasts incarcerated in the local prison, through her Dominican vocation as a *Mantellata*, a Sister of Penance of St. Dominic.

Blessed Margaret of Castello

Chapter 5. "A Holy Calling"

The Mantellata

"God...calls us with a holy calling, not according to our works but according to His own purpose and grace."

2 Timothy 1: 8-9

"A Holy Calling"

A "Holy Calling" the
Gentle Margaret
Longed for.

A "Holy Calling" the
Courageous Margaret
Sought.

A "Holy Calling" the
Prayerful Margaret
Heard.

A "Holy Calling" the
Caring Margaret
Embraced.

A "Holy Calling" the
Mantellata Margaret
Lived.

As described in the previous chapter, Blessed Margaret had in the monastery, similar to her time of enclosure next to the chapel in the forest, attempted to live a contemplative life of prayer and penance; this was, she believed, her way of serving the Lord. Margaret, we are told, was overjoyed at the opportunity to become a novice with the community of nuns housed at the Monastero di Santa Margherita in *Citta di Castello*. She tried to live the monastic calling to the best of her ability, which, for her, meant to follow the community's "Rule" as perfectly as possible; Margaret never did things half-way. But, as we learned, Margaret's efforts, rather than pleasing her religious Sisters, in fact, infuriated them. The Professed Nuns, it appeared, had grown quite comfortable in adhering to a relaxed version of the "Rule." The attempt to seek perfection by the newly arrived novice Margaret was an affront to their spirituality, to their perception of how the monastic rule should be lived and how the nuns wished that modification of the "Rule" to continue. The clash of wills between the older nuns' complacency and their young novice's enthusiasm became Margaret's undoing.

A Holy Calling
A Vocation of Service

After her expulsion from the Monastero di Santa Margherita, accompanied by renewed experiences of poverty and homelessness, as well as a judgment of failure by some, Margaret was again dealing with the question of where the Lord was leading her. As noted by author Barbara Sartori, "it matters little that biographers state that being expelled by such a petty group of nuns gives a sense of pride instead of humiliation, the reality is that poor Margaret is faced with yet another rejection. Back to wandering."[1] Initially Blessed Margaret's path forward seemed directed only to patient acceptance of God's will; she, nonetheless, needed to find some means of survival in the city.

Although criticized by some local citizens for her failure to fit in at the Monastero di Santa Margherita, Margaret, "demonstrating heroic and charitable restraint...never told why the nuns had asked her to leave the cloister."[2] Slowly, however, through no word of Margaret's, the townsfolk of *Citta di Castello* began to understand from whence came the conflict between the novice's earnest desire to serve God and the monastic nuns modified understanding of their rule of life. Before too long, Margaret's reputation as a holy young woman was restored.

As it happened, the local church where Margaret loved to attend Morning Mass was the Chiesa della Carita, a parish under the charge of the Dominican Friars. Thus, the Chiesa della Carita was also home to a Dominican Lay Community called the Sisters of Penance of St. Dominic. Through attendance at daily Mass, Margaret came to know the community well. Fr. Augustine Thompson noted that many of the pious laity of the era "drifted toward the mendicants" because they were available: "Margherita of *Citta di Castello* went to services daily at the

---

[1] Barbara Sartori, *Beata Margherita di Citta di Castello* (Milano, Italy: Paoline Editorale Libri, 2011), 50-51.
[2] Janice McGrane, *Saints to Lean On: Spiritual Companions for Illness and Disability* (Cincinnati, Ohio: St. Anthony Messenger Press, 2006), 9.

Dominican Church, where she could find a priest to hear her daily confession."[3]

Fr. Bonniwell reported that some of the Sisters, "knowing of Margaret's desire to join a religious order, suggested that perhaps membership in the Lay Order of Penance of St. Dominic might be the answer."[4] Author Ivan Innerst suggests that meeting the Sisters of Penance of St. Dominic provided for Margaret in "the later years of her short life, by some grace, what she might most have wished for, what for her would have seemed reward enough for her torturous journey through the years."[5]

The "Order of Penance of St. Dominic" was the penitent community which had been formalized from the early days of the Dominican Order, when "groups of lay people began to want to live in a more rigorous way the new spirituality of the mendicant orders. Thus, they had made their way to the first experiences of secular consecration before its time; men and women who, while continuing to live in the world, had chosen the path of penance and prayer."[6] The women penitents, "without being nuns, had vowed in a special way to God. Even in their dress (they) differed from the fashion of the time. They had their head covered by a white veil, a leather belt tight at the waist, and on the shoulders, a black cape, reaching to the feet. That's why the people called them the Mantellate."[7] From the time of St. Dominic, the lay penitents sought to support the Catholic faith against the assault of the heretics. Blessed Margaret did not have to face the "substantial presence of heretics" in *Citta di Castello*; however, "the conversion of hearts was an undeniable priority."[8]

It was others who initially suggested that Blessed Margaret might find her religious vocation in the community of the Dominican Sisters of Penance. Nevertheless, Margaret, as so many previous times in her young life, was open to embracing this new path as a blessing and a gift from God. Her joy lay in the fact that, although she would not be a vowed nun, as the women in monastic communities, she would, in this vocation, be able to dedicate the rest of her life completely to the service of her

---

[3] Augustine Thompson, *Cities of God: The Religion of the Italian Communes, 1125-1325* (University Park, Pa.: The Pennsylvania State University Press, 2005), 296.

[4] William R. Bonniwell, *The Life of Blessed Margaret of Castello:1287-1320* (Charlotte, N.C.: Tan Books, 2014), 65.

[5] Ivan Innerst, *Saints for Today: Reflections on Lesser Saints* (San Francisco: Ignatius Press, 2000), 82.

[6] Sartori, 62.

[7] Ibid.

[8] Ibid.

Beloved Lord. This was now, to Margaret, clearly His calling; this was for Margaret, truly, a holy calling.

The Sisters of Penance of St. Dominic

Prior to describing the Sisters of Penance of St. Dominic, the Mantellate, to which Blessed Margaret of Castello belonged, it should be acknowledged that some contemporary scholars question the historicity of previous accounts of the birth of the Dominican Penitent Order, especially the identified authorship of the Penitent Order's "Rule" by Master Munio De Zamora. While this opinion is noted in the following pages, citations from the writings of early Dominican authors are also included. This is done in an attempt to trace the published history of the medieval Dominican lay penitent movement, the movement which ultimately guided and supported Blessed Margaret's apostolic ministry to the sick and the outcast.

In his work *Cities of God: The Religion of the Italian Communes, 1125-1325*, Augustine Thompson, O.P., presents a carefully crafted history of laypeople in northern Italy "seeking a more intense Christian life."[9] Many of these 12th and early 13th-century lay persons called themselves "*Penitenti*" (Penitents), which was generally understood to identify those who "had more or less spontaneously taken up a life of asceticism."[10] Their ascetic practices were sometimes initiated individually but more frequently were guided by the spiritual direction of a "church or monastery."[11] The ascetics were formally identified as Brothers and Sisters of Penance, in 1227, by a proclamation of Pope Gregory IX.[12]

Members of the association, many affiliated with the newly created mendicant Orders, lived at home with their families but did make a commitment to certain devotions and met periodically in groups for Masses or sermons.[13] Some of the penitents wore a habit, the colors of which were guided by the Order with which they associated: gray for the Franciscans and black "for Dominican-sponsored penitents."[14] The penitents' daily prayers were adapted to the Divine Office of the Church; however, the penitents' autonomy also allowed "devotions suited to their own particular tastes."[15]

---

[9] Thompson, 69.
[10] Ibid.
[11] Ibid.
[12] Ibid., 70
[13] Ibid., 74.
[14] Ibid., 82.
[15] Ibid., 89-90.

The Order of the Brothers and Sisters of Penance of St. Dominic, Blessed Margaret of Castello's lay community, was an outgrowth of the first Dominican Friars' communities founded in the 13th Century. The Dominican Brothers and Sisters of Penance were lay men and women whose rule had been written by the Master of the Order.[16] The early lay community, or "third order" as it was called at the time, is described by Friar Martin Gillet:

> Wherever a convent of Friars was established, friends of the Order, both men and women, inspired by their spirit, nourished by their teaching, and edified by their example, endeavored to live according to the Dominican spirit and to promote the Dominican apostolate. The name of 'Third Order' was given to societies of men and women who, under the spiritual direction of the Fathers, wished in their own way and in the degree possible to them to share the religious and apostolic life of the Dominican Order.[17]

During Blessed Margaret's era of the late Thirteenth and early Fourteenth Centuries, there was seen "an enormous increase in the demand for ways in which lay people could express their piety and (one way) in which this demand was met was the Third 'Order of Penance'...The Dominicans were the first actually to set up an 'Order of Penance' that would formally be part of the (Dominican) Order under the jurisdiction of the Master of the Order; this was done in 1285."[18] The Church of the Thirteenth Century "showed a marked development of the institutional side and one of the first great orders of friars was the Dominicans."[19]

The Dominican laity, initially identified as "The Brotherhood of the Militia of Jesus Christ," or simply "The Militia of Jesus Christ," had existed from the beginning days of the Order; thus, "when the Master General, Munio De Zamora, St. Dominic's sixth successor, decided to give a definite constitution to the Third Order in 1285, all he had to do was to

---

[16] Arrigo Levasti, *My Servant Catherine*, Trans. Dorothy M. White (Westminster, Md.: The Newman Press, 1954), 25.

[17] Martin S. Gillet, *The Mission of St. Catherine*, Trans. Maria T. Lopez (St. Louis, Mo.: B. Herder Book Company, 1946), 53-54.

[18] Simon Tugwell, "Dominican Laity" in *Early Dominicans: Selected Writings*, Ed. Simon Tugwell (Mahwah, N.J.: Paulist Press, 1982), 432-451, 432.

[19] Ernest Barker, *The Dominican Order and Convocation: A Study of the Growth and Representation in the Church During the Thirteenth Century* (Berkley, Ca.: University of California Libraries, 1913), 7.

unify and revise the rules which had long been in force in the brotherhoods of Penance, linked from an early date to the Dominican Order, by having placed themselves under the guidance of the Preachers."[20]

In her 21st-century analysis entitled *Munio of Zamora: The Ordinationes*, Maria Lehmijoki-Gardner argues that Fr. Munio De Zamora's 1285/1286 "Rule" for the Dominican Third Order, identified as the *"Ordinationes,"* was written specifically for the penitent women of Orvieto and "was not the formal penitent rule hitherto attributed to Munio, but a set of simple, and at times awkwardly organized guidelines."[21] Lehmijoki-Gardner notes that "the *'Ordinationes'* offered rather detailed guidelines concerning the reception of Dominican penitents or *vestitae* into their association. It also discussed, at length, penitent women's liturgical and devotional observances, and their social obligations toward their sisters. Other aspects of the text were less clearly defined."[22] Maiju Lehmijoki-Gardner disagrees, however, that Munio De Zamora was the sole author of the Dominican Penitent Rule, which was approved by Pope Innocent VII in 1405, asserting that "Munio...was credited with the creation of the formal 'Dominican Order of Penance,' although he, in fact, wrote only a set of simple *'Ordinationes'* at the request of the *vestitae* of Orvieto."[23]

The "Militia of Jesus Christ" has been, as noted, commonly regarded as the original form of the Dominican Third Order:[24] the militia "were truly knights wearing the white tunic and the black cloak, and pledged themselves to fight in the defense of the faith...(they) had the direct benefit of St. Dominic's direction."[25] The "Militia of Jesus Christ," a kind of military order, established by Saint Dominic, was "composed of men living in midst of the world but steadfast in the faith who would assist in defending the Church against fanatics who would attack it and its followers."[26] Saint Dominic also enlisted the wives of the early "Brethren of the Militia of Jesus Christ" to assist as much as possible in ways such as "prayers, alms and good works, for the freedom of the church."[27]

---

[20] Ferdinand D. Joret, *Dominican Life* (London: Sands & Co., 1937), 57.
[21] Mariju Lehmijoki-Gardner, Ed. and Trans., *Dominican Penitent Women* (Mahwah, N.J.: Paulist Press, 2005), 39.
[22] Ibid.
[23] Ibid., 40.
[24] Joret, 56.
[25] Ibid.
[26] Dominicans, *Summary of the Rule of the Third Order* (San Francisco: J.B. McIntyre, 1886), 7.
[27] Ibid., 8.

In describing the "necessity for establishing a Third Order," in the time of the Blessed St. Dominic, Pere Jean Baptiste Feuillet OP explained that the Albigensian heretics of the era, at times, even used physical force in their battle against the faith. In France, Italy and Spain, Saint Dominic encountered:

> An immense number of heretics, who, not content with spreading their errors, and drawing over all whom they were able to infect, had arrived at such an excess of impiety and avarice, that they dared even to despoil the Church itself, and to appropriate its property to their own sacrilegious uses; to use violence against those who were consecrated to God, and to establish their pestilential errors by the shedding of Christian blood...
> Our sainted patriarch (thus)...undertook to establish an order composed of men of exemplary piety, who should take up arms when lawfully commanded, in order to oppose themselves to the sacrileges and the violence of the heretics.
> This was the beginning of the Third Order. It embraced persons of every condition but those who were married were not received without the written and formal consent of their wives, who thereby pledged themselves to permit their husbands to take up arms and expose their lives whenever the pressing necessities of the Church might call for their assistance. He prescribed for them a rule of life, and fixed a certain number of Pater Nosters and Ave Marias to be daily recited in place of the canonical hours. He gave them a modest habit of black and white...
> It was called, at first, the Militia of Jesus Christ; but after the death of its sainted founder, those who embraced it were called the 'Brothers of Penance of St. Dominic'. This name is given them in a bull addressed to them in the year 1228 by his Holiness Pope Gregory IX.[28]

Pere Feuillet commented on the "antiquity of the Third Order":

> When St. Dominic saw that the wives of those who had joined themselves to the Third Order were inclined to practice all its pious exercises no less than their husbands, he associated them

---

[28] Jean Baptiste Feuillet, *Manual of the Brothers and Sisters of the Third Order of Penance of St. Dominic* (London: Burns and Lambert, 1852), 3-5.

also to his consecrated militia; not indeed to follow the army, or to fight, but to give themselves up to prayer, to the works of mercy, and the practice of all the Christian virtues; engaging them to follow the same rule and form of living that he had before prescribed to their husbands...(so that) early in the 13th century the Order was thus multiplied in an extraordinary manner"...

This rule, indeed was not written...(therefore) the sisters of Italy urgently besought the Venerable Father Munio De Zamora...to reduce this rule into writing...He complied with their request, (writing) the rule which St. Dominic had only given verbally. It is thus clear that the Venerable Father Munio was not the author, but merely the editor and compiler of this rule, for one cannot believe that the Third Order, which was in so flourishing a state in the year 1228, which Pope Gregory IX honored...had existed without a rule or statutes until the year 1285...

The sisters of the Third Order... of Italy expressly assure us that he (Munio De Zamora) only reduced to writing the statutes which St. Dominic had given for the guidance of the brethren and sisters"...This is sufficient to prove the antiquity of the Order, and that it received its rule of living from the Blessed St. Dominic its founder.[29;i]

The "Militia of Jesus Christ" was the "third branch of a single order (which included) both men and women religious and the laity."[30] It was suggested that:

Actually the Order of Preachers was linked with the laity from its very inception, in a quite natural way by reason of its establishment in cities. It always made room for them...Pursuing its apostolic thrust, the Order of Preachers was bound to encounter the evangelical movement of the laity, who in Italy, had organized themselves into an "Order of Penance". These lay groups, divided into local fraternities, addressed their spiritual concerns to the new contemporary mendicant orders.[31]

The members of the Dominican "Order of Penance":

---

[29] Ibid., 9-10.
[30] Guy Bedouelle, *Saint Dominic: The Grace of the Word* (San Francisco: Ignatius press, 1995), 212.
[31] Ibid.

A Holy Calling

Were to bear witness to a love of truth proper to the Order of Preachers in the thirteenth century. Munio De Zamora's Rule made this clear in unequivocal terms: "Let them excel in virtue and guard their reputations. Let them in no way leave themselves open to suspicion or heresy, but on the contrary be true sons of St. Dominic in the Lord, filled to the utmost with strong and ardent zeal for Catholic truth, in ways in keeping their own life."[32]

In essence, Guy Bedouelle observed: "the Laity were here being given an ecclesiastical mission, were being placed at the service of preaching the truth in accordance with their own life."[33]

Lay men and women members of the "Third Order of Penance of St. Dominic," while not taking formal vows, did make a religious profession. By this profession "the Tertiary is introduced, is fixed, into a superior state of life. Although it falls short of the state in which those who take the triple vows of religion are established and settled, nevertheless it imitates that state in its quality and duration."[34] They profess to follow the Rule of the Third Order for the duration of their lives.

The early "Rule" for the community of "The Brothers and Sisters of the Third Order of Penance of St. Dominic" consisted of some twenty-two chapters which contained specific directives on such topics as: "Qualities of those to be Received (into the Order)," "Habit of the Brethren and Sisters," "Manner of Profession," "Permanence of the State," "Recitation of the Canonical Hours (and other Prayers)," "Confession and Communion," "Keeping Silence in Church," "Showing Reverence to Ecclesiastical Superiors," "Fasts and Abstinence," "Going Out of the Brethren and Sisters," "Correction and Assembly of the Brethren and Sisters," and "Visiting and Relieving the Sick."[35] Importantly, the final chapter of the "Rule," entitled "Of the Obligation of this Rule or Manner of Life," states that "the constitutions and ordinances of this Rule do not oblige the brethren and sisters in any way under sin, but only under penalty of the fault."[36]

In a "Summary of the Rule of the Third Order of St. Dominic," the history of the Third Order explains that when St. Dominic's first "Brotherhood of the Militia of Jesus Christ" was no longer needed to

---

[32] Ibid., 213.
[33] Ibid.
[34] Joret, 28.
[35] Feuilllet, 21-47.
[36] Ibid., 47.

battle the heretics of the era, and the group "lost its military character, the combat changed from an earthly into a purely spiritual one. When the men who were in the 'Militia' died, their widows, accustomed to religious life which they had led, renounced marriage and persevered unto death in their usual practices."[37] Following this, "the name of the association was changed to The Brothers and Sisters of Penance of St. Dominic; the community was later simply referred to as Dominican Tertiaries,[38] or the Third Order of St. Dominic."

Now that an armed "militia" was no longer relevant, the "Third Order of St. Dominic" "changed its aim to form a vast crusade against the spiritual enemies of God and man."[39] Thus, myriad men and women, single and married, "put on the livery of St. Dominic and grafted themselves on his Order, to share the toils and the privileges" of the Dominican Order.[40] They no longer needed "to leave the world in order to reach the measure of the saints. The chamber became a cell and the house a monastery."[41] It is suggested that women tertiaries "in particular" have "enriched' the Order with their ministries":

> The convent went to them as they could not go to the convent. They turned some hidden corner of the house of their father or consort into a sanctuary of the invisible Spouse, whom they loved above all else. Who has not heard of St. Catherine of Siena, and of St. Rose of Lima, those two Dominican stars that beamed on the old and the new world? Thus, the Spirit of God works according to the times, and proportions its aids to the miseries of man. After having flourished in solitudes, it now blooms on the highways.[42]

In the Thirteenth and Fourteenth Centuries, Third Order lay men and women generally wore a Dominican habit, as described in the "Manual of the Brothers and Sisters of the Third Order of Penance of St. Dominic":

> Let all, both the brothers and the sisters be clothed with white and black stuff, which, neither in its appearance nor in reality should shew forth too much costlinesss, as becometh the

---

[37] Dominicans, 9.
[38] Ibid.
[39] Ibid., 11
[40] Ibid.
[41] Ibid., 12.
[42] Ibid.

Christian modesty of the servants of the Lord. Let the mantle be black, as also the capuces of the brethren; but the tunics white, with sleeves extending to the wrists and closed. Let them have only leathern belts, which the sisters shall wear over their tunics. In their purses, their shoes and the like, let them put away all worldly vanity. Let the veils and bands of the sisters be of white linen, or hempen cloth.[43]

The habited brothers and sisters of Blessed Margaret's community in the Fourteenth Century were often recognized in the conduct of the ministries directed by the Rule and guidelines for the community of Brothers and Sisters of Penance of St. Dominic:

Every Christian, as such, in indispensably obliged to serve his neighbor, to whom he is bound by the holy tie of charity; but this active serviceable charity is more especially the spirit of the Order of St. Dominic, and ought ever to animate its children. Charity is the very end for which the Order was instituted; it devotes all those who embrace it to the salvation of their neighbor, with this difference only, that whereas the Religious of the First Order labour to advance this object by the ministry of preaching...the brethren and sisters of the Third Order advance it on their part by the practice of works of mercy toward the afflicted. It is their duty to visit the sick, to exhort them to penance and to patient suffering of their afflictions, to prepare them for receiving the last sacraments...to serve them with diligence, and if they be poor, to obtain for them temporal necessaries and comforts;...they may (also) be seen waiting upon the poor and the sick in the hospitals (and) visiting and consoling prisoners.[44]

In Blessed Margaret's time, the Sisters of Penance of St. Dominic could be found in Italian cities such as Florence, Pisa and Siena, as well as in smaller towns such as *Citta di Castello*; together with prayer and penance, their active ministry was directed toward visiting and caring for the ill and the infirm.[45] The Sisters' apostolate was involved primarily

---

[43] Feuillet, 23.
[44] Ibid., 15-16
[45] Levasti, 26.

in: "serving in hospitals, visiting and caring for the sick in their homes, ministering to prisoners and comforting those in spiritual distress."[46]

The community of Sisters of Penance of St. Dominic in *Citta di Castello*, although residing in their own homes, or those of friends, wore the earlier described habit which consisted of a white tunic and veil; over the tunic the Sisters added a black mantle which gave rise to their popular title among the people: the Mantellate. Most of the Mantellate were older women who were widows and unable to enter a cloistered religious order. Individual communities of Sisters of Penance met periodically in local Dominican churches or chapels for prayer and to receive spiritual guidance from the Friars.[ii]

The *Mantellata*

Because of Margaret's young age, approximately 22 or 23 years, there was some concern about her joining the Sisters of Penance and becoming a *Mantellata*" in this community consisting primarily of older widows. Nevertheless, after a committee of sisters examined Margaret's "faith, character and reputation" and presented a positive report, she was "notified, to her unbounded joy, that she was acceptable as a member" of the Mantellate.[47] It has been suggested that the decision "was historic because, as far as records show, it was the first instance of a young, unmarried woman being permitted to join the 'Order of Penance of St. Dominic.'"[48] However, this latter suggestion appears to be inaccurate as there was, some years earlier, also a "young, unmarried woman" accepted as a Sister of Penance of St. Dominic, Blessed Giovanna (Jane) of Orvieto.

Giovanna of Orvieto was born in 1264, twenty-four years before Blessed Margaret of Castello, and died in 1306, fifteen years prior to Margaret's death. We are told that Giovanna "decided to enter the Third Order of St. Dominic", as a Mantellata, as young adult.[49] As with Blessed Margaret, "because of her youth, the Dominicans delayed in accepting her. Only after a long period of prayer and fasting was she able to win the privilege of putting on the Third Order habit...Once a member of the Order, she so much desired, she set her goal at the highest sanctity and worked at attaining it. She prayed all morning and part of the afternoon,

---

[46] Ibid.
[47] Bonniwell, 66-67.
[48] Ibid., 67.
[49] Mary Jean Dorcy, *St. Dominic's Family: Over 300 Famous Dominicans* (Charlotte, N.C.: Tan Books, 1983), 136.

leaving herself only enough time to do enough work to care for her few needs and some alms to give to the poor."[50]

Blessed Giovanna "lived as a Dominican Penitent, or as her legend addresses her, a *vestita*, for about 22 years."[51] "Not unlike many other religious laywomen," Giovanna came from a troubled background. She lost both parents at the age of five years, and at twelve was "forced to support herself": "Giovanna earned her undoubtedly meager living as a dressmaker and a domestic servant."[52] Similar to Blessed Margaret of Castello, Blessed Giovanna of Orvieto frequently stayed in the residences of her benefactors: "As a Dominican *vestita*, Giovanna lived for several years in the upper floor of the home of her wealthy mistress, Ghisla, and many of her supporters came from wealthy families of Orvieto."[53] Giovanna:

> was a *vestita* at a time when women sought Dominican guidance but the Dominican Life of Penance had not yet been institutionally established and penitent women did not have an official position within the Order. The sixth Master General of the Dominican Order, Munio De Zamora, wrote his set of simple religious guidelines, the Ordinationes, for the *vestitae* of Orvieto in 1286...it is probable that Giovanna was among the women of Orvieto who received Munio's Ordinationes.[54]

Blessed Giovanna would have been around the age of twenty-two when the "Rule," or *Ordinationes*, for the Sisters of Penance of St. Dominic was written by the Master of the Order; she died at age 42. Again, as with Blessed Margaret, a number of healing miracles were credited to the intervention of Giovanna both prior to and following her death.[55] Two incidents of healings attributed to Blessed Giovanna during her lifetime, are reported in the following anecdotes: "A noble lady, named Toscha, whose son was ill, sent a messenger to ask the Virgin to pray for her son. After the prayers were completed, the saint sent the lady a message, 'Know that your son is healed.' When the mother set out to find out about the matter, she found her son to be totally cured";[56] and

---

[50] Ibid.
[51] Lehmijoki-Gardner, 59-86.
[52] Ibid., 59.
[53] Ibid.
[54] Ibid., 60.
[55] Ibid., 73-74.
[56] Lehmijoki-Gardner, 73.

"A young man named Giacomo had the tertian fever (Malaria), for which some barley water was being prepared. The Blessed Giovanna took the water from the fire where it was cooking, and, lifting it up, she said: 'You will no longer drink this water!' Her words were proven true by the healing that followed."[57]

A number of extraordinary healings also occurred after Giovanna's death; several anecdotal examples include:

- "A sick boy was standing by the bier on which the still unburied saint lay. On the suggestion of his mother, he touched the Virgin's hand. He was immediately freed from his illness."[58]
- "There was a certain paralyzed woman whose extremities were constantly shaking and had totally lost their strength. A few devout persons made a vow on her behalf to the Saint Giovanna and the extremities of the woman's body recovered their strength and were totally healed."[59]
- "When a certain religious man was having an intense pain after fracturing his foot, he devoutly invoked the saint's name, and was at that moment freed."[60]
- "Another woman, named Sibilla, who was ravaged by a continually strong fever for a year, invoked the Virgin's name and (she) was totally healed."[61]
- "A certain woman had a son who was suffering bitterly from spasms. He meticulously followed all the prescriptions assigned by the doctors and he was making no progress. After a vow to the Virgin, he was completely freed from his illness."[62]

Blessed Giovanna of Orvieto "was one of the first Dominican laywomen to be venerated as a *beata*."[63]

Blessed Margaret of Castello was formally received into the community of the Sisters of Penance of St. Dominic in a...

> church filled with Dominican Friars, members of the Mantellate and other friends...(she was asked by the Prior) "What do you

---

[57] Ibid.
[58] Ibid., 79.
[59] Ibid.
[60] Ibid.
[61] Ibid., 80.
[62] Ibid., 81.
[63] Ibid., 59.

seek?" (and answered) according to the ritual: "God's mercy and yours." The Prior solemnly addressed her in these words: "Sister Margaret! You are about to become a member of the Order of St. Dominic. Such a step carries with it the gravest obligations. Henceforth, though you live in the world, you must not be part of the world...From now on, Sister, your greatest concern must be to serve God and your fellow man, out of love for God."
(Margaret made her profession): "To the honor of Almighty God, Father, Son and Holy Spirit, and of the Blessed Virgin Mary, and of St. Dominic and in the presence of you, most reverend Father, Prior of the Order of St. Dominic in *Citta di Castello*, I, Sister Margaret, do make my profession. And, I do promise that henceforth I will live according to the form and Rule of the same Order of Penance of St. Dominic until death."[64]

Sister Margaret then received the blessing, as a new *Mantellata*, from the Prior: "May He who has begun this good work in you perfect it until the day of Christ Jesus!"[65]

Father Bonniwell observed that after Margaret's reception into the Order, she no longer felt alone in the world: "Wearing the Dominican habit, she knew that finally she possessed what had been lacking in her life. Now, for the first time, she knew what it meant to be part of a family, a great religious family, whose numerous friars and nuns were truly her brothers and sisters by a tie closer than that of blood relationship."[66]

Through her reception as a member of the Lay Dominican Order, the later years of the life of Margaret of *Citta di Castello* were indeed blessed by a holy calling: "In the church where she attended morning Mass she had met the members of the Order of Penance of St. Dominic, the Third Order Dominicans, that same Order of which Saint Catherine of Siena was not long after to become a most illustrious member. These were women who, though unable to enter a convent, wore a religious habit and followed a religious rule of life in their homes."[67]

As Fr. William Bonniwell, author Ivan Innerst suggests that acceptance into the community was a treasured gift for Margaret:

> She could not have asked for more and her joy was unbounded. The new Dominican Tertiary, clad in her habit, was vowed to the

---

[64] Bonniwell, 67-68.
[65] Ibid., 68.
[66] Ibid., 69.
[67] Innerst, 83.

life she most wanted, one of study, penance, and prayer. Then, as if to fill to the brim her newfound cup of good fortune, she was given first one home for a time, and later a second with well-to-do families of the city under whose roof she might follow her rule. From within those walls a series of miracles, of healing, were to be reported in the course of the days that followed...(and)The untutored woman, displaying something of a miracle in her own life, too, was said to recite from memory the 150 Psalms, the Office of the Blessed Virgin, and the Office of the Holy Cross.[68]

Now, as a *Mantellata*, as noted above, Sister Margaret faithfully prayed the Divine Office and the Office of the Blessed Virgin Mary, and of the Holy Cross faithfully each day; although blind, Margaret learned to recite the "entire psalter."[69] And, each night, when she heard the Dominican Monastery bell tolling for the liturgical hour of "Matins," she would get up and recite the psalms of the hour in order to be in community with her Brothers in Christ. She often spent the remainder of the night in contemplative prayer. Margaret's perception of the life of a *Mantellata*, as posited by Fr. Bonniwell, was: "If I cannot live in a convent, at least I can follow as far as possible the routine of one!"[70]

After becoming a *Mantellata*, Margaret lived briefly with the wealthy Offrenduccio family who offered her a home. On the death of one of the members, and breakup of the house, Blessed Margaret was invited to live in the Venturino household, which was to be her last home on earth.

Venturinus and his wife Gregia lived in a large house not far from the Chiesa administered by the Dominican Friars. While financially comfortable, Venturinus and Grigia "never flaunted their wealth. Rather the proximity of the Preachers had educated them to the ideal of justice and sobriety which guided them to a wise use of money, considering charity toward others not only as a moral duty but a way to help establish...the kingdom of heaven."[71]

In providing a small garret room for her to occupy, Venturinus and Grigia "allowed Margaret to enjoy the tranquility that she wanted to deepen her relationship with Jesus, introducing her at the same time into a network of relationships, both within and outside the family."[72] This

---

[68] Ibid.
[69] Thompson, 358.
[70] Bonniwell, 71.
[71] Sartori, 53.
[72] Ibid., 58.

assisted Blessed Margaret in gaining "some independence while remaining within the limits imposed by her physical condition."[73] Venturinus and Grigia also did not "hesitate" to inform Margaret about "the main events of the city, thick stormy events, replete with quarrels, divisions adorned with injustice. Involving her in what was happening, Margherita had become aware of the needs of those who had now become her countrymen."[74]

Donna Grigia also familiarized Blessed Margaret with the needs of the local "poor, the sick, the elderly, prisoners, human cases which seemed to run counter to Divine goodness."[75] In this way Margaret began to prepare herself for her *Mantellata* ministry to the sick and the outcast. She was able, with the companionship of Grigia, to visit the ill and infirm and later to visit those desperately needy poor, incarcerated in the *Citta di Castello* prison (Blessed Margaret's ministries to the sick and to prisoners are described in the following chapter).

The Tertiary Vocation

In order to better understand the Dominican Tertiary vocation of Margaret of Castello, the lives of three other well-known Tertiaries are explored: Saint Catherine of Siena, also a medieval Sister of Penance of St. Dominic, born only 27 years after the death of Blessed Margaret; Saint Rose of Lima, who deeply loved and sought to emulate Saint Catherine and entered the Dominican Third Order a little over 200 years after Catherine's death; and Blessed Pier Giorgio Frassati, a young 20th-century Dominican Tertiary, who responded to God's call to serve the poor in his urban milieu. These three Tertiaries were chosen not only for their holiness of life and commitment to the charism of our Holy Father Dominic, but also because each, in his or her respective ministries, served the sick and the outcast, thus following in the footsteps of Blessed Margaret of Castello.

Catherine of Siena

Saint Catherine of Siena was born Caterina Benincasa in Tuscan Italy on March 25, 1347. Catherine was the 24th of 25 children born to Mona Lapa and Giacomo Benincasa; the Benincasas were a devout Catholic family, the parents committed to raising their children in the faith. Siena, the city of Catherine's birth, was described as one of the most unruly

---

[73] Ibid.
[74] Ibid.
[75] Ubaldo Valentini, *Beata Margherita De La Metola Una Sfida Alla Emarginazione* (Perugia, Italy: Petruzzi Editore, 1988), 42.

cities in Italy, filled with discord and discontent, yet it was, paradoxically, also the home of many holy people, thus being accorded the title "Vestibule of Paradise."[76] While there were a number of "elegant homes in Siena, owned by nobles and wealthy merchants, as well as modest middle-class dwellings, there were also underdeveloped sections of the city where disadvantaged citizens lived in poverty and squalor."[77]

As Blessed Margaret of Castello, Saint Catherine of Siena's spiritual life was initiated as a small child when, at the age of only six, she had a vision of Our Lord accompanied by the Apostles Peter and Paul; Catherine saw Jesus bless and smile at her. Catherine's confessor and first biographer, Blessed Raymond of Capua reported that following the vision, the young girl gave up her childhood games and began to immerse herself in prayer.[78]

Catherine lived in a small room at home, in distinction to Blessed Margaret's enclosure in a religious cell, but she did accompany her family to Mass each day at the Church of San Domenico. As well as spending time each day in prayer, young Catherine began to beg her father "to allow her to give some of the family's household provisions to the sick and the poor of the city."[79]

At the age of seven, just a year after her vision of Christ, Catherine, like Blessed Margaret, made a promise of virginity to Jesus, placing her pledge in the hands of Our Lady, who she asked "to give me as Husband Him whom I desire with all the power of my soul, your most holy Son, our one Lord Jesus Christ: and I promise Him and you that I will never choose for myself and other husband, and will always do all I can to keep my virginity unspotted."[80]

As Catherine matured there were repeated challenges to a religious commitment primarily from her parents who expected their daughter to marry, the more usual vocation for young Italian girls of her era. Nevertheless, she remained steadfast in her childhood calling, despite the cost of disappointing her dearly loved mother and father. From attending daily Mass at the Church of San Domenico, Catherine became familiar not only with the Dominican Friars but also with the community

---

[76] Gillet, 68-69.
[77] Mary Elizabeth O'Brien, *Catherine of Siena: A Sacred Covenant of Caring for the Sick* (Chicago, Ill.: New Priory Press, 2015), 3.
[78] Ibid., 9.
[79] Ibid.
[80] Raymond of Capua, *Catherine of Siena*, Trans. George Lamb (Charlotte, N.C.: Tan Books, 2011), 15.

of Dominican lay women, The Sisters of Penance of St. Dominic (The Mantellate).

Thus, at the age of around seventeen or eighteen, Catherine begged admittance to the community of Mantellate. As with Blessed Margaret before her, the Sisters of Penance were hesitant to admit Catherine because of her youth and inexperience; the community, similar to Margaret's day, consisted primarily of older widows. However, again as with Blessed Margaret, an evaluation of Catherine's spirituality and motives, led the community, with the blessing of the Dominican Friars, to admit her as a full member of the Sisters of Penance of St. Dominic.

Catherine was formally clothed with the black and white Dominican habit for which she had yearned. Although living at home, as was customary for the community, the new *Mantellata* embraced a rigorous daily schedule of prayer and penance, leaving her small room only to attend Mass or deliver food and alms to the poor. She spent the next three years essentially living as a contemplative *Mantellata* within the "enclosure" of her family home. Catherine was very much at peace and filled with joy in this regimen of solitary prayer and fasting, spending many hours in intimate conversation with God.

At age 21 or 22, however, the saint, heard the Lord's call to a more active ministry. God said to Catherine: "On two feet you must walk and on two wings you must fly to heaven"; Catherine now understood that if she was to love God completely, she must serve her neighbor as well as serving the Lord.[81] God told Catherine that the unselfish love of neighbors "is the means I have given you to practice and prove your virtue. The service that you cannot render me, you must do for your neighbors."[82] Now, also as Blessed Margaret, who was forced to leave her contemplative existence, Saint Catherine was called to leave the solitary reclusive life of her room.

Thus, although earlier paths had differed, both Margaret and Catherine, began in their early twenties, to engage in active ministry to the sick and to outcasts as mandated by their vocation as members of the community of Sisters of Penance of St. Dominic. Both young *Mantellatas*, dressed in their black and white Dominican habits, now began to walk the streets, one in *Citta di Castello*, the other in Siena, seeking to bring care and consolation to those who were ill and infirm, especially to the sick poor and to the outcasts of society.

---

[81] O'Brien, 31.
[82] Catherine of Siena, *The Dialogue*, translation and introduction by Suzanne Noffke OP (Mahwah, N.J.: Paulist Press, 1980), 36.

Blessed Margaret of Castello and Saint Catherine of Siena both died at the age of thirty-three, having dedicated their lives to the service of God and of their neighbors (Note: For a more detailed description of Saint Catherine of Siena's ministry to the sick and the outcast see: Mary Elizabeth O'Brien, *Catherine of Siena: A Sacred Covenant of Caring for the Sick* (Chicago, Ill.: New Priory Press, 2015).

Rose of Lima

Saint Rose of Lima was born into a Spanish Colonial family in Peru in 1856; she had a reputation for extreme asceticism and also for the care of the sick and the outcast in her city. She was given the baptismal name of Isabel by her godmother but several months later, "as she slept in her cradle, her mother and several others...having perceived on her countenance a beautiful rose, called her from that time, by no other name than Rose."[83] At her confirmation, the Archbishop of Lima, Toribio de Mogrovejo, gave the child "the name of Rose."[84] When the saint got older, she developed some scruples on learning that Rose had not been her baptismal name; She felt that keeping the name "Rose" might indicate vanity. Saint Rose brought her anxiety, in prayer, to the Virgin Mary who provided consolation to the young woman, "assuring her that the name of Rose was pleasing to her Son, Jesus Christ."[85]

Rose's initial devotion and small spiritual practices began as a child when she "patterned her life after what she had learned of the life of Saint Catherine of Siena."[86] As Rose grew into adolescence she developed a wellspring of spirituality and spiritual practices which were not well received by her mother, Olivia (Maria de la Olivia), who was counting on a noble wedding for her daughter. A prosperous marriage would help alleviate the family's current state of poverty. As with Blessed Margaret and Saint Catherine, Rose, as a young child of five, had taken a private vow of virginity "without telling anyone...Olivia would have been very angry."[87] Rose's mother had not even an "inkling" of Rose's vow and "consoled herself daily in her poverty that Rose would wed illustriously."[88] Olivia spent much time in creating elaborate dresses for

---

[83] Leonhard Hansen, *The Life of Saint Rose of Lima* (N.Y.: P. J. Kennedy & Sons, 1847), 22.
[84] Ibid.
[85] Ibid., 23.
[86] Kevin Vost, *Hounds of the Lord* (Manchester, N.H.: Sophia Institute Press, 2015), 194.
[87] Sister Mary Alphonsus, *St. Rose of Lima: Patroness of the Americas* (Charlotte, N.C.: Tan Books, 1982), 82.
[88] Ibid.

Rose in order to present her in a favorable light to young men of aristocratic background.

In the meantime, Rose was seeking to live a quiet life of prayer and penance; she asked to use "the discipline" for mortification and was given permission from her parents. It needs to be noted, however, that in Rose's era, the "discipline," consisting of several light, waxed cords, was fairly mild and commonly used by the laity; it was not as traumatic as sometimes thought. Primarily Rose's "teenage years were spent immersed in prayer and chores within her family household."[89]

As she grew older, Rose participated in the "Flores family's charity to the sick poor," distributing herb medicines to those in need. The saint also soon "found herself being asked to tend wounds and give advice beyond her capacity...she had to look to someone who knew how to diagnose and treat the diseases which she met most commonly among the poor who crowded the patio of her home each morning."[90] After study with a medical practitioner, "Rose became a competent diagnostician and learned how to treat many diseases."[91] Rose's caregiving ministry began to "assume the earmarks of a profession (but) it was always a joy beyond measure. Through it she became known as the "mother of the poor."[92]

While outwardly trying to placate her own mother, Olivia, who was still attempting to find her a suitable husband, Rose privately embraced prayer and various mortifications of the flesh. Things came to a head with a visit to the family by Archbishop Toribio who asked if Rose had decided on a vocation; he affirmed that his blood sister was currently "in heaven" in her cloistered life with the "Poor Clares"; Olivia was not pleased with the Archbishop's hinting and insisted that Rose would find her vocation in the "married state."[93] Some months later, Archbishop Torribio died, and Rose began to pray intently about her vocation and about the Archbishop's earlier suggestion of the Monastery of St. Clare. In the end, however, it appeared that God had His own plan for Rose's future.

As the story goes, Rose was seated one day in her garden and suddenly she was visited by a beautiful black and white butterfly which lighted on her heart; it left black and white (the Dominican colors) markings on her gown. Rose interpreted this as God's response to her

---

[89] Vost, 195.
[90] Sister Mary Alphosus, 134.
[91] Ibid., 135.
[92] Ibid.
[93] Ibid., 178.

prayers: "It means that God wishes me to be a Dominican Tertiary...I was just praying that he would make His Divine Will known to me when the butterfly came. As it rested on me, I had an interior light explaining what it meant."[94] The experience "confirmed in Rose's mind and heart her intention to follow in the footsteps of Saint Catherine and join the Third Order Dominicans."[95] All of Rose's desires and especially her attraction to penance "prompted her to follow the holy mistress she had chosen and become a Dominican of the Third Order."[96]

Although her mother immediately rebuffed the idea, Rose stood firm. She had longed for the cloister, which her mother would not consider, so God was presenting her with a calling to the Third Order of St. Dominic whose Rule allowed Tertiaries to live at home; this, she prayed, would appease Olivia. The mother, although unhappy, ultimately gave in. Olivia "consoled herself with the thought that Rose's entrance into the Third Order would be no impediment to her marriage."[97] Rose, however, had no plans for marriage but this was the only alternative to the longed for cloister and was a step into a form of religious life.

It was reported that, "At her clothing ceremony Rose received the full Tertiary habit: a long white tunic and scapular, a leather belt, a coif and white veil. Over her tunic she wore, when outside, a black mantle which extended to the bottom of the white tunic. Although still living at home, she looked like a religious novice."[98] In that era "the habit was worn outwardly by Tertiaries, whether living cloistered or not, so that there was nothing strange in her being formally clothed."[99]

"'What do you ask' said the priest, Fr. Velazquez, as Rose knelt before him: 'The mercy of God and yours,' she responded, in the manner of the Dominican investiture ritual."

Father Velazquez then spoke about the Tertiaries:

> He mentioned the original name of the Third Order of St. Dominic, the "Militia of Jesus Christ," and told those assembled in the chapel that the soldier's obedience and valor, his devotedness and loyalty must characterize the Tertiary. Then he spoke of the actual name of the Third Order, "Brothers and Sisters of Penance of St. Dominic." This indicated its spirit. The

---

[94] Vost, 194-195.
[95] Ibid., 196.
[96] F.M. Capes, *St. Rose of Lima: Flower of the New World* (Middletown, DE.: 1899), 93.
[97] Vost, 196.
[98] Ibid., 197.
[99] Capes, 96.

members of the Third Order were to be brothers and sisters to one another in charity, but brothers and sisters dedicated to a life of penance, supernatural restraint...(Rose) would be obligated to certain morning and night prayers of the Rule, to the keeping of certain fast and abstinence days, to the recitation of the Little Office of Our Lady and the Office of the Dead at prescribed times. Moreover, she would be bound to practice the virtue of charity with special zeal, visiting the sick and devoting herself to works of mercy.[100]

Rose initially "sought to be more alone and begged to be allowed to build a regular little 'cell' for herself at the bottom of the family garden."[101] This was the saint's refuge in solitude; she left her cell only for three reasons: "to go to church, to help sick friends or relations and to visit or find out poor and miserable women whom she made it one of her duties and pleasures to nurse."[102] Rose also prayed the Divine Office "every day while living in her hermitage";[103] she also loved and prayed the Little Office of the Blessed Virgin.

Over time Rose was able to persuade her mother to allow a back room of their home to be turned into a small infirmary where she could care for the sick poor who came seeking her help. We are told that "all kinds of miseries found their way to this little adobe room, but she had a remedy for each...No disease was too loathsome for her to treat, although her stomach might turn. Sometimes she would leave the sick for a few minutes, retch painfully, then come back smiling...from day to day she fought her repugnance; but she never lost it till her death."[104]

In caring for the sick:

> Rose's heart was particularly tender, as it went out beyond her own race to the poor Indians of Peru, despised, downtrodden and often ill-treated by her haughty fellow-countrymen. It appears that in Lima, while she lived, numbers of wretched Indian women, diseased as well as outcast and neglected, were to be found, and it was chiefly to seek these out and help them that Sister Rose began, at times, to leave her solitude.[105]

---

[100] Sister Mary Alphonsus, 199.
[101] Capes, 102.
[102] Ibid., 104-105.
[103] Ibid., 120.
[104] Sister Mary Alphonsus, 237.
[105] Capes, 121-122.

Because Rose treated patients from all races and social background, her infirmary had a "revolutionary impact" on Lima's society:

> In the humble room built behind her father's house, the young Tertiary upset the most cherished prejudices of her time and class. Until she began her work of mercy, race pride and an exalted sense of their dignity had kept Spanish ladies from tending the sick of subject peoples...they confined their care to the sick poor of their own race...But Rose's heart knew no barriers of race, color or class. Her interracial infirmary was a revolution in love.[106]

Saint Rose of Lima died young, as Blessed Margaret and Saint Catherine, at the age of only thirty-one; she was canonized in 1671.

Pier Giorgio Frassati

Pier Giorgio Frassati was born in 1901 to a prominent family in Turin, Italy. Growing up, Pier Giorgio was only an average student but was very committed to Catholic action and social justice; because of these interests he became a member of the local St. Vincent de Paul Society which was dedicated to helping the poor, especially those who were ill and infirm or outcasts. It was reported by "all his associates in the St. Vincent de Paul Society that Pier Giorgio was first to volunteer for any mission to the poor, that he was endlessly patient with difficult people, and that every cent of his money went to relieve the needs of the poor."[107]

Although viewed as an adventurer and fun-loving comrade by his friends, Pier Giorgio was also well-known for his dedication to those who were suffering. He was described as "a rich young man, who was able to put 'the last' first in his life and (who) devoted himself to the poor and needy, understanding that the least of our brothers and sisters on this earth are first in God's heart."[108]

It was clear that "Pier Giorgio showed through his actions that he believed that in serving the homeless, the naked, the hungry, he was serving Christ who said 'Truly, I tell you, just as you did this to one of the least of these who are members of my family, you did it to me' (Mt.

---

[106] Sister Mary Alphonsus, 238,
[107] Dorcy, 576-577.
[108] Maria Di Lorenzo, *Blessed Pier Giorgio Frassati: An Ordinary Christian* (Alexandria, Va.: Pauline Books and Media, 2004), 67.

25:40)."[109] Pier Giorgio's witness was badly needed in his home country as he grew up in an era of "reconstruction in Italy, the post war years when so many young people were drifting away from their faith and joining various socialistic or atheistic societies."[110]

Pier Giorgio never limited his love and care for the poor to a "general group"; he is described as loving and caring for each person he met, seeing in that individual "the very face of Christ."[111] He is, however, quoted as saying: "I see a special light around the sick, the poor, the less fortunate, a light we do not possess."[112] Every week Pier Giorgio "visited four or five families and brought not only material assistance in the form of coupons with which to buy bread for the week, or clothing, blankets, medicine, firewood and coal for heating, but also, above all, spiritual support."[113] Pier Giorgio's charity was "unconditional":

> He did not pass judgements on anyone; he did not need to know if the people he helped had a police record; he did not ask questions to find out if they agreed with his way of thinking. People were poor and they needed help; that was all that mattered to Pier Giorgio. They were the poor whom he was called to love with the heart of Christ.[114]

On the Feast of St. Dominic, in 1922, Pier Giorgio "joined the Third Order Dominicans," taking the name Girolamo; he "entered the society that he felt would best combat the evil influence (of the era) and better his own spiritual life."[115] He also realized that "to bring to others 'the fruits of contemplation' made a positive demand on people who were in a position to spread the truth."[116] The Dominican affiliation would also continue to support his vocation to care for the sick and the outcasts of his city. An engineering major in college, Pier Giorgio dreamed of one day traveling to a developing country as a lay missionary where "he could combine his professional skill with the lay apostolate";[117] he also

---

[109] Ibid., 72.
[110] Dorcy, 576.
[111] Di Lorenzo, 73.
[112] Ibid.
[113] Ibid., 74.
[114] Ibid., 75.
[115] Dorcy, 576.
[116] Ibid.
[117] Ibid., 577.

hoped to use his family inheritance "to build a home for destitute people in Turin."[118]

Pier Giorgio Frassati, as the other Tertiaries described above, died very young at the age of 24; the diagnosis was poliomyelitis. His "last words would be to ask his family to be sure to check his coat so they could deliver some medicines, he had in one pocket, to a sick man in need, and in another, a pawn ticket he had obtained to help another poor friend reclaim a precious item he had pawned in order to eat."[119]

Even Blessed Pier Giorgio's early death seemed related to his ministry to those in need: "the doctors concluded that his polio had probably been contracted through his interactions with the sick and the poor, but Pier Giorgio would not have had it any other way. Christ showed us and Saint John told us, 'Greater love has no man than this, that a man lay down his life for his friends' (John 15:13). Pier Giorgio knew this and he did this."[120]

At his beatification, Blessed Pier Giorgio Frassati was labeled by Pope John Paul II as the "Man of Eight Beatitudes."

This chapter has focused on the vocation of Blessed Margaret of Castello, a Sister of Penance of St. Dominic, or *Mantellata*, one of the earliest Dominican Tertiaries. The experiences of three other well-known Tertiaries has been included to help elucidate the Dominican spiritual journey of Blessed Margaret; these included: Saint Catherine of Siena, Saint Rose of Lima, and Blessed Pier Giorgio Frassati. In the following pages, Blessed Margaret's vocation as a *Mantellata* will be explored with focus on her two specific ministries: first, Margaret's care of the ill and infirm in the streets of *Citta di Castello* and in their homes, and, secondly, her support and ministry to outcasts incarcerated in the local prison.

ENDNOTES - Chapter 5. "A Holy Calling"

[118] Ibid.
[119] Vost, 211.
[120] Ibid., 225.

[i] In a 1913 work entitled "The Dominican Order and Convocation: A Study of the Growth of Representation in the Church During the Thirteenth Century," Sir Ernest Barker suggests in a footnote that it is "dubious whether the 'Third Order' was instituted by St. Dominic himself" (Barker, 2013, p. 17). Actually, this thinking does not conflict with the comments as cited above. Pere Jean Baptist Feuillet only observed that St. Dominic informally guided the first brethren of the "Militia of Jesus Christ," pointing out that the "rule" "was not written"; that the "rule" attributed to Dominic had only been given "verbally."

[ii] For more information on the early history of the Sisters of Penance of St. Dominic, or Mantellate, some suggested works include: F.D. Joret, *Dominican Life* (London: Blackfriars Publications, 1958); Jean Baptiste Feuillet, *Manual of the Brothers and Sisters of the Third Order of Penance of St. Dominic* (London: Burns and Lambert, 1852); Sir Ernest Barker, *The Dominican Order and Convocation: A Study of the Growth of Representation in the Church During the Thirteenth Century* (London: Oxford University Press, 1913); Dominicans, *Summary of the Rule of the Third Order of St. Dominic* (San Francisco: J.B. McIntyre, 1886), Guy Bedouelle, *Saint Dominic: The Grace of the Word* (San Francisco: Ignatius Press, 1995), Augustine Thompson, *Cities of God: The Religion of the Italian Communes, 1125-1325*, (University Park, Pa.: The Pennsylvania State University Press); and Mariju Lehmijoki-Gardner, *Dominican Penitent Women* (Mahwah, N.J.: Paulist Press, 2005).

Blessed Margaret of Castello

Chapter 6. "Love One Another"

Serving the Sick and the Outcast

"I give you a new commandment that you love one another, just as I have loved you."

John 13:34

"Love One Another"

To the cobblestone streets
of the impoverished city
Margaret came
To bring her love
As Jesus
Loved.

To the desolate homes of
The sick and the poor
Margaret came
To bring her love
As Jesus
Loved.

To the barren cells of the
cheerless prison
Margaret came
To bring her love
As Jesus
Loved.

To the anxious,
the lonely,
the abandoned,
the unloved,
Margaret came
To bring her love
As Jesus
Loved.

Blessed Margaret of Castello's ministry of serving the sick and the outcast was truly a lived experience of the Gospel mandate to "love one another" as Jesus loved us (John 13: 34). Margaret, despite her own physical afflictions, was filled with love and compassion for others, especially for the sick and the outcast. After responding to the Lord's call to become a "Sister of Penance of St. Dominic," a Dominican *Mantellata*, Blessed Margaret never wavered in her commitment to the sick poor and the outcasts incarcerated in the local prison of *Citta di Castello*. Margaret was described as having been seen, at all hours of the day and night, limping with the assistance of her small walking stick, to the homes of the sick who were in need of her nursing care, as well as to the jail where poor prisoners were left starving and with few clothes to protect them from the cold and damp of the fetid cells.

What was it that urged Margaret along the path of such challenging ministries? The answer lies in the blessed's deep desire to follow Christ; to be His servant in whatever way He would allow. In serving the poor, especially the sick and the imprisoned, Margaret understood, that she was indeed serving her Beloved Lord (Matthew 25: 35). Margaret was truly a minister; Margaret was also truly a mystic.

Margaret as Mystic
"If Only You Knew What I Carry in My Heart"

From the time of her birth, we are assured by the Medieval Biographer, the earliest author of Blessed Margaret of Castello's legend, that Margaret was a mystic. She was, in his words, "nourished by a Divine light, so that standing on earth she might see heaven."[1] Margaret was "from infancy...freed for Divine training";[2] even in childhood she believed "herself chosen by God, who contemplated through her, while her tender mind was radiated by the light of God."[3] The Medieval Biographer explained that the reason Margaret was subjected to suffering and persecution during her early years was "because God wanted her to have a fervent Divine training."[4]

Father William Bonniwell describes the young Margaret's mind as "luminous." While he admitted that some of her extraordinary understanding resulted from the teaching of Chaplain Giacomo Cappellano, he added: "there can be no question that it was, in a far

---

[1] *Blessed Margaret of Castello OP: A Medieval Biography* (Trans. Carolina Accorsi) (Fatima, Portugal: Dominican Nuns of the Perpetual Rosary, 1994), 16.
[2] Ibid., 17.
[3] Ibid.
[4] Ibid., 14.

greater degree, due to Divine grace."[5] Fr. Bonniwell also suggested that Margaret's early development of intelligence cannot help but remind us of that of other well-known mystics: "St. Catherine of Siena, St. Catherine De Ricci and St. Rose of Lima, when they were the same age."[6]

During the period from childhood through adolescence, it appeared that Blessed Margaret was called to be solely a mystic; that is, one seeking union with God through a life of contemplation, prayer and penance. Her vocation, it seemed, was to be lived in enclosed solitude in settings such as the anchorhold (cell) next to the Chapel of St. Mary of the Fortress of Metola, the underground vault in the family Palazza at Mercatello or, finally as a nun in the Monastero di Santa Margherita at *Citta di Castello*. However, as with two other Dominican Tertiary mystics, St. Catherine of Siena and St. Rose of Lima, Margaret was ultimately led to a vocation of caring for the sick and the outcast: her call was to ministry to the ill and infirm in the streets of *Citta di Castello* and in their homes, and ministry to those incarcerated in the local prison. This was the apostolic calling which occupied the final decade of her brief life. Blessed Margaret was indeed, both mystic and minister.

It was, however, Blessed Margaret's mystical spirituality which provided the catalyst, as well as the foundation, for her ministry to those in need. To date only one quotation has been handed down, by word of mouth, from Margaret's lips, containing the words: "If only you knew what I carry in my heart." Several years after her death and burial in the Dominican Church in *Citta di Castello*, "Margaret's remains were moved, and when her coffin was opened her body was found incorrupt. At a primitive autopsy procedure, it was discovered that her heart contained three precious stones marked with images of her favorite meditations."[7] The "stones" seemed, miraculously, to demonstrate the meaning of the above quotation, "If only you knew what I carry in my heart."

Blessed Margaret's Medieval Biographer first addressed the appearance of the stones in describing the 14th-century examination of the internal organs of Margaret's body; he reported that the trachea was attached to the Blessed's heart and when opened: "three wonderful pebbles leaped out, each having different images impressed on them."[8]

On one, the Medieval Biographer related, was:

---

[5] William R. Bonniwell, *The Life of Blessed Margaret of Castello: 1287-1320* (Charlotte, N.C.: Tan Books, 2014), 19.
[6] Ibid.
[7] Sarah Gallick, *The Big Book of Woman Saints* (N.Y.: Harper San Francisco, 2007), 115.
[8] *Blessed Margaret of Castello OP*, 37.

Sculpted a very beautiful woman with a golden crown, which certain ones interpreted was the effigy of the gloriously blessed Virgin Mary who Blessed Margaret worshipped with immense devotion. On another one a little boy was seen in a cradle with sheep around him. Certain ones said this signified the Nativity of Christ. On a third stone was sculpted the image of a certain bald man, with a white beard and a golden staff, in front of whom a certain woman was kneeling dressed in the habit of the preachers. And they said this was Blessed Joseph and Blessed Margaret. On the side of this pebble was drawn a certain very white dove which they said represented the Holy Spirit, with whose aid Mary conceived the Son.[9]

The "kneeling" woman "dressed in the habit of the preachers" has been consistently identified as "probably Margherita herself."[10]

In a contemporary article, medieval scholar Cordelia Warr explored the relationship between devotional images, visions and the body, comparing the interpretation of the 14th-century finding of "three stones" in the heart of Blessed Margaret of Castello and that of finding the image of the Crucified Lord Jesus in the heart of Saint Clare of Montefalco.[11]

Clare of Montefalco was born some 20 years earlier than Margaret in Perugia, Italy; she died about a dozen years before Blessed Margaret. Clare, as Margaret, was initiated into a profound spiritual life at the age of six, "at which time she insisted on following her older sister Jane into a monastery" where she was later elected Abbess.[12] Saint Clare developed a deep devotion to the Crucified Savior; she once reported that "Jesus appeared to her as a beautiful young man, searching for a place to set down His cross. That place was Clare's heart."[13] When she was dying, one of Clare's nuns "tried to make the sign of the cross over her and was reprimanded by Clare herself with the words: 'Why do you make the sign of the Cross over me?' 'Did I not tell you that I have within my heart the Cross of my Crucified Lord Jesus?'"[14] After she was

---

[9] Ibid., 37-38
[10] Heather Webb, *The Medieval Heart* (New Haven, Ct.: Yale University Press, 2010), 219.
[11] Cordelia Warr, "Re-reading the Relationship Between Devotional Images, Visions and the Body: Clare of Montefalco and Margaret of Citta di Castello," *Viator* 38:1 (2007): 217-249.
[12] Gallick, 247.
[13] Webb, 171.
[14] Ibid., 170.

anointed, Clare told her nuns: "You will find...the cross of Jesus graven on my heart."[15]

As with Blessed Margaret, an internal examination of Clare's heart was carried out after the saint's death; for Clare, the dissection was done by a group of her nuns. The nuns anticipated that "Clare's repeated avowal that she had the Crucified Christ in her heart could be taken literally and that her heart had physically changed to mirror her religious experiences."[16] Such thinking reflected the "understanding of the somatic nature of female spirituality" common in the era.[17]

As one of Clare's nuns severed a tendon that extended through the heart, "all saw to their great astonishment, the figure of the Crucified, formed in flesh and intersected with veins, lying in a cavity which itself was in the shape of a cross."[18] On hearing of this, the local Vicar General of the Diocese came to the Monastery of Santa Croce, as a representative of the Bishop, "convinced that it was all mere women's fancy, and...he angrily dashed a knife or razor through one of the two parts (in Clare's heart) by way of making short work of such delusions. His consternation gave place to an act of faith as, on the two fresh surfaces now disclosed, he saw no less distinctly the figure of his Crucified Master and the instruments of his suffering."[19] The Vicar's astonishment was heightened as he saw images not only of the Crucified Lord but also other "emblems of the mysteries of the passion...the pillar, the crown of thorns, the three nails, the lance, the reed and the sponge."[20]

In her discussion of the findings in hearts of Blessed Margaret and Saint Clare, Cordelia Warr reminds us that the legends of the lives of both women were "filtered" though the writings of early hagiographers "who did not know their subjects personally";[21] however, images related to the legends of the saints and blesseds of the era were important "instruments for the instruction of the unlettered who could learn from them rather than from books."[22] And, Warr points out, "physical changes

---

[15] William Lloyd, *Saints of 1881: or Sketches of Lives of St. Clare of Montefalco, St. Laurence of Brindisi, St. Benedict Joseph Labre, St. John Baptist De Rossi, 1882* (Whitefish, Montana: Kessinger Publishing LLC, 2010), 19.

[16] Warr, 225.

[17] Ibid.

[18] Lawrence Tardy, *Life of St. Clare of Montefalco, Professed Nun of the Order of Hermits of St. Augustine*, 2nd Edition. Trans. Joseph A. Locke OSA (Cincinnati, Ohio: Benziger Brothers, 1897), 165.

[19] Lloyd, 21-22.

[20] Tardy, 167.

[21] Warr, 220.

[22] Ibid., 218.

to the body were not viewed only as psychosomatic manipulation; they could also be the result of a physiological process."[23]

In a *vita* of Clare of Montefalco, authored by Berenger de Saint-Affrique, "the change in Clare's heart is presented as an interiorization of her visualization of the passion."[24] The images of the Holy Family, as identified by observers of Margaret of Castello's heart, were believed to have been the result of Margaret's daily meditation on "the parturition of the Blessed Virgin, the Nativity of Christ, and on Joseph's assistance."[25] "Of these," Warr added, "while she lived, (Margaret) spoke frequently...(and) like Clare of Monefalco, the affective nature of her piety, whilst alive, led to its somatic indication being discovered after her death."[26]

In distinction to the initial autopsy carried out in the monastery, by the Augustinian Nuns, after Saint Clare of Montefalco's death, those involved in the examination of Blessed Margaret of Castello's organs reflected "a clear desire to ensure both that there were suitable witnesses to the procedure and that appropriate symbolism was called into play."[27] We are told by the Medieval Biographer that people gathered from everywhere "anxious to see the relics of Blessed Margaret."[28] Some of these included the older Dominican Brothers and many clergy and seculars, as well as certain doctors; city Magistrate Jacal of Burgo and Ugolinus Virides also hastened to the sepulcher of Blessed Margaret.[29] Margaret's autopsy was conducted before these witnesses, in front of the main altar of the Dominican Church in *Citta di Castello*.

The removal of Blessed Margaret's internal organs, the first step in the autopsy process, which took place before the Dominican Church altar, linked "her body to the Church as the body of Christ... symbolically, Margaret was placed nearest to the heart of Christ."[30] Cordelia Warr adds that from a practical perspective, Margaret's dissection may also have been carried out in front of the Church's main altar as this location "would afford the best opportunity for a widely witnessed event."[31]

Warr's description of the stones is similar to that of the Medieval Biographer: "The first stone contained the face of a woman with a crown

---

[23] Ibid., 230.
[24] Ibid.
[25] Ibid., 232.
[26] Ibid.
[27] Ibid., 233.
[28] *Blessed Margaret of Castello OP*, 36.
[29] Ibid.
[30] Warr, 233.
[31] Ibid.

of gold who was identified as the Virgin Mary. In the second stone there was a little child in a crib surrounded by cattle; the Nativity of Christ. In the third stone was Saint Joseph: a man with a beard and a halo. Next to the saint was a small kneeling figure of a young girl, Margaret, wearing the habit of the Order of Preachers."[32] Cordelia Warr notes that "the description of the stones varies slightly in two extant *vitae*": the *recensio maior* and *recensio minor* in that "the author of the *recensio maior* provides more information," re: such details as whether the religious images were carved into or engraved on the stones.[33;i]

After the discovery of the "three stones" in Blessed Margaret's heart, people were reminded that Margaret had, during her lifetime, said: "Oh, if only you knew what I carried in my heart."[34] Cordelia Warr notes that "there is a clear parallel here to Clare of Montefalco's repeated assertion that, 'I have Jesus Christ Crucified inside my own heart'; however, she adds, Margaret did not specify what was in her heart."[35]

Finally, Warr speculates that "the identification of the objects found in Clare and Margaret's hearts may also be interpreted as a projection of the expectations of the faithful: "Margaret and Clare's 'interior images' can be understood as having been 'imposed' on them by their contemporaries."[36] While images "were not necessary to Clare, who rejected them, and Margaret, who could not see them, they were perceived as important to those who knew and followed these holy women."[37]

Although it may seem particularly strange that "interior images" should be found in the heart of Blessed Margaret of Castello, who had been blind from birth, Cordellia Warr asserts that this "can be interpreted as a result of Margaret's intellectual vision."[38] Warr points out that in one of the early medieval biographies (the *recensio minor*) "the seven-year-old Margaret is described as 'blind with the eyes of the body but bright and luminous with the eyes of the mind.'"[39]

Clearly, the finding of images of the Crucified Jesus in the heart of Clare, and of the Holy Family in the heart of Margaret, were attested to by myriad distinguished witnesses present either during or immediately after the individual examinations. The miraculous nature of the

---

[32] Ibid., 234.
[33] Ibid.
[34] Warr, 234.
[35] Ibid.
[36] Ibid., 238.
[37] Ibid., 235.
[38] Ibid.
[39] Ibid.

discoveries must be guided by an understanding of the spirituality of the era, the popular piety of the people and the documented mysticism of both Saint Clare of Montefalco and Blessed Margaret of Castello.

Mysticism

There are numerous definitions of "mysticism," but it is generally considered to be a "way of life, as an individual's direct unmediated experience of God";[40] a mystic, then, "is a person who has, to a greater or lesser degree, had such an experience."[41] From "the beginning of Christianity" many attempted to "experience the presence of God" in their lives "in a direct and personal way";[42] in the twelfth century there was a "flowering of mystical expression which intensified in the later Middle Ages."[43] During this era, "the growth of autobiographical accounts of visionary experiences of Christ in that century hinted at the visionary explosion" of the later medieval period "especially among women."[44]

The female visionary is generally described as:

> celibate; her vocation, her commitment to virginity or to chaste widowhood, exempted her from the charge of female weakness or corruption...celibacy altered her status, moving her upward toward a position of potential authority. Visions set the seal on that authority and for a number of reasons, the most important being that visions gave an individual woman a voice and a belief in herself as chosen to speak and also gave her an experience of inner transformation that she felt compelled to communicate to others.[45]

Blessed Margaret of Castello's reported visions of Jesus during Mass essentially "set the seal" on her authority as a mystic. Near the end of her life, Margaret revealed to her confessor that whenever she attended

---

[40] Barbara M. Dossey, "Florence Nightingale: A 19th Century Mystic," *Journal of Holistic Nursing* 28:1 (2010): 10-35, 11.
[41] Ibid.
[42] Carl A. Volz, *The Medieval Church: From the Dawn of the Middle Ages to the Eve of the Reformation* (Nashville, TN.: Abingdon Press, 1997), 175.
[43] Ibid.
[44] Bernard McGinn, "The Changing Shape of Late Medieval Mysticism," *Church History* 65:2 (1996): 197-219, 197.
[45] Elizabeth A. Petroff, *Medieval Women's Visionary Literature* (N.Y.: Oxford University Press, 1986), 5-6.

Mass she could "see Christ Incarnate on the Altar."[46] Although this perception was initially challenged by the confessor, Margaret insisted: "Since I am obliged to speak, I must repeat what I have said before: 'From the Consecration until the Communion, I do not see the priest, the Crucifix, the Missal or anything else, but I do see Christ our Lord.'"[47] When the priest theologian asked Margaret what the Lord looked like when she saw Him at Mass, she replied: "Oh Father, you are asking me to describe Infinite Beauty."[48]

As well as Blessed Margaret, there were a number of other important thirteenth-century women mystics such as: "Hadewijch of Flanders, Mechthild of Magdeburg and Marguerite Porete of Hainault...who reflected a new beginning in Christian mysticism."[49] The concept of a "personalized and emotional notion of mystical union with Jesus" was prominent among such women.[50] The mysticism of these medieval women frequently included conceiving of the spiritual life as divided into three states or ways—the *purgatio*, *illuminatio*, and *unio*—the purgative way, in which one purges the self of most non-spiritual ideas or cares; the illuminative way, in which one's life is illuminated by the light of Christ; and the unitive way, which brings one to a state of perfect union with God.[51]

European women identified as medieval mystics came from a number of different geographical locations and pursued a variety of vocations. As well as the three mystics mentioned above, Hadewijch, a former Beguine and hermit; Mechthild of Magdeburg, a Dominican Tertiary; and Marguerite Porete. We might also add: Catherine of Siena and Rose of Lima, both Dominican Tertiaries; Angela of Foligno and Margaret of Cortona, Franciscan Tertiaries; Hildegard of Bingen, a Benedictine Abbess; Catherine De Ricci and Beatrijs of Nazareth, cloistered nuns; Margery Kempe, a married woman and mother; and Julien of Norwich, an anchoress. Most of these women "did not come from the lower orders of society."[52]

---

[46] Bonniwell, 96.
[47] Ibid., 97.
[48] Ibid.
[49] William K. Grevatt, "Exploring the Sacred Medieval Psyche: The Flowering of Feminine Mysticism, 1200-1350," *Psychological Perspectives* 56:4 (2013): 404-421, 404.
[50] Jerome Kroll, *The Mystic Mind: The Psychology of Medieval Mystics and Ascetics* (N.Y.: Routledge, 2005), 2.
[51] Dorothee Soelle, *The Silent Cry: Mysticism and Resistance* (Minneapolis, Mn.: Augsburg Fortress Press, 2001); Monica Furlong, *Visions and Longings: Medieval Women Mystics* (Boston: Shambhala, 1997).
[52] J. Ward, *Women in Medieval Europe: 1200-1500* (London: Longmans, 2002), 192.

Among women medieval mystics "piety often developed during childhood" with some becoming nuns as young as five and seven.[53] Thus, Blessed Margaret's childhood religious devotion would not have been considered outside the norm for her era.

Women mystics of the Middle Ages viewed their lives of renunciation as constituting an imitation of Christ. Many "went to extremes in their austerities and asceticism...the ultimate aim (being) to follow Christ and to identify with the suffering of the human Jesus, especially in His Passion and Crucifixion."[54] Individual austerities often revolved around such practices as limiting one's diet (extreme fasting and/or complete abstention from certain foods) and modification of apparel (the wearing of a 'hair shirt' or chains underneath external clothing).

Again, Margaret of Castello's adoption of the religious practices of fasting on "bread and water" and the wearing of a "haircloth" would not have seemed abnormal for her time.[55] For Margaret, as for most other mystics "suffering was seen as an element in penitential discipline, and penance for sins committed was regarded as essential preliminary and accompaniment to a holy life. The writings of the mystics portrayed penance as an inherent part of religious development."[56]

Blessed Margaret of Castello, a Dominican Tertiary, as St. Catherine of Siena and St. Rose of Lima, can be categorized as a mystic, not only for the continued seeking of union with Christ in her religious devotions, but also for the earlier described visions and for the healing miracles attributed to her intervention. The Medieval Biographer posited an explanation for Margaret's visions of the Lord: "although she was blind, in church when the body of Our Lord, Jesus Christ, was consecrated, and whenever this sacred mystery took place, Margaret saw Christ Incarnate...Jesus wanted to show himself to the one who had been deprived of vision in order that He might shine in an earthen vessel crafted by Divine clemency."[57]

In terms of this vision of Jesus, when Blessed Margaret related it to her confessor, he first attempted to understand it as a "spiritually imagined" vision rather than a "true" vision because of Margaret's blindness. When the confessor shared his interpretation, however, Margaret corrected him, insisting that she did indeed see Christ as "Infinite Beauty"; at this response, "the last shadow of doubt fled from

---

[53] Ibid., 191-192.
[54] Ibid., 193-194.
[55] *Blessed Margaret of Castello OP*, 18.
[56] Ward, 196.
[57] *Blessed Margaret of Castello OP*, 30-31.

(Margaret's confessor's) mind, and with awe he recalled the words: 'Blessed are the clean of heart for they shall see God.'"[58] We are told that Margaret was so great a mystic to whom God had revealed "sublime secrets of heaven" and "the great mysteries of the Gospel," that ultimately canons and theologians of *Citta di Castello* "wanted to meet her to ask for some doctrinal explanations."[59]

It is documented by several biographers that a number of miracles, attributed to Margaret's intervention, occurred both during her earthly life and after her death. Following Blessed Margaret's formal entrance into the Sisters of Penance of St. Dominic, the Mantellate, she was invited by several well-to-do families in *Citta di Castello* to share their homes. One of the miracles, recorded by the Medieval Biographer and others, occurred in the home of Venturinus and his wife Gregoria (identified as Gritia in "A Medieval Biography"). This miracle was related to the extinguishing of a serious fire in the home. Margaret had been staying in a little room in an upper portion of the house when suddenly a great fire broke out in one of the lower rooms. Immediately Gritia called out to Margaret to come down and save herself. Blessed Margaret, however, simply told Gritia not to be afraid but to trust in God, and take Margaret's cloak and throw it on the fire. The Medieval Biographer reported that "Gratia threw the mentioned cloak on the fire; suddenly, in the presence of the crowd which had come together from everywhere to help, the heavy fire was miraculously extinguished."[60]

A second miracle, related by the Medieval Biographer, concerned the healing of an eye. A Sister named Venturela discovered that she had a tumor in one eye and thought she was losing vision from the problem. She went to a doctor who was not encouraging about whether her sight could be restored; the physician also asked Venturela for money which she did not possess. Venturela then sought out Blessed Margaret and begged her for healing. When Margaret touched the eye with her thumb, "in an instant, the tumor vanished from the eye and thus the eye was cured without cost."[61]

Several other miracles were described by the Medieval Biographer; these and a great variety of healings which took place after Blessed Margaret's death, through her intervention, are described in Chapter Seven.

---

[58] Bonniwell, 98.
[59] Ubaldo Valentini, *Beata Margherita De La Metola Una Sfida Alla Emarginazione* (Perugia, Italy: Petruzzi Editore, 1988), 50.
[60] *Blessed Margaret of Castello OP*, 26-27.
[61] Ibid., 28.

Blessed Margaret of Castello's identification as a mystic is clearly based on the reports of her spiritual gifts described above: the reported visions of seeing Christ at the consecration of the Mass, the healing miracles attributed to Margaret's intervention both before and after her death, as well the witness of repeated physical levitations while in ecstatic prayer, especially when praying for those incarcerated in the *Citta di Castello* prison.

While there is limited information documenting Blessed Margaret's mysticism, descriptions of the spiritual experiences of three other Dominican medieval mystics, two of whom lived during Margaret's era, can help elucidate her experience as a medieval mystic; the three mystics are Saint Catherine De Ricci, Blessed Henry Suso, and Mechthild of Magdeburg.

Saint Catherine de Ricci

Saint Catherine de Ricci (1522-1590) was born Alexandra De Ricci to a patrician Italian family. As Blessed Margaret of Castello, she developed a devout prayer life while yet a child; her particular spiritual attraction was the Passion of Christ. As a pre-teen age girl she expressed the desire to enter a Dominican Monastery of strict observance, the Convent of St. Vincent in Prato, Tuscany, but she was met with significant opposition from her father. After Alexandra experienced a serious illness which threatened her life, however, her father relented and gave his consent for her to enter the Monastery of St. Vincent.[62]

Alexandra received the Dominican habit at the age of fourteen and was given the name of Catherine, in religion. As a novice, however, she became so "lost" in "celestial visions" that the Sisters in the community began to question her fitness for religious life:

> For in her ecstasies she seemed merely sleepy and at times stupid. Her companions did not suspect her of ecstasy when she dozed a community exercises, spilled food or broke dishes. Neither did it occur to Sister Catherine that other people were not, like herself, rapt in ecstasy. She was on the point of being sent home when she became aware of the situation and told her confessor. He insisted that she tell her superiors.[63]

---

[62] *The Lives of St. Catherine of Ricci of the Third Order of St. Dominic, St. Agnes of Montepulciano, B. Benvenuta of Bojan and B. Catherine of Raconi* (London: Richardson and Son, MDCCCLII, 1852), 15.

[63] Mary Jean Dorcy, *St. Dominic's Family: Over 300 Famous Dominicans* (Charlotte, N.C.: Tan Books, 1983), 325.

After explaining the visions to her Sisters, Catherine, the young novice, was not questioned again.

When Sister Catherine was "twenty years old, she began weekly ecstasies of the Passion which were to last for twelve years. She received the Sacred Stigmata which remained with her always."[64] She was also the recipient of many other wounds related to Christ's Passion and was "mystically scourged and crowned with thorns."[65] The "astonishing ecstasy" of each week "began about two on Thursday afternoon, and ended at six o'clock on Friday evening, and she passed these twenty-eight hours on her knees...without moving and without food or rest." Catherine's ecstasies were examined by the head of the Dominican Order[66] who declared: "There is nothing to doubt about this soul, but everything to revere."[67]

As with Margaret of Castello, Catherine, "despite her intense mystical life of prayer and penance, lived a busy life," serving as Prioress of the Convent for several years.[68] Again, as with Blessed Margaret, Sister Catherine was highly respected by local citizens for her holiness: "Troubled people...from the town came to her for advice and prayer, and her participation in the Passion exerted a great influence for good among all who saw it."[69]

Following Catherine's death, many healing miracles occurred for those who visited her tomb seeking intervention; there were cures similar to those experienced by individuals who visited Margaret of Castello's tomb, as related in Chapter Seven.

Blessed Henry Suso (1295-1366)

Blessed Henry Suso was a German Dominican Friar and poet. He was born Heinrich von Berg, to a noble family but later, in humility, adopted his mother's name of Suso. As with Blessed Margaret of Castello, Blessed Henry left his home to begin a religious life at a young age.

Henry was not a very happy child at home and was sent to enter the Dominican Novitiate at only thirteen. With the Dominicans, Henry found peace and joy in both the religious ritual and in the community setting. At the age of eighteen, however, he experienced a mystical ecstasy which

---

[64] Ibid.
[65] Ibid., 326.
[66] *The Lives of St. Catherine*, 46.
[67] Gallick, 62.
[68] Dorcy, 326.
[69] Ibid.

changed his life. Henry suddenly envisioned himself as a "great sinner and should do great penance":

> The penance he performed for the next sixteen years became notorious, even in that age of extremes; an iron chain, and an undershirt studded with nails, were the most memorable of the methods he used…(he tortured) himself into submission to make himself ready for the Grace of God, which he felt that he so little deserved. At the end of sixteen years, he was favored with another vision telling him that the physical phase of his suffering was over, but to be prepared for mental torments.[70]

Sister Mary Jean Dorcy observed that despite all of "the intense purification being accomplished in his soul," Henry still carried out all of his routine priestly duties of preaching, teaching and hearing confessions.[71] Blessed Margaret of Castello, as Blessed Henry, was also engaged in an active ministry of care of the sick and the outcast while embracing a devout regime of prayer and penance as a Dominican *Mantellata*.

Blessed Henry had apparently achieved a reputation for being somewhat accident prone; challenging incidents continually happened in his life: "He fell into rivers and almost drowned. He became innocently involved in family feuds and was nearly killed for interfering. People tried to poison him. As Prior he ran the house finances into such a snarl, that no one could untangle them."[72] Nevertheless, Sister Dorcy admitted that "Some of the finest poetry in medieval German poured from the pen of this gifted man, during the years when life was most difficult for him."[73]

Some of Blessed Henry's writings were preserved by the nuns for whom he had provided spiritual guidance. His most well-known work is the "Little Book of Eternal Wisdom," a "classic of spiritual writing."[74] Henry also composed numerous other "treatises on the mystical union of the soul with God, all written with the same poetic language and the same intensity of feeling."[75]

---

[70] Ibid., 165.
[71] Ibid.
[72] Ibid., 166.
[73] Ibid.
[74] Ibid., 167.
[75] Ibid.

Blessed Henry Suso had a devoted group of followers, especially those identified with a movement called the "Friends of God." He was beatified in 1831.

Mechthild of Magdeburg (1207-1293/94)

Mechthild of Magdeburg was a Thirteenth-century German mystic who, like Blessed Margaret of Castello, developed, as a young child, a profound spiritual life. At the age of only twelve, she "left home to live as a Beguine and for fifty years she pursued this form of life."[76] The Beguines "were women who led lives of voluntary poverty, chastity and religious devotion...in Mechthild's time in Germany, Beguines usually lived in communal houses, sustaining themselves through support from their families, gifts and work...(such as) nursing."[77]

It was also around the age of twelve that Mechthild reportedly was "greeted" by the Holy Spirit"; these visions occurred daily for almost thirty years.[78] Mechthild's confessor was a Dominican, Henry of Halle, who guided her in the taking of private vows as a Dominican Tertiary; under his direction, Mechthild "reached a very high state of mystical prayer."[79] Mechthild, as Blessed Margaret, had lived a more contemplative life during her early years; then, as Margaret, she became a Dominican Tertiary in adulthood.

It was the Dominican, Friar Henry, who advised Mechthild to write down her mystical experiences; he urged her "to write the book 'out of God's heart and mouth.'"[80] The result was the classic work *Das Fliebende Licht der Gottheit*, "The Flowing Light of the Godhead," described as an "expression of mysticism,"[81] composed of seven books, in which Mechthild created a dialog between God and the soul. After the initial portion of the manuscript was circulated in Germany, criticisms of her writing forced Mechthild to leave Magdeburg and relocate in a "new home at Helfta" with a community of Cistercian nuns; "she spent the rest of her life at Helfta and completed her book there."[82]

While it is reported that Mechthild "followed the rules" of the Cistercian Convent while she lived there, the evidence is "that she

---

[76] Ibid., 106.
[77] Mechthild of Magdeburg, *Mechthild of Magdeburg: The Flowing Light of the Godhead* (Mahwah, N.J.: Paulist Press, 1998), 1.
[78] Ibid., 4.
[79] Dorcy, 106.
[80] Mechtild, 4.
[81] Ibid., 12.
[82] Gallick, 330.

remained a Dominican Tertiary and did not become a Benedictine Nun.[83] Mechthild was a Christian medieval mystic who is believed to have died around the years 1293 or 1294.

With the exception of writing, which Margaret's blindness hindered, the reports of prayer, penance and spiritual visions, described for the above three mystics, mirror those of Blessed Margaret of Castello. All three, as Blessed Margaret, combined the religious callings of both mystic and minister. As well as experiencing mystical manifestations of spiritual phenomena, they each engaged in an apostolic ministry: Catherine De Ricci served as Prioress of her convent, especially caring for the sick of the community; Blessed Henry Suso consistently practiced priestly duties of teaching and preaching; and Mechthild of Magdeburg, worked to support herself and her religious community while living as a Beguine.

Margaret as Minister

Blessed Margaret of Castello's move into the apostolic dimension of her vocation, that is, the ministry of caring for the sick and the outcast, is described in terms of her role as a "wounded healer" and minister to prisoners.

In discussing European women from the 13th to the 16th Century, medieval scholar Jennifer Ward noted that "All women probably had to care for the sick at some time in their lives."[84] Clearly this was evident in the *Mantellata* vocations of Tertiaries St. Catherine of Siena and St. Rose of Lima. Therefore, reports of Blessed Margaret of Castello's ministries to the sick and the outcast are not surprising. Medieval women such as Catherine, Rose and Margaret had no formal training in caring for the ill and infirm; their nursing knowledge was probably learned within the home or from neighbors and friends. What is particularly unique about the caregiving of Blessed Margaret is the fact that she embraced a ministry to the sick despite her own severe physical afflictions. Margaret was truly, in the language of 21st-century ministry, a "wounded healer."

A "Wounded Healer"

The current understanding of a "wounded healer" is generally attributed to the classic work of Henri J.M. Nouwen's *The Wounded Healer: Ministry in Contemporary Society*. The book was first published in 1972, but remains today a frequently cited publication in discussions of

---

[83] Dorcy, 106.
[84] Ward, 99.

ministry to the ill and infirm. In explaining his rationale for exploring the meaning of a "wounded healer," Nouwen observed that if current ministry "is meant to hold the promise of (the) Messiah, then whatever we can learn of the Messiah's coming will give us a deeper understanding of what is called for in ministry today."[85] He goes on to ponder how the Messiah can be recognized and responds with an "old legend in the Talmud," which Nouwen suggests may provide the beginning of an answer:

> Rabbi Yoshua ben Levi came upon Elijah the prophet while he was standing at the entrance of Rabbi Simeron ben Yohai's cave...He asked Elijah, "When will the Messiah come?"
> Elijah replied, "Go and ask him yourself."
> "Where is he?"
> "Sitting at the gates of the city."
> "How shall I know him?"
> "He is sitting among the poor covered with wounds. The others unbind all their wounds at the same time and then bind them up again. But he unbinds one at a time and binds it up again, saying to himself, 'Perhaps I shall be needed: if so I must always be ready so as not to delay for a moment.'"[86]

As the Messiah, "always prepared for the moment when he might be needed," Henri Nouwen observed, so it is with ministers: "they must bind their own wounds carefully in anticipation of the moment when they will be needed...(they) must not only look after their own wounds, but at the same time be prepared to heal the wounds of others. They are both wounded ministers and healing ministers."[87,ii]

Surely Blessed Margaret of Castello's care for the sick and the outcast reflected the image of the Messiah who did not "unbind" his wounds all at the same time. Descriptions of Margaret making her way through the streets of *Citta di Castello* to reach the homes of the sick poor and the prison, picture her as "limping" and using a walking stick due to her shortened leg. These errands of mercy must indeed have cost Blessed Margaret dearly as she was forced to expose the "wound" of her lameness for all to see. Yet this challenge, as well as those of her blindness and curvature of the spine, did not prevent the caregiving

---

[85] Henri J.M. Nouwen, *The Wounded Healer: Ministry in Contemporary Society* (N.Y.: Image Doubleday, 2010), 87.
[86] Ibid., 87-88.
[87] Ibid., 88.

missions. Margaret, emotionally, kept her afflictions "bound up" as it were, so as to be always ready to leave if she were needed and "not delay for a moment."

The concept of the "wounded healer" is in common use in contemporary discussions of the insights and attributes of those who care for the ill and the infirm. The term generally "refers to a person whose personal experience of illness and/or trauma has left lingering effects on him, in the form of lessons learned that later served him in ministering to other sufferers, or in the form of symptoms or characteristics that usefully influenced his therapeutic endeavors."[88] The wounded healer is also described as an "archetype that suggests that healing power emerges from the healers own woundedness."[89] The paradigm of the wounded healer points out that "wounded and healer can be represented as a duality rather than a dichotomy. Woundedness lies on a continuum, and the wounded healer paradigm focuses not on the degree of woundedness but on the ability to draw on woundedness in the service of healing."[90]

When we consider Blessed Margaret of Castello's degree of woundedness, it was indeed significant. Yet her committed ministry to the sick and the outcast reflected an incredibly powerful and empathetic ability to "draw on" her woundedness "in the service of healing." Clearly Margaret's "healing power" did emerge from her own woundedness.

For a health care provider, woundedness can "enrich understanding of the importance of empathy."[91] When we recognize our own woundedness, "alienation, separation, isolation or loneliness, explore the effects of this and accept it as part of membership in the human condition, we are able to use that woundedness to help us relate to others. Understanding our own frailty turns it from burden to resource for healing."[92] Discussions exploring the concept of the "wounded healer" in ministry to the sick abound in the healthcare and pastoral care literature.[93]

---

[88] Stanley W. Jackson, "Presidential Address: The Wounded Healer," *Bulletin of the History of Medicine* 75:1 (2001): 1-36, 1.

[89] Noga Zerubavel and Margaret O. Wright, "The Dilemma of the Wounded Healer," *Psychotherapy* 49:4 (2012): 482-491, 482.

[90] Ibid.

[91] Galia Benziman, Ruth Kannai, and Ayesha Ahmad, "The Wounded Healer as Cultural Archtype," *Comparative Literature and Culture* 14:1 (2012): 2-9, 2.

[92] Elizabeth Niven, "The Wounded Healer: What Has the Concept to Offer Nursing?" *Nursing Ethics* 15:3 (2008): 287-288, 287.

[93] Tony MacCulloch and Mona Shattell, "Reflections of a 'Wounded Healer,'" *Issues in Mental Health Nursing* 30:2 (2009): 135-137; Deborah K. Mayer, "Wounded

Blessed Margaret, as a "wounded healer," now undertook a new dimension of ministry in her vocation as a member of the Sisters of Penance of St. Dominic, a *Mantellata*. Margaret "committed herself to visiting people in the city who were ill or dying; this small woman making her way through the streets at all hours of the day and night became a common sight in *Citta di Castello*."[94] Instead of making her bitter, Margaret's physical afflictions led her to becoming "one of the most generous and sympathetic people in Castello...her courage, patience and deep devotion (to the sick, the dying and to prisoners) won her the affection of everyone in the town."[95]

When Sister Margaret received the habit of the Dominican Third Order she was reminded that it would be a "solemn pledge and a constant reminder" that she had "dedicated herself without reserve or conditions to the love and service of God."[96] Margaret embraced the concept with tenderness and compassion, especially for those who were poor and sick. Father Bonniwell asserted of Margaret that: "her heart is so overflowing with love of others that she has no time to think of herself";[97] he explained:

> Despite attempts on the part of well-meaning friends, the blind girl continued her austerities and her unending missions of mercy. No sick person was too far away for her to limp to; no hour of the day or night was ever too inconvenient for her to hasten to those in agony. If the sick were in want, she would leave nothing undone to obtain for them the medicine and food they needed.
>
> To the dying, she tried to impart resignation and courage. If they were unrepentant, she would plead piteously with them to make their peace with God; when her pleas brought no response she would turn to prayer. It was rare that even the most hardened

---

Healers," *Clinical Journal of Oncology Nursing* 12:4 (2008): 547; Philip S. Nolte and Yolanda Dryer, "The Paradox of Being a Wounded Healer: Henri J.M. Nouwen's Contribution to Pastoral Theology," *Hervormde Teologiese* Studies 66:2 (2010): 1-8; Vincent M. Corso, "Oncology Nurse as Wounded Healer: Developing a Compassion Identity," *Clinical Journal of Oncology Nursing* 16:5 (2012): 448-450; Serge Daneault, "The Wounded Healer," *Canadian Family Physician* 54: 9 (2008): 1218-1219.

[94] Janice McGrane, *Saints to Lean On: Spiritual Companions for Illness and Disability* (Cincinnati, Ohio: St. Anthony Messenger Press, 2006), 10.

[95] Thomas J. Craughwell, *This Saint Will Change Your Life* (Phila.: Quirk Books, 2007). 136.

[96] Bonniwell, 69.

[97] Ibid., 73.

sinner succeeded in resisting her efforts and after every such struggle, Margaret would betake herself, pale and exhausted, to the church to thank God for His mercy.[98]

Fr. Bonniwell reported that when the residents of *Citta di Castello* saw Blessed Margaret so frequently "limping her way to the sick and the dying", they were astonished "that anyone so afflicted should occupy herself with the miseries of others. But eventually the realization of Margaret's heroic self-denial and her all-absorbing love of her fellowman" brought about an attitude of reverence and veneration among the people.[99] "Margaret's fame," he observed, "spread abroad, and wherever it went, it was like a benediction passing over the land."[100]

When Blessed Margaret accompanied other Tertiaries "in fulfillment of their charitable actions" she "often stopped to talk to the poor, aware that they were in need of spiritual comfort as well as material support. She spent long hours with them, talking about their lives…(and) the torments of earthly existence."[101] How consoling these talks must have been coming from "Little Margaret" who knew so well the sufferings of the poor and the "torments of earthly existence". Margaret could now share the love of God which she so treasured with those who needed her message and they could trust the words coming from one who knew their sorrow personally.

Margaret continued to devote time to prayer and penance but she did not "neglect her mission among men and continued to carry out its work of charity as provided in the rule of Dominican Tertiaries."[102] Amazingly, Blessed Margaret seemed to move about the city with a "mastery that seemed to nullify the difficulties of her blindness."[103] It seemed as if "a mysterious forces guided her and helped her in making known to others the joy she felt in her heart."[104] Blessed Margaret's fame "soon breached the city walls and many came from far away to meet her and ask for help. The poor of the city were the first to trust her and will always be those who will have a special place in her prayers. Even the

---

[98] Ibid., 100.
[99] Ibid. 74.
[100] Ibid.
[101] Ubaldo Valentini, *Beata Margherita De La Metola Una Sfida Alla Emarginazione* (Perugia, Italy: Petruzzi Editore, 1988), 45.
[102] Ibid., 50.
[103] Ibid.
[104] Ibid.

prisoners, initially skeptical, will discover the power of her word and admire her testimony and her greatness."[105]

One of the primary roles of the Sisters of Penance of St. Dominic, the Mantellate, as most people of the era referred to them, was this care of the sick poor; thus, it would be a natural ministry for a young Sister, such as Blessed Margaret, herself living with multiple physical afflictions, to undertake. As noted in the literature on the concept of the "wounded healer," the "wounded" minister or caregiver is particularly sensitive to the "wounds" of others and seeks to alleviate their pain and suffering, conditions with which the healer him or herself is intimately familiar. Margaret's deep compassion for the sick and for prisoners came from a wellspring of her own experiences with physical affliction and the suffering of being isolated and imprisoned.

Margaret's care for and commitment to the sick, the outcast, and the poor may well have been born in her heart as a small child. Although, living in a noble castle during those early years, she was primarily mentored and taught by the family chaplain, Fra Giacomo Cappellano. One of a medieval castle chaplain's roles was that of "almoner"; he and his staff were responsible for "gathering the left-overs from the table and seeing that they were distributed among the poor."[106] The almoner was also expected to "visit, for charity's sake, the sick, the lepers, the captive, the poor, the widows and others in want...to distribute clothing, money and other gifts."[107] Fra Cappellano's witness would, no doubt, have made a deep impression on his small pupil with the "luminous" mind.

We do not have a record of precisely what caregiving tasks Blessed Margaret engaged in during her visits to the sick in their homes. We can, however, derive some understanding of her ministry to the ill and infirm from the conditions of medieval medicine and nursing. In small towns and villages, such as *Citta di Castello*, we are told that it was lay practitioners, such as Margaret, who provided most of the care for the sick or injured:

> Most people did not have access to the expensive services of the physician or surgeon. Surgical procedures might be performed instead by a barber, who also extracted bad teeth, in addition to his work trimming hair and shaving beards. For curing diseases,

---

[105] Ibid.
[106] Joseph Gies and Frances Gies, *Life in a Medieval Castle* (N.Y.: Harper Perennial, 2015, 105.
[107] Ibid., 106.

most people likely turned to a practitioner of folk medicine, who might be a professional or semi-professional, or in some cases was no more than a neighbor or family member. Women, in particular, learned traditional medical practices as part of their training of running a household.[108]

As well as serious diseases such as leprosy, the overall health of the poor in the Middle Ages was severely impacted by such factors as: "unevenness of diet, poor sanitation, infrequent bathing, and the general hardship of life":[109] "The lack of fresh fruit and vegetables for much of the year contributed to the high incidence of scurvy. Poor sanitation led directly to the proliferation of disease, as well as fostering vermin that carried disease…(and) personal injury was also a very common health risk."[110]

In the medieval era, practical treatments and folk remedies "went hand in hand with the belief that prayer could cure the sick."[111] As well as prayerful invocations and pilgrimages made in search of healing, more simple home grown medicinal remedies abounded; common among these were the use of plants and herbs. Many "monasteries, convents and manor houses had herb gardens for growing plants that could be used in Medicine."[112] There was, at the time, "a vast store of knowledge about the uses of herbs…for regulating health (and) every woman knew about them."[113]

All women in Blessed Margaret's medieval society were expected to know, not only about herbal remedies, but also about the administration of a variety of other folk medicines for healing a variety of ills. Women were considered generally better suited to serve as medieval healers as they had "the most comprehensive knowledge of caring for and healing the sick…(they) had inherited a rich catalog of healing traditions and tried-and-true herbal remedies handed down from generation to generation. The range of potions and methods went far beyond the proverbial Chamomile tea… to relieve and cure symptoms."[114]

---

[108] Jeffrey L. Singman, *The Middle Ages: Everyday Life in Medieval Europe* (N.Y.: Sterling, 2013), 64.
[109] Ibid., 62.
[110] Ibid.
[111] Ian Dawson, *Medicine in the Middle Ages* (N.Y.: Enchanted Lion Books, 2005), 8.
[112] Ibid., 22.
[113] Philip Warner, *The Medieval Castle* (London, Penguin Books, 1971), 206.
[114] Clemente Manenti, *Castles in Italy: The Medieval Life of Noble Families* (Cologne, Germany: Konemann, 2001), 106.

Whenever someone in the community became ill, "women...were the first line of defense. Unable to afford any other type of healer, peasant families turned to women among them who could help a sick family member."[115] In sum, "secular society expected women to be intimately involved in caring for the bodies of others (especially the young, the sick, and the dying). Women assisted in childbirth, prepared corpses for burial and carried out ritual mourning for the dead."[116]

As with St. Catherine of Siena, Blessed Margaret was no doubt in great demand for poor families experiencing illness or injury among their members. Margaret would have been able to treat with herbal or other folk remedies (we are told that she brought medicine and food to the sick poor); cleanse wounds that needed tending; bathe the sick who were feverish; and provide any other material comforts that might aid in an ill person's healing. These were often critically important services for while it is suggested that physicians "practiced" in larger cities and in court, "villagers were left to their own devices" for treatment; even the barber-surgeons were "rarely seen in the villages."[117]

While it may seem difficult to conceptualize a blind young woman caring for the sick, it must be remembered that Margaret had been forced to manage this physical challenge from birth. For one such as Blessed Margaret, who has totally lost the use of sight, there is generally a heightened ability of the other senses, especially those of hearing, touch and smell. The use of these senses, which had been fined tuned in Margaret from infancy, would have proved invaluable in ministering to the sick. Margaret could listen with the "ear of her heart" to an ill person's symptoms, often hearing subtle messages not verbalized vocally. Her refined sense of touch could identify physical injuries or anomalies without being able to directly visualize them. And, the heightened sense of smell could help the blind caregiver diagnose certain physiological changes not usual to normal bodily functioning.

Because of the association between prayer and healing, ill individuals of the middle ages sometimes made pilgrimages to religious shrines; for the very poor, however, such a journey was often not possible but Blessed Margaret, as a Dominican Tertiary, brought not only

---

[115] Kate Kelly, *The Middle Ages: 500-1450, The History of Medicine* (N.Y.: Facts On File, 2009), 73.

[116] Caroline W. Bynum, *Fragmentation and Redemption: Essays on Gender and the Human Body in Medieval Religion* (N.Y.: Zone Books, 1991), 197.

[117] Frances Gies and Joseph Gies, *Life in a Medieval Village* (N.Y. Harper & Row, 1990), 121.

physical care and healing on her errands of mercy to the sick poor but also the gift of spiritual care and consolation.

Interestingly, the literature suggests that "the vast majority of surviving evidence for health care, medicine and attitudes to Illness in early medieval northern Italy comes not from traditional medical texts "but from other works including hagiographical sources."[118] The legend of Blessed Margaret of Castello and that of St. Catherine of Siena, fit in the latter category. Perhaps one of the reasons for healthcare information being recorded in hagiographical texts is the fact that many "religiously affiliated women managed...the daily experience of health and illness" for marginalized populations in the medieval era.[119] Significant numbers of these woman were Tertiaries of Roman Catholic religious orders such as Margaret and Catherine.

In a classic history of nursing, the authors point out the importance of the Church's influence in medieval healthcare, noting that "since the care of the sick is an act of mercy, it is not at all surprising to find that many saints personally nursed the sick...(especially) countless thousands of poor."[120] The secular orders, to which the Tertiaries who cared for the sick belonged, achieved particular growth in the 12th and 13th Centuries.[121] The secular Tertiaries, such as the women in Blessed Margaret's Mantellate community, undertook care of the sick poor as their primary ministry.[122]

Ministry to the Outcast
Medieval Prisoners

As well as ministering to the sick, in the streets and in their homes, Blessed Margaret, having herself been an "outcast," had a heart filled with love and compassion for the outcasts of society incarcerated in the *Citta di Castello* prison. As Italian author and journalist Barbara Sartori observed: "Margherita felt especially the call to bring Jesus to another category of patients: those injured in soul, more than in the body. *Citta di*

---

[118] Clare Pilsworth, "Beyond the Medical Text: Health and Illness in Early Medieval Italian Sources," *Social History of Medicine* 24:1 (2013): 26-40, 26.

[119] Sara Ritchey, "Affective Medicine: Later Medieval Healing Communities and the Feminazation of Health Care Practices in the Thirteenth-Century Low Countries," *The Journal of Medieval Religious Cultures* 40:2 (2014): 113-143, 113.

[120] Gladys Sellew and C.J. Nuesse, *A History of Nursing* (St. Louis: The C.V. Mosby Company, 1951), 128.

[121] M. Adelaide Nutting and Lavinia L. Dock, *A History of Nursing*, Volume I (New York: G.P. Putnam's Sons, 1935), 257.

[122] Lucy R. Seymer, *A General History of Nursing* (New York: The Macmillan Company, 1949), 45.

Castello, with all its internal quarrels and grudges, produced many wounds that ended up in corrupt relationships between people, between families. But there was a physical place where all these disagreements gathered, mingling to bursting: the prisons."[123] With "overcrowding" and the lack of "real opportunities" for the prisoners, the conditions of the prisons in the 14th Century were devastating. There was "torture," "living in those caves filthy and dark; often men, women and children forced close together gave rise to all kinds of ugliness...corruption of body and spirit (was) a real threat. In the prisons there were murderers and criminals. But there were (also) those who stole from starvation. As in society, the law of the strongest applied here."[124]

Barbara Sartori graphically described Margaret's prison ministry:

> It took some courage to enter the jails, face to face with humanity lost and abandoned. Only Christian charity dared so much. Margaret could perhaps get to be exempted from visiting detainees. But was it not here, where God was, more often than not, called on with curses, that there was more need for love and forgiveness? So, with the other penitents (Mantellate), down in the basement, she braved the horror of the stench and cries of derision, to be close to these derelicts. She brought food, clothes. She brought especially consolation...Such was the intensity of her praying, even among the spiteful laughter and curses, (she) fell into ecstasy and rose from the ground. The anger gave way to wonder (and some) recovered the ability...to take back their lives...to discover (themselves) men and women loved by God and worthy of being welcomed back, as the parable of the (prodigal) son (into) the embrace of the merciful Father.[125]

Overall, conditions in the medieval prisons of the era were, as described above, devastating. Diseases, such as "Gaol (Jail) Fever," were prevalent. The etiology of these fevers was often unclear but it was thought that a cause might be "the foul air and the pestilential savour, whether arising from the 'noisome smell' of the prisoners or from the damp of the ground and the filth of the house."[126] Typhus and plague

---

[123] Barbara Sartori, *Beata Margherita di Citta di Castello* (Milano, Italy: Paoline Editorale Libri, 2011), 77-78.
[124] Ibid.
[125] Ibid.
[126] Christopher H. Collins and David A. Kennedy, "Gaol and Ship Fevers," *Perspectives in Public Health* 129:4 (2009): 163-164, 163.

symptoms, as well as the signs of scurvy, were ubiquitous among the impoverished prisoners.

Scholar of "medieval prisons," Guy Geltner, distinguishes between those inmates who had external financial and social support and those who were indigent. Wealthy prisoners were described as "having attendant pursuits" and receiving visitors during incarceration while "the poor cried for mercy."[127] Geltner points out that some of the institutions were initially designed to house private debtors and wealthy tax-evaders; however, over time, they became long term prisons for those "who could not pay for their upkeep, let alone improve the conditions of their captivity."[128]

For the "non-professional poor and those who lacked powerful patrons," Guy Geltner notes, "the consequences of arrest could be dire" and terrifying.[129] As witness, he cites the example of one Venetian who "embarked on a self-imposed four-year exile, 'fearing prison more than death,' and a local young man named Marco (who) was apparently so terrified that he pleaded to convert his six-month prison sentence into serving on a galley, 'or wherever it would please the lord doge' for three years."[130]

Geltner, whose research explored life in medieval Italian prisons during the early 14th Century, the period when Blessed Margaret's ministry took her to the *Citta di Castello* jail, explained how day-to-day "prison life was a struggle."[131] Some inmates passed their time by "decorating their cells with graffiti...they lamented their fate, composed prayers, recorded deaths, blasphemed...conspired to escape or plotted revenge against personal enemies or the government";[132] he added: "inmates routinely turned on one another, and rape, brawling and stabbing were common."[133]

Most jails had no kitchens or infirmaries and food and medicine had to be brought to prisoners by relatives or bought from the guards; the poor who had no family, friends or financial resources were left to starve

---

[127] Christopher H. Collins and David A. Kennedy, "Gaol and Ship Fevers," *Perspectives in Public Health* 129:4 (2009): 163-164, 163.
[128] Guy Geltner, "A Cell of Their Own: The Incarceration of Women in Late Medieval Prisons," *Signs* 39:1 (2013): 27-51, 36.
[129] Guy Geltner, *The Medieval Prison: A Social History* (Princeton: Princeton University Press, 2008), 60.
[130] Ibid., 60-61
[131] Ibid., 68.
[132] Ibid.
[133] Ibid., 69.

unless a religious group came forward to provide for their needs.[134] It was to the impoverished prisoners incarcerated in the *Citta di Castello* jail, that Blessed Margaret brought not only food, medicine and clothing but also the love and compassion of Christ.

Blessed Margaret's sensitivity to the plight of the poorest prisoners was directly related to her own past experiences of isolation, especially her time of "imprisonment" in the underground vault of the family palazzo. While Margaret was living with Venturinus and Gregoria, she became intimately aware of the needs and agony of the *Citta di Castello* prisoners from hearing the townspeople express concern over their situation. She began to strongly desire to extend her ministry of caring for the sick in the city to the outcasts lingering in the prison, as she was told there was no one to care for them when they were ill. The problem was that the prison "was viewed as an unsafe environment for women."[135] At the time "medieval prisons were brutal and inhumane. Prisoners were shackled, ill fed and sometimes kept underground. Prison wardens readily accepted bribes to provide well-off prisoners with food while ignoring the poorer prisoners. Sanitary conditions were abominable allowing disease to spread rapidly."[136]

Fear, however, did not dissuade Blessed Margaret from the ministry. One day, after returning from caring for the sick in their homes, Margaret sought advice from Ventuinus and Gregoria about visiting the Prison. They initially responded negatively, describing the prison as a terrible place which was not safe for women visitors. Blessed Margaret's answer was that this seemed even more reason to initiate a prison ministry. Margaret related stories she had heard of the dreadful conditions in the local prison; the fact that many of the cells were damp and cold without light or fresh air; that prisoners had to sleep on the ground and were without adequate clothing or food. She also had been told that there was no medical care even for those who were seriously ill or the dying. Margaret added that, according to local reports, the prisoners were "chained day and night to the walls as if they were savage wild beasts (and) because of the inhuman treatment, they get, a number of them have ceased to believe in God."[137]

Blessed Margaret continued to relate anecdotes describing the questionable character of the jailers who "demanded money each time a

---

[134] Ibid., 73.
[135] Lucinda Vardey, *Traveling with the Saints in Italy: Contemporary Pilgrimages on Ancient Paths* (Mahwah, N.J.: Hidden Springs, 2005), 155.
[136] McGrane, 11.
[137] Bonniwell, 83.

prisoner was unchained, as well as selling charitably donated food to prisoners who had no one to bring them food."[138] Because of lack of sanitary conditions the prisons were a breeding ground for disease: "every year fully half the prisoners died of jail fever."[139] Margaret especially wanted to minister to the impoverished sick prisoners who had no one to care for them in their illness.

Ultimately, Blessed Margaret's desire to minister to the *Citta di Castello* prisoners was supported by her hosts Venturinus and Gregoria, and Gregoria began accompanying her on these missions of mercy. Thus, Margaret, Gregoria and several other Mantellate began to visit the prisoners bringing them food, clothing, medicine and, most importantly the love and support of God. "Every day," it is reported "these white-robed heroines could be seen entering the prison, their arms laden with as many bundles as they could carry. But of all their gifts, none approached in value their restoring to the prisoners a consciousness of their dignity as human beings."[140] Blessed Margaret and her *Mantellata* Sisters brought not only material comfort and support but most importantly spiritual comfort and support reflected in their tender care and compassion.

At times, upon witnessing a prisoner's suffering, Margaret "would think of Christ's suffering and levitate, rising in the air above the dank prison floor. Her frequent visits and levitations (attracted) the townspeople to come to the cells…In this way, Margaret was able to help the prisoners and raise the consciousness of others about the conditions in prison."[141] At the times of her levitations, Margaret "fell into ecstatic prayer and prisoners reported that when she was in that state…she became beautiful and beatific."[142]

An anecdote is told about one of Blessed Margaret's prayerful visits to a prisoner called Alonzo:

> On one of Margaret's frequent visits to the city prison, something happened that caused quite a stir in the town. It seemed that one of the prisoners, a man named Alonzo, went into a wild rage when he learned that his son, living in utter destitution, had died of starvation. He was inconsolable and even tried to kill himself.

---

[138] Ibid.
[139] Ibid.
[140] Ibid., 84-85.
[141] James Heater and Coleen Heater, *The Pilgrim's Italy: A Travel Guide to the Saints* (Nevada City, Ca.: Inner Travel Books, 2008), 209.
[142] Vardey, 155.

He was cursing and crying at the same time. Margaret stood beside him in intense contemplation, her arms raised to heaven, as she dwelt upon a merciful God. In the midst of all the prisoners and Sisters, Margaret levitated several feet, remaining in the air for some time. When she descended Margaret's face was glowing. The reaction of all present, including Alonzo, was immediate and breathtaking. They called upon God to forgive their sins and made a firm resolve to turn their lives to Him. Margaret's mystical vision with God had converted the most hardened sinners."[143]

The importance of Blessed Margaret's spiritual and religious support of 14th-century prisoners is reflected in current literature which continues to document the value of ministry to those incarcerated in contemporary penal institutions. Today, as in the past, prison chaplains and volunteers provide "an array of services such as counseling, religious teaching, assisting with adjustment to prison, visiting those in isolation and helping inmate's families."[144] Prison ministers "simultaneously" minister and are ministered to in the prison setting;[145] the "Incarnate Presence of God is in the interaction between the minister and the prisoner" in his or her anguish and alienation.[146]

A study of the value of spiritual and religious intervention, in prison, from the inmates' perspective, revealed the importance of this support on both intrinsic and extrinsic orientations; intrinsic factors included; dealing with guilt, finding a new way of life, dealing with the loss of freedom, and extrinsic factors were: safety, material comforts, access to outsiders and inmate relations."[147] The concept of safety, of concern in the 14th Century, remains relevant today as reflected in the words of a prison chaplain: "I have been in two riots in high violent units where my life was threatened. I've been verbally abused and threatened by inmates and staff. I have broken up group fights in the Chapel and I have

---

[143] Alex La Perchia, *Food for the Soul* (N.Y.: University Press of America, 2015), 59.
[144] Richard Tewksbury and Sue C. Collins, "Prison Chapel Volunteers," *Federal Probation* 69:1 (2005): 26-30, 49, 26.
[145] Alicia Vargas, "Who Ministers to Whom: Matthew 25: 31-46 and Prison Ministry," *Dialog: A Journal of Theology* 52: 2 (2013): 128-137, 128.
[146] Stephen T. Hall, "A Working Theology of Prison Ministry," *The Journal of Pastoral Care and Counseling* 58:3 (2004): 169-178, 169.
[147] Todd R. Clear, Patricia Hardyman, Bruce Stout, Karol Lucken and Harry R. Dammer, "The Value of Religion in Prison: An Inmate Perspective," *Journal of Contemporary Criminal Justice* 16: 1 (2000): 53-74, 58-71.

witnessed a killing in my Sunday service."[148] However, as with Blessed Margaret, fear did not hinder the chaplain's continued ministry.

In what might perhaps be considered a recognition of Margaret of Castello's respect for the lives of medieval prisoners, one contemporary U.S. prison has initiated a Lay Dominican chapter. The chapter membership is comprised of 35 inmates, "17 of whom have made their final profession in the Lay Dominican Order."[149] It is reported of the prison Tertiaries: "They wake each morning to pray the Liturgy of the Hours and chant it again before they go to sleep. They pray the Rosary, spend time in contemplative prayer and gather each Sunday to discuss the Gospel. In almost every way they are like members of other chapters of the lay fraternities of St. Dominic, except they are incarcerated."[150]

It appears that the Dominican charism of Blessed Margaret of Castello, lovingly introduced to 14th-century Italian prisoners, now lives on in the experience of those incarcerated in 21st-century American penal facilities.

This chapter has summarized Margaret of Castello's gifts as both mystic and minister. As a mystic, Margaret was blessed with a profound devotion to God exemplified in prayer and penance, the experience of repeated spiritual visions of Christ during Mass, and the manifestation of the Lord's love demonstrated in the variety of miracles attributed to her intervention. As a minister, Blessed Margaret tirelessly embraced the *Mantellata* vocation of caring for the sick and the outcast.

"Little Margaret" of Castello truly lived the scriptural commandment of Jesus that we love others, as He has loved us (John 13: 34). Her own physical afflictions in no way hindered Margaret from hastening to the desolate homes of the sick poor and to the fetid cells of the depressing prison. Wherever she recognized a need, Blessed Margaret was there as the small and humble ambassador of God's loving care and tender mercy.

---

[148] R.N. Ristad, "A Stark Examination of Prison Culture and Prison Ministry," *Dialog: A Journal of Theology* 47:3 (2008): 292-303, 294.

[149] Christine Williams, "Norfolk Inmates Seek Christ in Lay Dominican Chapter," *The Pilot* (2007): 1-3, 1.

[150] Ibid.

ENDNOTES: Chapter 6. "Love One Another"

[i] According to Cordelia Warr, "two versions of Margaret of Castello's 'legenda' exist: the *recensio maior* and the *recensio minor*. Both appear to have been compiled between 1347-1349 and 1400. The *recensio minor* was probably written by a Dominican toward the end of the fourteenth century. The author of the longer version of Margaret's life, which may have been composed shortly after 1350, cannot be positively identified...Since the earliest of these vitae was compiled at least thirty years after Margaret's death it seems unlikely that either author knew her personally, although it has been argued that both versions of the vita rely on an earlier source and may, therefore, have their roots in information provided by Margaret's contemporaries" (Warr, 2007, p. 221).

[ii] Notes in a contemporary copy of the "Talmud," observe that the illness from which those sitting with the Messiah were suffering was Tzaraas, a disease whose symptoms include discolored patches of the skin (Leviticus, Chapter 13); and explain the response of Elijah: "He unties one (bandage) and ties one. Each of the others unties all his bandages at the same time, cleans all his sores, and then reties all the bandages. The Messiah, however, unties only one bandage at a time; he cleans that sore and re-ties the bandage before proceeding to the next one. He does not allow two sores to be exposed at the same time. He does not want to delay even the amount of time it takes to tie two bandages" (*Talmud Bavli, Tractate Sahhedrin* (3A), Mesorah Publications, Ltd, Brooklyn, N.Y., 1990-1993).

Blessed Margaret of Castello

Chapter 7. "Unless a Grain of Wheat Falls"

The Healing Miracles

"Unless a grain of wheat falls into the earth and dies, it remains just a single grain; but if it dies it bears much fruit."

John 12: 24

"A Grain of Wheat"

As the tiny grain of wheat,
"Little Margaret" fell
softly into the
earth.

The comforting wind caressed
her small form with its
caring tenderness.

The worshipping birds gentled
their song in a hymn
of thanksgiving.

For Margaret had now been
transformed:

Transformed to stand
graceful and tall
as a blessed
of God;

Transformed with eyes
Shining and joyous
at the sight
of His
Majesty;

Transformed at last into
the radiant beauty
she was born to
become.

Blessed Margaret of Castello

As described in the previous chapter, Blessed Margaret of Castello lived her Dominican religious vocation fully, as both mystic and minister, seeking only to love God and her neighbor as deeply and completely as possible. From her childhood days, when she was indeed "Little Margaret," Blessed Margaret never allowed her physical afflictions to deter her from embracing what she trusted the Lord was asking of her. Margaret truly deserved the title "blessed" from her earliest years until the time of her death. Although a number of healing miracles have been described as resulting from Blessed Margaret's care and compassion during her lifetime, even more healings have been attributed to Margaret's intervention following her death. While Margaret of Castello was called from this earthly life after only thirty-three years, the blessed "grain of wheat" which fell into the ground, did indeed continue to "bear much fruit" in eternal life.

As Margaret's fragile body began to weaken, she told the friends who had supported her that she believed she would not be with them much longer; she was losing the battle to "keep body and soul united": "The signs were unmistakable. Margaret was by now so transformed that she had completely forgotten self and thought only of God and His glory."[1]

As "Little Margaret" became more ill:

> the city tightened around her when they foresaw her imminent end. Donna Grigia and the Tertiary Sisters prayed for her (and) worried about the state of her health deteriorating more and more, because she did not have any regard for her body and continued to subject it to repeated penance. The house of Donna Grigia and Venturino became a place of sad pilgrimages for news about the health of the blessed. In the church of the Friars Preachers people met in prayer and, in all the churches of the city prayers rose up for the blind (Margherita) of Metola.[2]

The Medieval Biographer reported that as Blessed Margaret's "illness progressed, she had the preaching Brothers called, so that she might receive the sacraments."[3] The Biographer added: "After the sacraments had been received, I do not say with how much devotion,

---

[1] William R. Bonniwell, *The Life of Blessed Margaret of Castello:1287-1320* (Charlotte, N.C.: Tan Books, 2014), 98.
[2] Ubaldo Valentini, *Beata Margherita De La Metola Una Sfida Alla Emarginazione* (Perugia, Italy: Petruzzi Editore, 1988), 53
[3] *Blessed Margaret of Castello OP: A Medieval Biography* (Trans. Carolina Accorsi) (Fatima, Portugal: Dominican Nuns of the Perpetual Rosary, 1994), 32.

breathless with Christ she returned her gracious spirit to God. The Mother of God...presented Margaret to her Son, in glory, in the year of the Incarnation, April 13, 1320."[4]

During her final reception of the Holy Eucharist, Blessed Margaret was surrounded by a family of Preaching Brothers, and Sisters of Penance of St. Dominic, the Mantellate Community, as well as by dear friends who had cared for her over the years. As Margaret's faithful Dominican biographer, Fr. William Bonniwell, imagined the scene:

> The Friars and the Mantellate began the prayers for the dying, but Margaret did not hear them. She was rapt in loving contemplation of the God who had come to her in the Holy Eucharist. She could not bear to be separated again from Him whom she loved so completely; she longed to be dissolved and to be with her Eternal Love forever. Flesh and blood could no longer hold so ardent a soul, and Margaret's spirit, freed at last from its shackles, soared aloft to her God.[5]

Following Blessed Margaret's death, her body was washed and clothed in the religious habit of the Mantellate. It was a Dominican tradition to observe poverty both during life and in death; therefore, no coffin was provided for the burial. Margaret's small body would simply be covered by her black Dominican mantle which she had so treasured in her lifetime and in which she would now go forth to meet her Blessed Lord. As a Dominican, Blessed Margaret had wished to be buried in a Dominican Church, the Chiesa della Carita in *Citta di Castello*. The Preaching Brothers carried Margaret's body in procession, planning to bury her in the Church's cloister cemetery where other Mantellate had been buried. Unexpectedly, however, a great crowd of mourners had assembled outside of the Church to greet their beloved Margaret.

When her friends and supporters learned of the Friars intention to bury Margaret in the cloister cemetery they cried out in protest. The mourners begged that their Blessed Margaret be buried in the sepulcher in the Church, as a saint, because that is what they believed she was. A cry arose from the crowd: "Let her be buried not in the cloister, but in the church. She is holy and reputed holy by all!"[6] While the Prior of the Dominican Friars hesitated to violate the norms of burial in the Church, a

---

[4] Ibid., 33.
[5] Bonniwell, 99.
[6] *Blessed Margaret of Castello OP*, 33.

miraculous healing occurred which seemed to confirm the wishes of Margaret's mourners.

A father and mother brought to the Church their young daughter who was both mute and afflicted with a crippling spinal disease which prevented her from walking. The distraught parents begged Blessed Margaret, as one who had herself been crippled, to heal their disabled child; they placed the little one on the ground beside Margaret's body. According to witnesses, one of Margaret's hands reached out to touch the child and the tiny girl, who had never been able to walk or speak, stood up and shouted: "I have been cured through the merits of Blessed Margaret."[7] Margaret's holiness had been confirmed for the Prior and her body was thus taken by the Friars into one of the chapels of the Dominican Church of Chiesa della Carita.

Beatification

The term "beatification" is derived from the Latin *beatus*, meaning "blessed," and *facere*, from the verb "to make." An individual who has been "beatified" is considered to have been, by the grace of God, made "blessed." There are three titles which the Roman Catholic Church has identified as being necessary prior to naming one a "saint"; these are: "Servant of God," "Venerable," and "Blessed." In order to achieve the first two titles, a person must be judged to have lived with significant, even heroic, virtue during his or her lifetime. Surely, Margaret of Castello fit easily into these first two categories of holiness. In order for one to be labeled "Blessed," however, usually a confirmed miracle must be attributed to the individual's direct intervention.[8]

After a person is declared "Blessed" they may be honored by the Church and a feast day is assigned on which to celebrate his or her holy and devout life. While the contemporary canonization process has, according to the code of canon law, been somewhat streamlined, the canonization procedure in the medieval era of Blessed Margaret of Castello, "did little to encourage the Church to declare lay men and women as saints. Indeed, the most underrepresented group in the ranks of the canonized" was the laity.[9]

---

[7] Ibid., 34; Bonniwell, 104.
[8] Sarah Gallick, *The Big Book of Woman Saints* (N.Y.: Harper San Francisco, 2007), 2-3.
[9] Richard Gribble, "Saints in the Christian Tradition: Unraveling the Canonization Process," *Studies in Christian-Jewish Relations* 6:1 (2011): 1-18, 11.

Incorruptibility

After Margaret's death, many witnessed miracles, which occurred through her intervention, were reported; nevertheless, "steps toward Beatification initiated by the Dominican Order languished."[10] However, "during the 16th century, interest in her cause was rekindled with the discovery of her incorrupt body."[11] Margaret's "exhumation was undertaken in the presence of many witnesses who were awe-stricken when the coffin was opened. While the clothing on the body had crumbled to dust, the body itself was found to be perfectly preserved, as though Margaret had just died...The body was thoroughly examined by physicians, who declared that no chemicals had been used to preserve it."[12]

As a result of this finding, and the reporting of many more miracles, the cause for beatification which was embraced "with a renewed interest, came to a successful conclusion on October 19, 1609, when the Church officially recognized Margaret's sanctity, pronouncing her a '*beata*' and designating April 13, as her feast day."[13] Presently, "the body of Blessed Margaret, which has never been embalmed, is dressed in a Dominican *Mantellata* habit and lies underneath the high altar of the Church of San Domenico at *Citta di Castello*, Italy."[14] Margaret's body is said to remain in a remarkable condition for having never been embalmed.

The Healing Miracles

After Blessed Margaret's death more than 200 healing miracles were documented "in confirmation of her heroic sanctity."[15] The affidavits testify to permanent cures for persons who had experienced a variety of illnesses or injuries. Margaret who was so committed to ministering to the sick and the outcast during her lifetime continued to care for those who were suffering from illness and injury even after she had been re-born into eternal life.

Many of the healings attributed to the intervention of Blessed Margaret after her death took place at her tomb. In discussing "holy persons and holy places" in medieval Italy, historian Augustine

---

[10] Joan C. Cruz, *The Incorruptibles: A Study of the Incorruption of the Bodies of Various Catholic Saints and Beati* (Charlotte, N.C.: Tan Books, 2012), 81.
[11] Ibid., 81.
[12] Ibid., 81-82.
[13] Ibid., 82.
[14] Ibid.
[15] Ibid. 81.

Thompson, O.P., observed that "as diverse as the lives of the communal saints, were the local rituals and practices at their shrines."[16] The tomb of a holy person "provided the most direct access to the saint."[17] At "Saint (sic) Margherita of *Citta di Castello*'s shrine, which like many others was raised on pillars, the sick regularly slept under the arca, hoping for cures."[18]

A number of Blessed Margaret's medieval healings, validated by witnesses identified as "notaries," were included in the appendix to Ubaldo Valentini's work, *Beata Margherita De La Metola: Una Sfida Alla Emarginazione*. Several of the blessed's miracles have already been mentioned, for example, the extinguishing of a great fire, by Margaret's mantle, in the home of Venturinus and Gregoria; the healing of Sister Venturella's eye tumor; the cure of the mute and crippled child at the Chiesa della Carita; and the miracle of the inscribed stones found in Margaret's heart.

Some other post-mortem miraculous healings, occurring through Blessed Margaret's intervention, and documented by Ubaldo Valentini included those of:

- Frederico di Villa Santa Cecilia, in Curia S. Angelo, in Vado, whose arms were paralyzed and his joints so afflicted that he could not walk unless assisted by someone or using a stick. After making a vow to Blessed Margaret, he was "perfectly healed," 19 May, 1320, as witnessed by a notary.[19]
- Donna Alda, wife of Angelo from Perugia, who declared before Ser Giovanni Cambi, notary, that she could not move her hand and left arm for three months but after visiting Margaret's tomb, was healed.[20]
- Giovanni Cambi di Verciano, Curia di Monte S. Maria, who before the notary Ser Goro and witnesses, declared under oath that he had been struck by fever and could not move his neck and head in any way from September until the following May. But after praying to Blessed Margaret he fell asleep and when he awoke immersed in sweat, he stood up completely healed.[21]

---

[16] Augustine Thompson, *Cities of God: The Religion of the Italian Communes, 1125-1325* (University Park, Pa.: The Pennsylvania State University Press, 2005), 209.
[17] Ibid.
[18] Ibid., 211.
[19] Valentini, 231.
[20] Ibid.
[21] Ibid., 233.

- Guglielmo di Francesco who declared before the notary and witnesses that he could barely walk without excruciating pain which the doctor could not heal, but after he stood at Margaret's tomb for a long time praying and declaring himself a sinner and asking for healing, was instantly cured as if he were never sick.[22]
- This healing was further discussed in Augustine Thompson's *Cities of God*: "The notary Ser Guglielmo di Francesco, who had an unhealed broken leg, came to the tomb of Santa Margherita in the choir of the Dominican Church at *Citta di Castello*. He prayed, shed tears of repentence, and swore on the Gospels that 'as much as human frailty permitted' he would avoid sexual sin. He was immediately healed and made it his special vocation to spread the saint's cult, repeating, 'with tears', the story of his healing to all and sundry. He filed a deposition regarding his cure, notarized by Giovanni di Francesco, at Margherita's shrine."[23]
- Dina, figlia di Iacobuzio, who declared before witnesses and the notary, that she had suffered from cancer of the face for 9 months with no relief from the doctors but after prayers to Blessed Margaret she was completely healed.[24]
- A noblewoman of Gubbio who was for many years paralyzed on the right side of her body, and was not able to visit Margaret's grave because of her infirmities, but after a vow and prayer to the blessed, reported that she had received perfect healing.[25]
- Signora Pera, who for fifty days suffered pain in her leg and thigh and could not move without the help of others, and who prayed and visited the tomb of Blessed Margaret and the next day felt completely healed.[26]
- A farmer who went out to cut wood in the forest was assaulted by bears who tore his body but after his wife, remembering the miracles done by Blessed Margaret, prayed with devotion and invoked the help of Blessed Margaret, then the farmer opened his eyes and found himself healed in an instant.[27]
- A robust young man, who during the harvest, counting on the strength of his body, raised a big barrel on his chest which was crushed by the weight and he could hardly breathe. A "godly

---

[22] Ibid., 235.
[23] Thompson, 204: cited from *Vita Beatae Virginis de Civitate Casetlli*, 10, 30.
[24] Valentini, 235.
[25] Ibid., 245.
[26] Ibid., 237.
[27] Ibid.

woman" who was nearby, taken by compassion, told him to pray to Blessed Margaret. The young man prayed, saying: "Do not consider my sins." He was healed perfectly and regained his strength as before.[28]

Overall, Ubaldo Valentini specifically identified more than 50 cures achieved through Blessed Margaret's intervention. So other healings or alleviations of suffering were reported for persons with such afflictions as: a paralyzed foot, a swelling in the chest, a fistula in the shoulder, a five-year-old paralyzed from birth, a shin and calf injury, left sided body paralysis, breast cancer, a complicated birth and a contracted left arm.[29]

A final dramatic healing was recorded which described the resuscitation of a young child who "fell from a high balcony onto the stones of *Citta di Castello* but was restored to life and health by Blessed Margaret of Castello."[30]

Medieval Christians believed that "the saints were endowed with healing powers and that this power resided in their relics, both bodily remains and personal possessions, after they had died and gone to heaven: Given the saints proximity to God, Christians held that the saints could serve as intercessors, bringing their requests before the Almighty, just as a king's counsellors might intervene on the part of an earthly petitioner."[31]

In the Middle Ages, however, those seeking a healing miracle "did not just register their request and stand by waiting for good things to happen."[32] Accounts of petitions for miraculous healing by a particular saint or blessed, almost always were accompanied by "a prayer, and act of veneration, a confession, a pilgrimage, or a presentation of gifts."[33] This is clearly demonstrated in Ubaldo Valentini's documentation of Blessed Margaret's healing miracles in such cases as: the "man who stood at Margaret's tomb for a long time praying," those making a "vow" or a promise related to their request, and the petitioner who prayed to Margaret begging her also "Do not consider my sins." Frequently a

---

[28] Ibid., 249.
[29] Ibid., 231-249
[30] Kevin O. Johnson, *Apparitions: Mystic Phenomena and What They Mean* (Dallas, Tx: author, 1998), 145.
[31] Deidre E. Jackson, *Marvelous to Behold: Miracles in Illuminated Manuscripts* (London: The British Library, 2007), 70.
[32] Roberta A. Scott, *Miracle Cures: Saints, Pilgrimages, and the Health Powers of Belief* (Berkeley, Ca.: University of California Press, 2010), 29.
[33] Ibid.

request for healing was carried out during a visit to the tomb of the saint or blessed to whom the petition is being made.

Medieval saints and blesseds, such as Margaret of Castello, were "recognized as possessing an extra measure of God's grace. One of the marks of such sanctity was the holy person's ability to perform miracles both before and after his or her death."[34] Blessed Margaret is believed to have performed the majority of her healing interventions after, rather than before, her death.

The concept of healing, which describes "a process that facilitates health and restores harmony and balance between the mind and the body,"[35] has been explored by theologians and health care professionals across the centuries. Since the time of Christ, many of His followers have continued the healing practices of Jesus and His early disciples. The documentation of many medieval religious healings is found in such sources as hagiographical writings and works prepared for canonization proceedings. The identification of numerous religious healings is included in the hagiographical works exploring the "legend" of Blessed Margaret of Castello.

A large percentage of the population of Western societies, approximately 70%, believe in miraculous healing,[36] many related to "the sovereignty of God over illness."[37] There is support for belief in the validity of Blessed Margaret's healing miracles on the part of the clergy and the citizens of *Citta di Castello* in the pictorial representations presented in a number of 17th-century lunettes found in the cloister of the Church of San Domenico (A detailed description of the "lunettes" and their commissioning by a Dominican Prior is discussed in Chapter 1).

Blessed Margaret's physical healings represented a reflection of her mystical spirituality described in the previous chapter. Belief in miracles, or "sudden occurrences that drastically affect nature or the human body, mostly the latter,"[38] was considered part and parcel of religious faith in the medieval era. A miracle has been defined as: "A religious wonder that

---

[34] Cathy J. Itnyre, *Medieval Family Roles: A Book of Essays* (N.Y.: Garland Publishers Inc., 1996), 103.

[35] Judy A. Glaister, "Healing: Analysis of the Concept," *International Journal of Nursing Practice* 7:1 (2000): 63-68, 63.

[36] Jacob Pawlikowski, Michal Wiechetek, Jaroslaw Sak and Marek Jarosz, "Beliefs in Miraculous Healings, Religiosity and Meaning in Life," *Religions* 6:3 (2015): 1113-1124, 1113.

[37] Andrew Village, "Dimensions of Belief About Miraculous Healing," *Mental Health, Religion & Culture* 8: 2 (2005): 97-107, 97.

[38] Esther Cohen, "Thaumatology at One Remove: Empathy in Miraculous Cure Narratives in the Later Middle Ages," *Partial Answers* 7: 2 (2009): 189-199, 189.

expresses, in the cosmic order (human beings and the universe), a special and utterly free intervention of the God of power and love, who thereby gives human beings a sign of the presence of his message of salvation in the world."[39]

Miracles may have a variety of purposes: they can be "functionalized as an argument for Christian belief, as a proof of the sanctity and the virtue of a person or relic, or as a didactic means in order to impress and to convince an audience of a theological message."[40] To speak of miracles in the middle ages, however, was to introduce phenomena that was "absolutely normal and a part of everyday life...natural phenomena, madness, battles, catastrophes, healing processes, everything could be interpreted as the intervention of God, and all these cases can be found in miracle narratives."[41]

Thus, "*miracula* became the term to designate phenomena that were considered contrary to or beyond nature. Between Augustine and Thomas Aquinas, miracles, signs and wonders were not discussed to a large extent. The reason for that...is the fact that miracles were so closely woven into the texture of Christian experience that there was no incentive to examine or explain the presuppositions that lay behind them."[42] "A marvel," Axel Ruth observes, is generally something extraordinary but not contrary to nature, whereas a miracle designates an intervention by God."[43]

The healing miracles of Blessed Margaret of Castello were not only proof of her personal sanctity but also served to inspire and uplift the medieval audience seeking concrete examples of God's mercy and compassion in their lives.

A "theory of miracles" was identified by renowned medieval scholar Sister Benedicta Ward, in describing the understanding of Augustine of Hippo who "argued that there is only one miracle, that of creation with its corollary of re-creation by the Resurrection of Christ. God, he held, created the world out of nothing in six days, and within that initial creation he planted all the possibilities for the future. All creation was, therefore, both 'natural' and 'miraculous'...the events of every day, the

---

[39] Rene Latourelle, "Miracle," pp. 690-709, in Eds. Rene Latourelle and Rino Fisichella (N.Y., N.Y.: The Crossroad Publishing Co., 2000), 701.
[40] Axel Ruth, "Representing Wonder in Medieval Miracle Narratives," *Modern Language Notes* 126:4 (2011): 89-114, 89.
[41] Ibid., 92.
[42] Ibid., 93.
[43] Ibid.

birth of man, the growth of plants, rainfall."[44] However, Sister Benedicta explained, "Augustine also held that men were so accustomed to these 'daily miracles' that they were no longer moved to awe by them and needed to be provoked to reverence by unusual manifestations of God's power."[45] Thus, some occurrences, or miracles, "that seemed to be contrary to nature were in fact inherent in it."[46] Benedicta Ward added: "The most usual channel for these 'hidden causes' to be made manifest was the prayers of the saints."[47]

Margaret of Castello's prayers of intervention, especially those seeking the Lord's healing of physical afflictions, reminded the sufferers and their witnesses of God's power and providence, as well as demonstrating the holiness and Divine guidance of Blessed Margaret.

In the Middle Ages, mystical union and the presence of God was seen as "a fact of experience, not a matter of 'theory' or 'belief.'"[48] In the later medieval era, miracles and rituals surrounding a saint's veneration, such as those expressed by the followers of Blessed Margaret of Castello, could fulfill "a number of interrelated functions which were intended to guarantee the social and political health of the community....The saint's cult served as an agency for the public expression of patriotic or communal fervor; the social harmony displayed in such civic rituals reduced intra-group or familial violence and emphasized the treasury of common values and history to which all citizens were heir."[49] Some of the common values, attributed to the devotees of Blessed Margaret of Castello, are reflected in the ministries created to honor Margaret's memory.

Ministries Dedicated to Blessed Margaret
"L'Istituto Beata Margherita Cieca della Metola" (Blessed Margaret of Metola Institute for the Blind)

The "L'Istituto Beata Margherita Cieca della Metola," or Blessed Margaret of Metola Institute for the Blind, was founded in 1920 by Monseignor (Canon) Giacinto Faeti.

---

[44] Benedicta Ward, *Miracles and the Medieval Mind: Theory, Record and Event, 1200-1215* (Phila.: University of Pennsylvania Press, 1987), 3.
[45] Ibid.
[46] Ibid.
[47] Ibid.
[48] Steven Justice, "Did the Middle Ages Believe in Their Miracles," *Representations* 103:1 (2008): 1-29, 1.
[49] Michael E. Goodich, "Miracles and Disbelief in the Late Middle Ages," *Mediaevistik* 1:1 (1988): 23-38, 23.

Msgr. Faeti's aim was the creation of a hospice for poor blind women in memory of Blessed Margaret of Castello. It was initially conceived as a purely charitable institution but then, "as the years passed (it) became a center of education and training with a qualified school for telephone operators."[50] In his book *Beata Margherita De La Metola: Una Sfida Alla Emarginazione*, Ubaldo Valentini has included several pictures of Institute guests and activities including: "Students of the Institute in prayer before the casket of the Blessed"; "The guests (students) in the cloister"; "A guest at work on knitwear; the reward of handwork"; "The blind girls struggling with studies"; "Life of the Institute: guests at work"; and "Recitation of the blind: 'The Revenge of the Gypsy.'"[51] The Institute closed around 1944.

"Dis-abilita Associazione Sportiva Dilettantistica Beata Margherita" (Blessed Margaret Amateur Sports Association for the Disabled)

The "Dis-abilita Associazione Sportiva Dilettantistica Beata Margherita" is a center located in *Citta di Castello*, Perugia, which provides for "recreational activities, sports and mobility for people with disabilities; athletic workouts 1 or 2 times a week and swimming; and participation in Para-olympics" for those with physical as well as mental and behavioral disabilities. The intended audience is males and females ages 14 to 62 years.[52]

Castello Nursing Simulation Learning Center (Learning Center for the Practice of Simulated Nursing Care Procedures)

The Castello Nursing Simulation Learning Center, an initiative of the School of Nursing of Aquinas College, Nashville, Tennessee (housed at Saint Thomas West Hospital) was formally blessed and dedicated on April 13, 2015, the Feast Day of Blessed Margaret of Castello:

> The center provides seminal opportunities for experiential learning using state-of-the-art interactive technology for developing and assessing the competencies of students in the cognitive, affective, and psychomotor domains of learning directly applicable to the practice of nursing in today's

---

[50] Valentini, 87.
[51] Ibid., 95-99.
[52] http://www.provincia.perugia.it/sportelloonline/sportellodelcittadino /guidadisabilita.

technology-driven health care systems....The Castello Center consists of twenty-four patient care settings that include instructional and practice units, debriefing areas, technology, equipment and software on the foundations of nursing, health assessment and for more advanced areas of nursing practice such as care of mothers and their newborns, infants and children and adults experiencing acute, critical and chronic episodes of alterations in health status in community outpatient centers and clinics, hospitals, residential care facilities, hospice care centers, schools and homes of patients.[53]

Three simulated home care rooms have been created in the "Castello Learning Center" and furnished to familiarize students with potential settings they will encounter when caring for clients in the community; these include "St. Mary's Nursery," "Maggie's Place," and "Ryan's Rumpus Room."

"St. Mary's Nursery" is dedicated to caring for infants and children. The room was named after "St. Mary's Orphanage," a facility founded in the 1860's by some of the first Dominican Sisters to arrive in Nashville. There is a painting on the wall, entitled "The Band-aid," which honors "special needs" children; it displays a young child placing a band-aid on the hand of Jesus and was inspired by a book, describing the life of a special needs child, entitled *His Name is Joel: Searching for God in a Son's Disability*, by Kathleen Bolduc. This setting and painting reminds nursing students that Blessed Margaret of Castello was also a special needs child, and like all of God's children, a masterpiece of His creative genius.

In "Maggie's Place," the room has been furnished similar to a typical patient's home setting where care in the community is provided. It contains personal items and clothing, comfortable furnishings, antiques, family photographs, a pet cat and a dog and an occasional wandering roach (who is also part of the community!). In this environment the nurse is welcomed as a guest in the patient's home where he or she can come to appreciate and understand family customs and cultural differences.

"Ryan's Rumpus Room" is designed to reflect a typical room for a child receiving care in the home, hospital or special care center. Furnished with stuffed animals, toys, games and appropriate wall coverings in bright colored and printed fabrics. The environment affirms

---

[53] http://www.aquinascollege.edu/aquinas-opens-expansive-nursing-simulation-lab-saint-thomas-west.

the unique dignity and developing personality of the child receiving care, while minimizing a focus on technology which can be frightening.

In his opening remarks at the Dedication and Blessing of the Castello Center, Professor and Dean of the Aquinas College School of Nursing, Brother Ignatius Perkins OP, PhD, RN, FAAN, explained that the importance of the Center "in developing the clinical competencies" of the students for nursing practice "is deeply embedded in the history of nursing as early as the first century when women and men went to the streets of the cities and towns to care for the sick, the unwanted, the unloved. Though not prepared to practice nursing as we envision it today." Brother Ignatius added, "These noble women and men applied principles of caring, healing and hope to all people in every nation. In their own time they took great risks in daring to journey to the peripheries of human life to care for the sick, dying and those who suffered with stigmatized illnesses. They brought the healing ministry of Jesus to the world. They accompanied the sick in their long and sometimes torturous journey to human freedom."

"We are reminded," Brother Ignatius noted, "that Margaret of Castello's life is emblematic of the charism attributed to St. Dominic and his Brothers and Sisters, 'consolers of the sick and those in distress.'" The Castello center "which we bless today is a unique center of learning leading to the formation of nurses as healers of the human person":

> It is a center where human dignity, freedom and human flourishing in the Catholic and Dominican tradition will govern learning and the formation of healers for our world, not the enshrinement of the technological imperative in health care.
>
> It is a center of caring and compassion, where faculty and students will work together to embrace the Dominican imperative to preach the Gospel, serve others and engage culture in truth and charity.
>
> It is a center of learning where students will come to the knowledge, application and synthesis as they develop competencies and confidence for caring for communities and populations of different cultures and in distant lands.
>
> And finally, it is a center of experience where students will come to understand how to bring caring, healing and hope to the well and the sick wherever they call home… "Maggie's Place," "Ryan's Rumpus Room," and "St. Mary's Nursing" (depict environments) where students can experience how they might provide care in a

variety of settings in the community, very different than what they will experience in a hospital environment.[i]

The opening of the "Castello Nursing Simulation Learning Center," at Aquinas College School of Nursing and Saint Thomas West Hospital, is not only an important accolade to the 14th-century ministry to the sick and the outcast embraced by Blessed Margaret of Castello, it is a reminder that nursing, as ministry, remains a critically important element in contemporary care of the ill and the infirm, especially for those living on the margins of society.

The creation of the "Castello Center" is also appropriate and timely in view of the emphasis on simulation learning in current schools of professional nursing. Articles on the value of simulation laboratories and the use of simulators for education abound in recent nursing journals. The appreciation of simulated learning is reflected in such comments as: "high fidelity simulators are becoming the tool of choice in preparing today's nursing students for the clinical setting";[54] "clinical simulation could potentially be used for the majority of clinical time in nursing education";[55] "Frontier Nursing University recently (opened) a new simulation lab where students can gain hands-on experience to prepare them for the clinical practicum in their home communities";[56] "simulation is a useful means of teaching psychomotor skills in a controlled laboratory environment prior to patient contact";[57] "simulation allows for the acquisition of skills through repeated practice and management of emergency situations without risk to patients or to the students";[58] students find that simulation lab "scenarios incorporating patient death and emotional debriefing are important to their learning in the clinical setting";[59] and through simulation, "students

---

[54] Gwen Leigh and Helen Hurst, "We Have a High-Fidelity Simulator, Now What? Making the Most of Simulators," *International Journal of Nursing Education Scholarship* 5:1 (2008): 1-9, 1.

[55] Laura T. Gantt, "Strategic Planning for Skills and Simulation Labs in Colleges of Nursing," *Nursing Economics* 28:5 (2010): 308-313, 308.

[56] *Frontier Nursing Service Quarterly Bulletin*, January 2013, 14.

[57] Deborah Y. Lewis and Ann D. Ciak, "The Impact of a Simulation Lab Experience for Nursing Students," *Nursing Education Perspectives* 32:4 (2011): 256-258, 256.

[58] Barbara G. Kaplan, Ann Connor, Erin Ferranti and Linda Spencer, "Use of an Emergency Preparedness Disaster Simulation with Undergraduate Nursing Students," *Public Health Nursing* 29:1 (2011): 44-51, 45.

[59] Jane D. Leavy, Calvin J. Vanderhoff and Patricia K. Ravert, "Code Simulations and Death: Processing of Emotional Distress," *International Journal of Nursing Education Scholarship* 8:1 (2011): 1-13, 10.

have the opportunity to practice selected skills prior to entering active patient settings."[60]

Surely Blessed Margaret of Castello, who spent the final decade of her life caring for the sick and the outcast, would approve and bless a mechanism such as the simulation laboratory, which will help students, who share her vocation of caring for the ill and the infirm, to serve their patients with heightened care and compassion. The Aquinas College School of Nursing's "Castello Nursing Simulation Learning Center," which honors Blessed Margaret's 14th-century legacy of caring for Christ, in the guise of the "least of our brothers and sisters," is indeed a gift to the practice of professional nursing in the 21st Century.

Religious Shrines to Honor Blessed Margaret of Castello in the United States
St. Patrick Church, Columbus, Ohio

Ever since the early 1930's, the congregation of St. Patrick's Roman Catholic Church, in Columbus, Ohio, has nourished a special devotion to Blessed Margaret of Castello. After a serious fire in the church, a shrine and Blessed Margaret guild were established by the Dominican Pastor, Fr. James McKenna. In the 1970's, when the church was renovated, the Shrine to honor Blessed Margaret was expanded into a separate chapel.[61]

The Shrine chapel contains a statue of Blessed Margaret of Castello which displays her physical afflictions and use of a cane for walking. There is also a reliquary in the chapel containing a relic of the heart of Blessed Margaret and a novena is prayed in her honor each week.[62]

The "Blessed Margaret Guild" was established to promote the cause of Margaret's canonization and to support a number of social justice programs, especially one which benefits the poor and underprivileged.[63]

St. Louis Bertrand Church, Louisville, Kentucky

In the Church of St. Louis Bertrand, Louisville, Kentucky, there is also a shrine to honor the memory of Blessed Margaret of Castello. The Shrine consists of a beautiful wood carved statue of Blessed Margaret with a bank of candles underneath. The St. Louis Bertrand Church

---

[60] "Nursing Students Practice Real World Situations in Simulation Labs," *The Maryland Nurse* 14:3 (2013): 5.
[61] http://littlemargaret.org/guild.html.
[62] Ibid.
[63] Ibid.

website identifies a "Novena Prayer" to Blessed Margaret, as well as a "Prayer for Canonization." Details of Margaret's life are included on the church's website; and a study of petitions to Blessed Margaret, reported to the Castello Shrine staff at the Church of St. Louis Bertrand, has been documented in the literature.

In the late 1980's, researcher Robert Orsi posed the question: "What happens when a sick person turns to a beloved holy figure in a moment of fear and pain, and sometimes doubt?"[64] As Orsi observed "devotion to the saints has been an essential component of the Catholic experience of sickness and suffering for centuries. Statues of the Saints stand on bedside tables of the sick and holy images are affixed to the walls over their heads."[65] "Despite the familiarity of these practices," he added: "the role of the popular cult of the saints in mediating the Catholic experience of sickness has received little careful attention."[66]

Robert Orsi also noted that "since the early decades of the 20th Century, Catholics have left a record" of their petitions, hopes and responses to prayer in letters and notes sent to Saint's shrines in the U.S.[67] In order to respond to his question of "what happens when one prays to a holy figure," Robert Orsi initiated a study of letters written to one particular shrine, that being the "Shrine of Blessed Margaret of Castello, founded in 1980 by the Dominican Fathers in Louisville, Kentucky."[68] Orsi argued that as Margaret's devotees wrote to her shrine at St. Louis Bertrand Church, in Kentucky from all over the world, they are representative of "the devotional culture of American Catholicism."[69] The letters reveal a great deal about the perceived importance of Blessed Margaret's intervention in the lives of her devout.

As expected, most of the letters identified a petitioner's request for or the result of Blessed Margaret's intervention in a health related issue. One woman wrote that a physician had just found a lump in her breast and she was terrified over the potential surgery; she admitted: "I am humanly very frightened"; another lamented "My daughter has gone through three surgeries, and then after a while she contracted lupus...I am very nervous and worried." A third writer admitted: "I am desperate. My dear friend has just found out that she has cancer of the bone

---

[64] Robert A. Orsi, "The Cult of the Saints and the Reimagination of the Space and Time of Sickness in Twentieth-Century American Catholicism," *Literature and Medicine* 8:1 (1989): 63-77, 63.
[65] Ibid.
[66] Ibid.
[67] Ibid., 63-64.
[68] Ibid., 65.
[69] Ibid.

marrow and it is affecting her kidneys and the prognosis is one to three years."[70]

It was also evident that the devout put themselves very much in Blessed Margaret's hands. A woman wrote: "The doctors would like to operate on me and I'm so scared about this upcoming event...I have prayed fervently for the intercession of Blessed Margaret and have felt better since then (but)... if it be the will of God let me conform to His holy desires."[71] A "man whose close friend is being operated on for cancer told the Shrine that he is praying to Margaret and is confident that she will not fail to help."[72] And, another woman reported that she had prayed a novena for Margaret's intercession because she had received a preliminary diagnosis of cancer of the liver; after exploratory surgery, however, the doctor found no cancer anywhere. The woman asserted: "I truly believe it was Blessed Margaret's intercession."[73]

Ultimately, Robert Orsi concluded that when the devout "turn to the saints, powerlessness is recast as dependence on the power and love of God and the saints; fear is transformed into love and trust; and despair is remade into faith."[74] The power of the letters analyzed in Orsi's research demonstrates the value and blessing of contemporary Catholic shrines such as the one honoring Blessed Margaret of Castello at St. Louis Bertrand Church, in Louisville, Kentucky.

Some 15 years after the 1989 publication describing his research on petitioner's letters sent to the "Blessed Margaret of Castello Shrine" at St. Louis Bertrand Church in Kentucky, Robert Orsi again visited the shrine in Kentucky, as well as Blessed Margaret's Shrine in Columbus, Ohio. He spoke with directors of both shrines to ask about the potential for a move to canonization for Margaret. Both Shrine Directors reported that they had submitted descriptions of healings, thought to be the result of Blessed Margaret's intervention, to Rome and were awaiting a response.[75]

At that time, Margaret's "cause" for canonization was being promoted in the United States at the two shrines described, St. Patrick's Church, in Columbus and St. Louis Bertrand Church, in Louisville, "both

---

[70] Ibid., 66.
[71] Ibid., 68.
[72] Ibid., 69.
[73] Ibid., 70.
[74] Ibid., 68.
[75] Robert A. Orsi, *Between Heaven and Earth: The Religious Worlds People Make and the Scholars Who Study Them* (Princeton: Princeton University Press, 2005), 41-44.

in the care of the Dominican Order and located in Dominican parishes."[76] As described by Robert Orsi:

> The Columbus Shrine is the oldest; devotion to Blessed Margaret there dates to the 1930's, the actual shrine to her was constructed in the 1950's, and it was renovated in the 1970's. The Shrine in Louisville was founded in 1980. (This shrine was moved for the period 1981-86 to Philadelphia when its director was re-assigned to a parish there but returned to Louisville when the Dominicans handed over the church to the Philadelphia archdiocese).
> Both shrines receive regular correspondence from people seeking healing for themselves or for loved ones from physical distress...parents of children 'with some kind of deformity'...are among the most regular correspondents to the shrines, especially the mothers and fathers of children with eyesight problems or Down Syndrome. People who are losing their eyesight are the Columbus Shrine's main petitioners, especially those suffering degeneration of their retinas....What people want from "Little Margaret," as her devout call her, is healing from physical distress, or if not this, then accompaniment in their sufferings.[77]

In his book dealing with the topic of Catholic devotion, Robert Orsi relates another story of healing; that of his "Uncle Sal" and his special relationship with Blessed Margaret of Castello. His physically challenged uncle, he observed, had "discovered Margaret in his devotional world, (and she) served as the 'articulatory pivot' through which Sal was able to express his emotions."[78] For Uncle Sal, Orsi asserts, "Margaret became a sign of his own presence. If there was someone up in heaven like him...then people like him could be recognized on earth."[79] "Little Margaret" had become for Sal, and for many such those who wrote to her Shrine at St. Louis Bertrand Church, a sign of hope, a sign of courage, and a sign of God's deep and abiding love for the "least of His brothers and sisters" in the world.

---

[76] Ibid., 43
[77] Ibid.
[78] Ibid., 45.
[79] Ibid., 46.

Religious Shrines to Honor Blessed Margaret in Italy
"La Chiesa di San Domenico"

The primary shrine to Blessed Margaret of Castello in Italy is located in *Citta di Castello*, Perugia at La Chiesa di San Domenico, the Church of St. Dominic. The renaissance gothic style church is located on the Via Luca Signorelli 8/06012. The Dominicans, who arrived in *Citta di Castello* in 1270, only 17 years before Margaret's birth, were first given charge of the church of San Pietro di Massa. The Friars moved for a time to La Chiesa Santa Maria della Carita and ultimately broke ground for La Chiesa di San Domenico around 1400. In La Chiesa di San Domenico, Blessed Margaret's glass encased coffin is located within and at the front of the main altar. Her incorrupt body, dressed in the Dominican habit of a 14th-century *Mantellata*, may be viewed by the faithful who come to honor her.

It has been suggested that, "although it hasn't been proven, the church may have been built over Blessed Margaret's favorite Dominican Church where she prayed and where she was finally accepted into a religious community."[80] That church was La Chiesa della Carita; it was the church where a Dominican Prior gave Blessed Margaret the black and white habit of the Sisters of Penance of St. Dominic. The ceremony was attended by many Dominican Friars, as well as members of Margaret's Mantellate community.

The Chiesa di San Domenico "has a single aisle and a cross-shaped choir, revealing a structure that is both severe and solemn."[81] Visitors to San Domenico may spend time praying privately in the presence of the incorrupt body of Blessed Margaret. The wonder of Margaret's life is "expressed in the marvel of her body's preservation, which astounds scientists who cannot explain its incorruptibility."[82]

"La Cappella Beata Margherita"

In the area between Metola and the town of Mercatello, there is a chapel, adjacent to a small cell, which is thought to be the place where Blessed Margaret prayed "for most of her childhood and teens. The chapel is cared for by local women, who tend its altar and light it's

---

[80] Lucinda Vardey, *Traveling with the Saints in Italy: Contemporary Pilgrimages on Ancient Paths* (Mahwah, N.J.: Hidden Springs, 2005), 165.
[81] James Heater and Coleen Heater, *The Pilgrim's Italy: A Travel Guide to the Saints* (Nevada City, Ca.: Inner Travel Books, 2008), 210.
[82] Vardey, 166.

candles. A terra-cotta statue of Margaret stands below a plaque" describing the chapel as a memorial to Blessed Margaret of Castello.[83]

Margaret's Legacy
Memorialization in Art: Painting, Sculpture, and Stained Glass

In the medieval era "there was no argument about what art was and precious little definition or discussion either. Art was not an isolated phenomenon, but was integrated in all forms of visual display and associated with numerous aspects of cultural behavior, custom and communication."[84] Art was used in churches to illustrate "Christian philosophy and dogma."[85] The Middle Ages, "into which Christianity was born, was (a time) in which visual imagery served an important role as communication as well as embellishment; as message as well as objects of adoration."[86] There was in such medieval art "a simplicity or directness of statement (and)...intensification of emotion."[87] Examples of the above description of medieval art are well represented in the "Lunettes," commissioned at the end of the middle ages to commemorate the life and miracles of Blessed Margaret for the edification of the faithful.

Although Blessed Margaret of Castello has never been formally canonized by the Church as a "saint," she is indeed considered to have achieved "sainthood" in the eyes of many followers. Thus, in the years since her death, a number of exquisite artistic representations of Margaret and of her personal spirituality have been created to inspire the faithful. The majority of these works are located in Italy, especially in the towns of *Citta di Castello* and Mercatello, geographic areas important in Margaret's legend. Selections of the artistic works are presented, pictorially, in the books by Italian authors Ubaldo Valentini and Barbara Sartori.

Valentini's work includes numerous photographs of paintings, sculpture and stained glass windows devoted to the memory of Blessed Margaret. Some of the paintings include:

- *Venezia Museo Civico Vetrario* (Venice Civic Museum): "*Maestro delle Effigi Dominicane*": Blessed Margaret in her white

---

[83] Ibid., 163.
[84] Veronica Sekules, *Medieval Art* (N.Y.: Oxford University Press, 2001), 2.
[85] Ibid.
[86] James Snyder, *Medieval Art: Painting, Sculpture, Architecture, 4-14th Century* (N.Y.: Harry N. Abrams Inc. Publisher, 1989), 329.
[87] Marilyn Stokstad, *Medieval Art* (Boulder, Co.: Westview Press, 2004), 329.

Dominican habit covered with the mantle of black as worn by the Sisters of Penance of St. Dominic, the Mantellate.[88]

- *Mercatello (Chiesa di S. Chiara* - Church of St. Clare): Blessed Margaret in habit, holding her heart within which are three round stones depicting the "inscribed stones" found in Margaret's heart after death and relating to her famous comment: "If only you knew what I carry in my heart."[89]
- *Mercatello (Chiesa Parrocchiale* - Mercatello Parish Church): Blessed Margaret kneeling in prayer before a Crucifix; and, *Mercatello (Chiesa Parrocchiale* - Mercatello Parish Church): Blessed Margaret kneeling, her heart exposed displaying the three engraved stones, with a painting of the Holy Family pictured on a table next to her.[90]
- *Perugia, Galleria Nazionale: Trittico* (Perugia National Gallery: Triptych): Blessed Margaret holding her heart with the three stones visible accompanied by two other Dominican saints.[91]
- *Citta di Castello, Chiesa San Domenico*: Blessed Margaret holding in her left hand a covered heart and in her right hand an image of the Holy Family; and, *Citta di Castello*, Chiesa San Domenico: Photo of the glass enclosed casket holding the incorrupt body of Blessed Margaret.[92]
- *Vanezia: Chiesa S.S. Giovanni e Paulo* (Venice: Church of Sts. John and Paul): Blessed Margaret is pictured with a small opening in her habit exposing her heart with three round stones and on a table at her side is a small image of the Holy Family.[93]

As well as the paintings listed above, Valentini pictured other art works honoring Blessed Margaret some of which included:

- *Citta di Castello, S. Domenico Vetrate* (Stained Glass): 2 stained glass windows with images of Blessed Margaret located in the Chiesa di San Domenico[94] and, *San Domenico, Citta di Castello,*

---

[88] Valentini, 154.
[89] Ibid., 157.
[90] Ibid., 158-159.
[91] Ibid., 160.
[92] Ibid., 163; 183.
[93] Ibid., 184.
[94] Ibid. 162.

- *Trittico Scuola Senese*:(Triptych Sienese School): Triptych showing Blessed Margaret with other habited Dominicans.[95]
- *Citta di Castello: Blessed Margherita Statua*: wood carved statue of Blessed Margaret.[96]
- *Mercatello, Altare e Monumento dedicate a Blessed Margherita*: 2 pictures, one of a church altar in Mercatello, and the other an outdoor stone monument, both dedicated to the memory of Blessed Margaret.[97]
- *Citta di Castello, Chiesa di Belvedere, Statua in Gesso di Beata Margherita*: statue of Blessed Margaret, in gypsum, located inside a *Citta di Castello* Church, Chiesa di Belvedere.[98]

In her 2011 book, *Beata Margherita di Citta di Castello*, Italian journalist Barbara Sartori also included several pages of photos of art works honoring Blessed Margaret; some of these included:

- *La Beata Margherita, Sacristia della Collegiata di Mercatello*: Blessed Margaret in the sacristy of the Collegiate Church in Mercatello picturing Margaret kneeling with hands folded before a Crucifix (this painting is also presented in Valentini's work).
- *Chiesa di San Domenico a Citta di Castello dove e Sepolta Margherita*: The altar in Chiesa San Domenico picturing Blessed Margaret's glass encased casket in front of/under the altar.
- *Margherita in Pregheira, Trittico Museo di Murano*: Blessed Margaret in prayer before an image of the Crucified Christ, holding her heart in both hands.
- *Altare della Beata Margherita, Chiesa di St. Patrick*, Columbus, Ohio, USA: Altar and statue in the chapel dedicated to Blessed Margaret at St. Patrick's Church in Columbus, Oh.
- *Statua Lignea della Beata Margherita*, Bertrand Church, Lousiville, Kentucky, USA: Statue of Blessed Margaret located at her shrine in the Church of St. Louis Bertrand, Louisville, KY.
- *Ceramica della Beata Margherita nel Centro di accoglienza San Giovanni, per disabili, Citta di Castello*: Ceramic image of Blessed Margaret in St. John's Reception Center for the disabled, in *Citta di Castello*.

---

[95] Ibid.
[96] Ibid.166.
[97] Ibid.
[98] Ibid., 167.

- *Monumento a Margherita nella cittadina di Mercatello*: Monument (outdoor) to Blessed Margaret in the town of Mercatello.[99]

As well as the statues described above, a "to scale" statue of Blessed Margaret welcomes students and faculty of Aquinas College School of Nursing to the recently dedicated and blessed "Castello Nursing Simulation Learning Center" at Saint Thomas West Hospital, Nashville, Tennessee. The hand carved statue, which stands approximately 3.5 feet tall, is made of wood and is crafted with Margaret dressed in the habit of a "Sister of Penance of St. Dominic," reflective of her *Mantellata* role of serving the sick and the outcast.

Although Blessed Margaret is not well known to many in the United States, the data in this chapter reflect the beauty and the power of her humble spirituality. This is demonstrated in the accounts of her many miraculous healings, the ministries dedicated to honor Margaret, and her legacy as memorialized in works of art including paintings, sculpture and stained glass. The legend of Blessed Margaret's life is a gift to be treasured; her care and compassion for the "least of our brothers and sisters," a witness to be admired and imitated.

Margaret spent the final decade of her young life serving the sick and the outcast. In our contemporary society, with its rampant philosophies of egoism, consumerism and materialism, we too are called to serve the sick and the outcast; to bring kindness and compassion to the poor and the marginalized living on the peripheries of our towns and cities.

How blest we are to have the legacy of Blessed Margaret of Castello to inspire and guide us as we seek, each in his or her own way, to love God and to love our neighbor.

---

[i] Permission has been granted to cite extensively from the Castello Center Blessing and Dedication remarks of Brother Ignatius Perkins OP, PhD, RN, FAAN, KHS, ANEF, FNYAM, FRSM, Professor and Dean, Aquinas College School of Nursing.

---

[99] Barbara Sartori, *Beata Margherita di Citta di Castello* (Milano, Italy: Paoline Editorale Libri, 2011), 48-49.

Epilogue

Margaret of Castello: Mystic and Minister

The aim of this contemporary exploration of the legend of Blessed Margaret of Castello was to attempt to let Margaret speak to us, from across the centuries, of her love, of her faith and of her compassion. The hope is that Blessed Margaret's 14th-century ministry to the sick and the outcast can serve to inspire 21st-century caregivers seeking to embrace a similar calling.

Blessed Margaret loved God with a passionate and fervent devotion and she treasured her neighbor as a reflection of God's love.

Margaret was a compassionate caregiver dedicated to alleviating the suffering of the poor, the sick and the outcast; she was, also, a passionate contemplative continually seized by the wonder of God's love.

May we be blessed by the witness of Blessed Margaret whose life and ministry can inspire and guide us to embrace and preach the Gospel message of Jesus.

Blessed Margaret pray for us!

Blessed Margaret of Castello

Index

John 12: 24, 165
John 13: 34, 133, 134, 162
John 15: 13, 130
Luke 9: 57-58, 83
Matthew 7: 7, 74
Matthew 10: 29, 74
Matthew 11: 28-30, 64
Matthew 12: 20, 59
Matthew 25: 35, 134
Matthew 25: 40, 129
1 Peter 3: 4, 1
1 Peter 4: 11, 81
2 Corinthians 4: 7, 47

Almoner, 22, 153
Anchoress, ix, 2, 12, 24, 26-35, 37, 39-43, 45-48, 51, 52, 53, 56, 57, 63, 67, 141
Anchorhold, 2, 25, 28, 31-42, 44, 46, 48, 49, 51, 56, 59, 64, 67, 101, 135
Anchorite, 24, 25, 31-34, 39, 41
Anchoritic tradition, 32
Ancrene Wisse, 28, 34, 38-41
Angela of Foligno, 31, 141
Antony, St., 53
Archbishop Toribio de Mogrovejo, 124, 125
Augustinian Friars, 51
Beatification, x, 130, 168, 169
Beatrijs of Nazareth, 141
Beguine(s), 141, 147, 148
Blessed Margaret Guild, 180
Bodily mortification, 50, 101-102, 125
Brothers and Sisters of Penance, 108, 109, 113, 114, 115, 167
The Brotherhood of the Militia of Jesus Christ, 109, 113
Caregiver, xiii, 85, 153, 155, 189
Catherine de Ricci, 135, 141, 144, 148

Catherine of Siena, St., ix, 54, 55, 56, 114, 119, 121-124, 126, 128, 130, 135, 141, 142, 148, 155, 156
Christ Incarnate on the Altar, 141
Christ's Passion, 51-52, 137, 138, 142, 144, 145
Clare of Montefalco, St., 28, 136-140
Cloister, 13, 55, 56, 106, 126, 167, 173, 176
Conversion of hearts, 107
Daughters of Charity, 56
Disability, 48, 93, 97, 98, 99, 101, 102, 177
Disibodenburg, 48, 49
Divine Office, 48, 92, 108, 120, 127
Divine providence, 57, 72-75, 91, 175
Dominic, St., xi, xiii, 1, 4, 107, 109-114, 119, 131, 162, 178, 184
Dominican Laity, 109
Dominican Nuns of the Perpetual Rosary, 2, 3, 37, 61, 134, 166
Dominican Tertiary, ix, 1, 4, 27, 44, 54, 64, 114, 119, 121, 126, 130, 135, 141, 142, 147, 148, 152, 155
Emilia, 16-19, 21, 22, 24, 26, 27, 29, 35, 38, 67-71, 73, 75, 76, 78, 81
Exodus, 53, 74
Failed miracle, ix, 5, 59, 60, 71, 72, 78, 96
Fasting, 38, 50, 101, 102, 103, 116, 123, 142
Feast of St. Dominic, 129
Forgiveness, 44, 75-79, 157
Fra Giacomo Cappellano, ix, 17, 19, 21-24, 30, 35, 36, 38, 40, 44, 52, 60, 63, 64, 65, 68, 69, 74, 79, 83, 86, 87, 90, 97, 101, 134, 153
Franciscan Shrine of Fra Giacomo, 60, 78

Francis of Assisi, St., 25, 70, 73
Friends of God, 147
Gaol Fever, 157, 158
Giovanna of Orvieto, Blessed, 116, 117, 118
Gregory IX, Pope, 108, 111, 112
Habit, 25, 108, 111, 119, 136, 139, 186
    Brethren and Sisters, 113
    Dominican, 114, 119, 123, 144, 184, 186
    Hermit, 34
    Mantellata, 46, 167, 169, 184
    Sister of Penance of St. Dominic, 14, 116, 184, 188
    Third Order, 116, 126, 151
Hadewijch of Flanders, 141
Hairshirt, 38, 60, 142
Healing miracle, 2, 12, 45, 69, 70, 117, 142, 144, 145, 165, 166, 169, 172, 173, 174
Heretic(s), 73, 107, 111, 114
Hermit, 25, 31, 33, 34, 53, 141
Hermitess, 33
Hildegard of Bingen, St., ix, 25, 26, 33, 42, 44, 48-51, 141
"Hinds Feet on High Places", 95, 96
Holy calling, 103, 105, 106, 108, 119
Holy Family, 138, 139, 186
Holy obedience, 94
Homelessness, 82, 83, 85, 86, 87, 103, 106
Humoral physiology, 50
Imitatio Christi (Imitation of Christ), 47, 142
Incorruptibility, 169, 184
Infinite Beauty, 52, 141, 142
Innocent VII, Pope, 110
Interior image(s), 139
John Paul, II, Pope, 130
Julien of Norwich, ix, 33, 42, 51, 52, 53, 141
Jutta von Sponheim, 48, 49
La Chiesa della Carita, 95, 184

La Chiesa di San Domenico, 27, 184
La Chiesa di San Francesco, 81
Laity, 23, 55, 206, 112, 113, 125, 168
Lay Dominican, ix, 2, 55, 119, 152
Lame Margaret of Magdeburg, ix, 33, 42-48
Legend, ix, xi, xiii, 2, 3, 4, 7, 10-14, 16, 24, 27, 31, 33, 35, 38, 45, 64, 79, 98, 117, 134, 137, 156, 173, 185, 188, 189
Legenda, 3, 4, 11, 31, 66, 71, 79, 80, 163
Man of Eight Beatitudes, 130
Mantellata, ix, 46, 50, 103, 105, 116, 119, 120, 121, 123, 130, 134, 146, 148, 151, 160, 162, 169, 184, 188
Mantellate, 107, 108, 116, 118, 123, 131, 143, 153, 156, 157, 160, 167, 184, 186
Margaret of Cortona, 31, 102, 141
Margareta Contracta, *see* Lame Margaret of Magdeburg
Margery Kempe, 141
Marguerite Porete of Hainault, 141
Mary Magdalen, St., 53
Massa Trabaria, 6, 16, 65, 68, 69
Master Munio de Zamora, 108, 109, 110, 112, 113, 117
The Medieval Biographer, 2, 3, 5, 16, 17, 21, 25, 35, 37, 38, 65, 68, 71, 72, 75, 90, 94, 101, 134, 135, 138, 142, 143, 166
Medieval Biography, 3, 4, 5, 25, 143
Medieval prisons, 12, 28, 156-159
The Militia of Jesus Christ, 109-114, 126, 131
Monastero di Santa Margherita, 91, 93, 96, 105, 106, 135
Moral theology, 50

Mystic, x, xiii, 32, 44, 48, 51, 54, 61, 62, 86, 134, 135, 140-144, 147, 148, 162, 166, 189
Mysticism, 5, 47, 140, 141, 144, 147
Novice, vii, 93, 94, 105, 106, 126, 144, 145
Novitiate, 96, 103, 145
Opus Dei, 92
Papal state, 16, 65
Parable of the Homeless Patient, 83
Parisio, 5, 8, 16-24, 26, 27, 29, 35, 37, 66, 67, 69, 70, 71, 73, 75, 76, 78, 81, 97
Penance, xiii, 4, 5, 24, 37-40, 42, 44, 50, 54, 57, 60, 61, 65, 90, 93, 105, 107, 115, 120, 123, 125, 126, 127, 135, 142, 145, 146, 148, 152, 162, 166
Penitenti (penitents), 107, 108, 110, 157
Pier Giorgio Frassati, Blessed, ix, x, 121, 128, 129, 130
Poor Clares, 125
The "Rule", 92-95, 105, 106, 108, 110-113, 115, 119, 126, 127, 131, 152
Sanctity of the blessed, 4
Santa Sabina, 4
"Showings", 51-53
Sister(s) of Penance of St. Dominic, 1, 2, 12, 14, 28, 46, 50, 55, 64, 103, 106-109, 111, 115-118, 121, 123, 130, 131, 134, 143, 151, 153, 167, 184, 186, 188
(Christian) solitude, 53, 56
Spirituality of solitude, 12, 33, 53
Stigma, 96, 97
Tertiary vocation, 12, 121
Theology of solitude, 53, 89
Theory of miracles, 174
Veridiana, St., 24, 25, 29, 35, 67
Vestita, 110, 117
Vincent de Paul, St., 56
St. Vincent de Paul Society, 128

Visionary, 50, 140
Vita, ix, 2, 6, 11, 25, 31, 44, 45, 47, 138, 139, 163
Wounded healer, ix, x, 12, 28, 148-151, 153
Woundedness, 150

Printed in Great Britain
by Amazon